The Two *cines con niño*

The Two *cines con niño*

Genre and the Child Protagonist in over Fifty Years of Spanish Film (1955–2010)

Erin K. Hogan

EDINBURGH
University Press

Edinburgh University Press is one of the leading university presses in the UK. We publish academic books and journals in our selected subject areas across the humanities and social sciences, combining cutting-edge scholarship with high editorial and production values to produce academic works of lasting importance. For more information visit our website: edinburghuniversitypress.com

Edinburgh University Press Ltd
The Tun – Holyrood Road
12 (2f) Jackson's Entry
Edinburgh EH8 8PJ

First published in hardback by Edinburgh University Press 2018

Typeset in Monotype Ehrhardt by
Servis Filmsetting Ltd, Stockport, Cheshire,
and printed and bound by CPI Group (UK) Ltd, Croydon, CR0 4YY

A CIP record for this book is available from the British Library

ISBN 978 1 4744 3611 3 (hardback)
ISBN 978 1 4744 3614 4 (paperback)
ISBN 978 1 4744 3612 0 (webready PDF)
ISBN 978 1 4744 3613 7 (epub)

Contents

Acknowledgements

On Rites of Passage

Writing a scholarly monograph is in many ways a rite of passage towards academic maturity. It has its preliminary, liminary, and postliminary steps and, what's more, missteps. It's a zig-zagging path that, for this monograph, has come to a conclusion thanks to the generosity and support of many individuals.

The Two cines was conceived as my doctoral dissertation at the University of California, Los Angeles (UCLA). I am grateful to my oral exams and dissertation committee – Professors Jesús Torrecilla, Roberta L. Johnson, Teófilo F. Ruiz, and Cristina Pons – and, especially, to my advisor Professor Adriana Bergero for her insight and patience. I am thankful for funding from UCLA's Graduate Division and Department of Spanish and Portuguese, specifically Ben and Rue Pine, and Spain's Ministry of Culture Program for Cultural Cooperation. The Filmoteca Española, especially Trinidad del Río, and Euskadiko Filmategia were enormously helpful. I appreciate the time and insight that filmmakers, screenwriters, and producers shared with me in conversations during my graduate and post-graduate research: Montxo Armendáriz, Ramón Barea, the late José Luis Borau, Roberto Brodsky, José Luis Cuerda, Ana Díez, Manuel Gutiérrez Aragón, José María 'Txepe' Lara, and Imanol Uribe. Many thanks to scholars Valeria Camporesi and María Pilar Rodríguez who met with me during my investigations. I am grateful to Marvin D'Lugo for inspiring my love for Spanish cinema through his undergraduate summer course at Dartmouth College.

In relation to the liminary transition from dissertation to book, I would like to recognise the support of a number of institutions and individuals. The University of San Diego (USD) and the University of Maryland, Baltimore County (UMBC) funded summer research, writing periods, and conference travel. I am grateful to Jessica Berman and Rachel Brubaker at UMBC's Dresher Center for their thoughtful help in navigating the academic publication rites of passage and for other mentoring and research support through the College of Arts, Humanities and Social Sciences and

Office of the Vice President for Research. For the Latin American cinema piece, I wish to acknowledge the generosity of Vania Barraza Toledo and the help of Gabriel Cea and Roxana Garcés from the Cineteca chilena, Celeste Castillo from Buenos Aires' Museo de cine Pablo Ducrós and Julia Choclin from Arte Video. I thank Jack Sinnigen for his mentorship and reading of chapter and proposal drafts. I would like to recognise my undergraduate research assistant, Colin Hrenko, for his fine proofreading of the manuscript prior to submission. I would also like to acknowledge the valuable suggestions of Nicoleta Bazgan, Ana Corbalán, Ana Oskoz, Denis Provencher, and Margarita Vargas. I am beholden to all my colleagues who believed in this project and to all the filmmakers, film archives, and production companies who have supported this academic enquiry.

I have been fortunate to benefit from intellectual exchanges with a number of experts whose perceptive scholarship I admire immensely. You can find them by name and in alphabetical order in *The Two* cines' bibliography. I would especially like to recognise Sarah Wright as a stellar scholar, consummate professional, and humble academic role model. Finally, during the postliminary phase, I thank Edinburgh University Press (EUP) and all those who circulate, adopt, and engage with this volume.

My adoption by friends, flatmates, classmates, and their families from Spain – Covadonga, Pablo, Elisa, Natalia, Mónica, and Ricardo – has enriched this project immensely. Cova, Belén, and María have been and become tireless supporters and collaborators.

This book is dedicated to my family: Janet and Charles; Catherine and Gene; Lindsey, Austin, and Grayson; and Alexander. Words cannot sufficiently express a lifetime's worth of gratitude.

Figure Permissions

1.1 Used with permission from Filmoteca Española.

1.2 *Demonios en el jardín* © 1982 LUIS MEGINO PRODUCCIONES CINEMATOGRAFICAS, S.A. Used with permission from Egeda.

2.1 *El pequeño ruiseñor* © 1956 MARTE FILMS INTERNACIONAL, S.A. Used with permission from Egeda.

2.2–2.6 *La mala educación* © EL DESEO, D.A., S.L.U. Used with permission from El Deseo.

3.1–3.3 *Tómbola* © Grupo M Asociados. Used with permission from Grupo M Asociados.

4.1 *Un rayo de luz* © 1987 VIDEO MERCURY FILMS, S.A.U. Used with permission from Egeda.

4.2–4.3 *El viaje de Carol* © Aiete-Ariane. Used with permission from Aiete-Ariane.

5.1 *Marcelino pan y vino* © 1987 VIDEO MERCURY FILMS, S.A.U. Used with permission from Egeda.

5.2 *Secretos del corazón* © VIDEO MERCURY FILMS, S.A.U. Used with permission from Video Mercury Films.

6.1 *El espíritu de la colmena* © 2005 VIDEO MERCURY FILMS, S.A.U. Used with permission from Egeda.

6.2 *Secretos del corazón* © VIDEO MERCURY FILMS, S.A.U. Used with permission from Video Mercury Films.

7.1–7.2 *Pa negre* © Faraig and Massa d'Or Produccions. Used with permission from Lucía Faraig and Massa d'Or Produccions

8.1 *Machuca* © Wood Producciones. Used with permission from Wood Producciones.

8.2–8.3 *El premio* © Paula Markovitch. Author made more than three attempts to contact the rights holder regarding fair-use reproduction.

8.4 *Infancia clandestina* © Historias cinematográficas. A author made more than three attempts to contact the rights holder regarding fair-use reproduction.

9.1–9.3 *Spanish Movie* © Telecinco Cinema, Think Studio. Used with permission from Mediaset, Telecinco, Think Studio.

Introduction
The Two *cines con niño*:
The Ventriloquism, Dialogism and Biopolitics of the Children of Franco in Genre Film

Franco, ese ventrílocuo

A retrospective piece from the traditionally centre-left Spanish newspaper *El País* on Francisco Franco's thirty-six-year dictatorship for the fortieth anniversary of his death on 20 November showcases the biopolitics of the military regime with a focus on the original child of Franco, his own daughter Carmencita (1926–2017), and Franco's ventriloquism of her. Manuel Jabois's 'Carmencita y el amor' (Carmencita and Love) from 22 November 2015 is an ironic declaration of love for the former dictator's daughter 'Nenuca' that departs from the now infamous newsreel, from the penultimate year of the Spanish Civil War, 'Franco en Salamanca II' (Franco in Salamanca II) (Amo 1996: 449–50).[1] The performance of the national family is a ventriloquist act that casts the dictator, demonstrated in fullest etymological expression, as ventriloquist who controls the speech of Carmencita, his child dummy. Franco dictates Carmencita's ideology-ridden lines that Chapter One will explore in further detail. As the dummy addresses the children of the world, Franco mouths her words. Carmen Polo, wife and mother, plays only a literally supporting role, with no lines, as the lap on which Carmencita sits. In accordance with Foucauldian and Agambenian biopolitics and in the metaphorical terms of ventriloquism, the child dummy's docile body and voice are incorporated into the mechanism of state power. The objectification and political instrumentation of Franco's only child and the greater children of Franco are distilled and anticipated in this early newsreel.

I use the phrase 'children of Franco' with the intention of denoting a generation and referencing the title of film scholar Marsha Kinder's 1983 article in which she explores the filmmakers who lived their formative years during the Civil War and the dictatorship and whose child protagonists reflect their directors' childhoods under Franco. Ryan Prout also observes of this population: 'It is commonplace of criticism of Spanish cinema to equate the prevalence of children in film of the 1970s and 1980s with the youthfulness of a country newly emerging from forty years of isolationism and *nacionalcatolicismo*' (2005: 154). We should recall that the representations and visual artwork of the children of the Spanish Civil War, *los niños de la guerra* or *generación de medio siglo*, predate Kinder's children of Franco by thirty years and are prevalent in the narratives of authors, including Ana María Matute, Carmen Martín Gaite, Rafael Sánchez Ferlosio, Rafael Azonca, Juan Benet, Juan García Hortelano, Medardo Fraile, José Manuel Caballero Bonald, and Ignacio Aldecoa, who were children during the war (Aldecoa 1983).

Francoist philosopher, politician, and diplomat Francisco Javier Conde also highlights the condition of Spaniards as children under Franco, depicting the dictator of the country as the father of Spain:

> '[E]l Caudillo es Héroe hecho Padre. Traduce el carácter genuinamente fundacional del caudillaje. Decir Pater Patriae es decir fundador de un orden y de una forma doctrina política nuevos. Mientras el vocablo héroe arguye el camino guerrero y heroico de la fundación, la palabra padre es término calificado para quien asume la cura y el bienestar de sus seguidores.' (Conde 1942: 35; italics in the original)

> [[T]he Commander as Hero made Father. It translates the genuinely foundational character of leadership. To say Pater Patriae is to say founder of the new order and political doctrine. While the word hero connotes a warrior's path and heroic foundation, the word father is a term used for the person who assumes the care and well-being of his followers.]

The biological father–daughter relationship between Franco and Carmencita translates to a broader paternalism towards the obedient Francoists or disobedient Republicans. It follows in Jabois's interpretation of Francoist propaganda, thus, that Franco infantilises Spaniards (2015: n.p.). In Jabois's estimation, Franco iconised his daughter as a site or even mascot of national significance. Carmencita was a 'pantano móvil' (mobile reservoir), or another example of a public work of propaganda like the reservoirs inaugurated all over Spain (ibid.). Jabois analogises Franco's use of Nenuca amidst his bombing campaigns of the Civil War (1936–9) to the humanising effect of Hitler's dog Blondi on the Führer (ibid.). Parodoxically, by dehumanising Carmencita, Franco would appear more human. In fact, this analogy points to the vampire-like quality of ventriloquism and biopolitics in which the dictator-ventriloquist utilises the voice and body of another for his own political survival. Issues of power and paternity (as well as violence, ownership, and identity) are the basis of the performance art (Connor 2001: 75, 88). The child dummy is an inanimate being animated by the ventriloquist's voice under the illusion that the child is acting of her own free will. Notably, the classic bit of the dummy's back talk, which I will explore in content chapters, is not available to Carmencita in this propagandistic newsreel.

This enquiry into the child protagonist's speech and voice distinguishes itself from a plethora of scholarship on the gaze: either the child's gaze or the spectator's gaze on the child (Larrosa 2007; Lebeau 2008; Thau 2011). Giorgio Agamben, Jorge Larrosa, and Vicky Lebeau remind us of the etymology of 'infancy', denoting the inability to speak. Agamben's philosophical exploration links speech and the voice: 'It is significant that the author should have arrived at his inquiry into the human voice (or its absence) precisely through a reflection on infancy' (1993: 4). Vicky Lebeau's consideration of the child takes up this etymology:

> Closer to the state of infancy, or *infans* (literally, without language), the small child tends to be discovered at the limit of what words can be called upon to tell, or to mean – a limit that then generates the questions of how to convey the child's experience in language, of what in that experience, of what in the image, falls outside of, and so resists, the world of words. (2008: 16; italics in the original)

The child's language in cinema is not his or her own; the child is ventriloquised. *The Two* cines asks, therefore, to what end does the cinematic child protagonist speak? By discussing the child protagonist's speech in terms of ventriloquism, we take as a given that the character's agency, or lack thereof, is staged and mediated. Carolina Rocha cautions: 'even when children and adolescents are protagonists and move the narrative development, young actors perform roles and scripts written by adults. Hence, their on-screen agency masks their subalternity in the film industry' (2011: 127). The scholar further explores the issue in an article on Brazilian cinema, 'Can Children Speak in Film?', inspired by Gayatri Spivak's question of the subaltern condition. Rocha advances: 'children are the object of the spectatorial gaze: they move the stories forward and communicate within the parameters set by the demands of the films' scripts, yet their "voices" remain muffled by the conditions of commercial cinema, in which adults not only control the plots, but also the production, shooting, editing, and distribution of films' (2014: 2). In our evaluation, the child protagonist remains bound by a ventriloquial power structure that is imbued with commercial and ideological factors and inflected with genre functions (Altman 1999).

Two Spains, Two *cines con niño*

We may consider 'Franco en Salamanca II' a prelude to the *cine con niño* (child-starred cinema), in which a ventriloquist character even kidnaps national treasure Marisol in *Tómbola* (Lucía 1962). A fully fledged and commercially successful *cine con niño* genre emerged in the 1950s[2] with the following characteristics:

> Inspired by the child protagonists of Italian neo-realism, this child cinema existed in Spain in various hybrid forms – in religious, folkloric, and musical formats – becoming well established in Hungarian Ladislajo Vajda's enormously successful *Marcelino pan y vino* (1954) and Antonio del Amo's *El pequeño ruiseñor* (1956). These were remarkably potent vehicles for Pablito Calvo and Joselito, the new, male child superstars of the 1950s (alongside many unsuccessful imitators) and were followed by their female counterparts in the 1960s, Marisol, Rocío Durcal, and Ana Belén. (Jordan and Allinson 2005: 19–20)

The Two cines focuses on the biggest and youngest child stars of the *cine con niño* and their earliest films: Pablito Calvo (1949–), Joselito (1943–), and Marisol (1948–). Defining the parameters of childhood is a complicated task and one that is informed by considerations of time, place, race, class, sex, and age. For our purposes, the child character includes the on-screen young person up to early pubescence but excludes adolescence (and therefore its stars Rocío Dúrcal, Pili and Mili, and Ana Belén). Since engagement with audiences and in intertextuality is key to genre filmmaking, *The Two* cines is inclined not to focus on stars (Maleni Castro, Cesáreo Quezadas 'Pulgarcito') and films (*El florido pénsil* (Porto 2002), *El coche de pedales* (Barea 2004)) that have demonstrated less resonance (in the box office, consumer culture, and intertexts) with spectators and filmmakers. The audience of the *cines con niño* is not limited to children.

Cine con niño features dovetail with state propaganda. Francoist censorship began in the first year of the Civil War and continued with the *Ley de prensa e imprenta* in 1937, the year of 'Franco en Salamanca II', remaining mostly unchanged until 1966 and finally abolished after Franco in 1977 (Craig 2001: 19). While *cine con niño* films were not exclusively for children, they represent both the importance of cinema, as propaganda, and of children, addressees of propaganda, to the dictatorship. Ian Craig argues that cinema played as important a role in the transmission of Francoist ideology as children's literature; 'the ideological principles contained in [the] declaration [on children's literature] then served as a prototype for the regulation of the other medium which the regime viewed as increasingly important in terms of its impact on the populace, the cinema' (2001: 66). *The Two* cines contends that the *cine con niño* engages in the ideological genre function in its transmission of state ideology but also in the ritual function (Altman 1999) through fleeting moments of back talk and stories of unity.

The Two cines con niño is a genre study of child-starred film in Spain that identifies, contextualises, and theorises the emergence of a *nuevo cine con niño* (new child-starred film genre) since the early transition to democracy (1973–) from Francisco Franco's military regime (1939–75) to 2010. I examine the child-starred cinemas in order to reveal how the genres address national concerns and engage with national and cinematic history, an understanding I share with film scholar Leo Braudy:

> [B]ecause of the existence of generic expectations – how a plot 'should' work, what a stereotyped character 'should' do, what a gesture, a location, an allusion, a line of dialogue 'should' mean – the genre film can step beyond the moment of its existence and play against history. (Braudy 1999: 618)

My cinematic corpus consists of *cine con niño* films by Ladislao Vajda, Antonio del Amo, and Luis Lucía followed by *nuevo cine con niño* features by Víctor Erice, Carlos Saura, Manuel Gutiérrez Aragón, Arantxa Lazkano, Montxo Armendáriz, José Luis Cuerda, Imanol Uribe, Guillermo del Toro, Juan Antonio Bayona, and Agustí Villaronga. Childhood set historically during the Spanish Civil War or post-war that also displays filmic retrospection towards the *cine con niño* defines the *nuevo cine con niño* genre. These terms exclude the presence of child characters who do not bear a protagonist's responsibility for advancing the action of the film.

The apparent agency of the child protagonist is central to *The Two* cines, insisting on the difference across what the child character does, what is done in the name of the child, and what is done to the child. This also rules out from primary examination the child or adolescent within a familial (either biological or adoptive) ensemble cast (*La gran familia* (Fernando Palacios 1962) and sequels, *La guerra de papá* (Antonio Mercero 1977), *Las largas vacaciones del '36* (Jaime Camino 1976), *El sur* (Víctor Erice 1983), *Las bicicletas son para el verano* (Jaime Chávarri 1984), *El embrujo de Shanghai* (Fernando Trueba 2002), *Los girasoles ciegos* (José Luis Cuerda 2008), *Pájaros de papel* (Emilio Aragón 2010)), the reminiscent adult who re-enacts his childhood (Carlos Saura's *El jardín de las delicias* (1970) and *La prima Angélica* (1974)) and documentaries of the childhood during the war and dictatorship (*Los niños de Rusia* (Jaime Camino 2001), *Els nens perduts del franquisme* (Montse Armengou and Ricard Belis 2002)).

The *nuevo cine con niño* is a diverse cinema comprised of and hybridised with subgenres: the coming-of-age or *bildungsfilm* (Deveny 2012), the often-nostalgic heritage film, the thriller, the literary adaptation, fairy tale and fantasy, the Gothic and horror film to film noir, the documentary, the auteur film, the children's film and combinations of these subgenres. The only *nuevo cine con niño* film to make a nod to the relatively more generically homogenous child musical, religious and folkloric films of the *cine con niño* is Pedro Almodóvar's *La mala educación* (2004) and its altar boy singer. Barry Jordan's and Rikki Morgan-Tamosunas's *Contemporary Spanish Cinema* from 1998 could not anticipate the advent of the new child-starred genre, which emerged in the late 1990s alongside the memory boom.[3] They file the early Erice, Saura, and Gutiérrez Aragón films of the 1970s and 1980s under their category of the 'personalized' historical memory film set within the private sphere of the family (Jordan and Morgan-Tamosunas 1998: 39–41). Other scholars, Román Gubern, José Enrique Monterde, Julio Pérez Perucha, Esteve Riambau, and Casimiro Torreiro, might even be disgusted by the robust re-appearance of child protagonists in Spanish cinema, having described in 1995 their ancestors as 'repelentes' (1995: 275) (repellent).[4] *The Two* cines con niño addresses the development of the *nuevo cine con niño* genre within its historical and film historical contexts, noting how the medium of the cinema brings the private to the public sphere.

The spoof film *Spanish Movie* (Javier Ruiz Caldera 2009), the focus of our concluding chapter, illustrates many of the elements that form the *nuevo cine con niño* genre with the remarkable inclusion of a cameo by Joselito. As the English-language title suggests, intertexts are not entirely Spanish but also Hollywoodian: Keenan Ivory Wayans's *Scary Movie* (2000) franchise and films with Spanish stars like Javier Bardem and Penélope Cruz. What is true of *Scary Movie* also seems to be the case for *Spanish Movie*: 'What happens in parody is, first there is a good movie, then there are fifty bad versions of that movie, and when the audience is tired of seeing those films, then that genre's right for parody' (Wayans cited in Alexander 2003: 144). I wish to rise above prejudices against genre films by refraining from evaluating *nuevo cine con niño* films in such negative terms. Although the production numbers of Hollywood and Spanish filmmaking do not compare, the relative bulk of features in the *nuevo cine con niño* mould coincides with Wayans's criterion for parody.

A weary comedian, journalist, and screenwriter, Pepe Colubi would likely beg to differ with me. Colubi's review of Ruiz Caldera's film in *El País* relates genre and nation and discusses genre convention in terms of stereotypes. For Colubi, child protagonists of films set during the Spanish Civil War and Franco's dictatorship have become synonymous with Spanish film: 'Del niño de la posguerra al terror que no se ve, repasamos los estereotipos que hacen país' (From the child of the post-war to unseen horror, we review the stereotypes that make the country) (2009: n.p.). Accordingly, these characters are not simply genre-making but even nation-making. Colubi dismisses cinematic repetition as a conglomeration of irritating stereotypes rather than as an indicator of genre formation. One item from his list of annoyances identifies some common elements of the *nuevo cine con niño*:

> La Guerra Civil a través de los ojos de un niño. Por mucho que le pese a José Luis Cuerda, el cansino espectador medio español cataloga, por pura acumulación, las películas ambientadas en nuestra Guerra Civil y su posguerra como todo un subgénero ibérico con varios elementos comunes: ausencia de escenas bélicas, pre-adolescentes salidos, tristeza vital, algún curilla, graves penurias y Maribel Verdú. (Colubi 2009: n.p.)

> [The Spanish Civil War through the eyes of a child. In spite of José Luis Cuerda, the tired and average Spanish spectator catalogues, by pure accumulation, the films set during our Civil War and post-war as an Iberian subgenre with various common elements: absence of war scenes, horny preteens, vital sadness, a priest here or there, grave scarcities and Maribel Verdú.]

First, the tone of Colubi's critique is a very common one used towards genre films, that may 'offend our most common definition of artistic excellence: the uniqueness of the art object, whose value can in part be defined by its desire to be uncaused and unfamiliar, as much as possible unindebted to any tradition, popular or otherwise' (Braudy 1999: 613). Patterns and repetition that are central to genre filmmaking get old for Colubi, Wayans, and others.

Second, however, the characteristics that Colubi enumerates do appear to varying degrees in *El espíritu de la colmena* (*Spirit of the Beehive* 1973, Víctor Erice), *Secretos del corazón* (*Secrets of the Heart* 1997, Montxo Armendáriz) and *El laberinto del fauno* (*Pan's Labyrinth* Guillermo del Toro, 2006). (Maribel Verdú in fact plays the resistance fighter Mercedes in Del Toro's film.) Nevertheless, in my inventory of *nuevo cine con niño* protagonists, I catalogue curious, rebellious, intrepid, heteronormative, and sexually naïve children who may either be victims of Francoism or the thorns in its side. The illuminating exception to this rule, *Pa negre* (*Black Bread* 2010, Agustí Villaronga), is the focus of Chapter Seven. It is the epitome of the 'genre film [that] lures its audience into a seemingly familiar world, filled with reassuring stereotypes of character, action, and plot. But the world may actually be not so lulling, and, in some cases, acquiescence in convention will turn out to be bad judgment or even a moral flaw' (Braudy 1999: 617). I argue, first, that more contemporary films depicting the Spanish Civil War (1936–9) and Franco's dictatorship (1939–75) have a dialogical relationship with the *cine con niño* and, second, that each Spain utilises the child protagonist for differing political and genre functions. Appropriation and dialogism, from the micro-scale of ventriloquial relationships among characters to the macro-scale of the adoption of the child protagonist and re-signification of *cine con niño* narrative hallmarks, are the structuring themes of my analysis. The child-starred cinemas are my focus, but I should note that political expropriation from Franco to post-Franco is not exclusive to this genre; it also occurs in the comedy (Jordan and Morgan-Tamosunas 1998: 64).

Through a comparative lens, I analyse common narrative strategies across the political divide of the two Spains, to which my title alludes, from Francoism's *cine con niño* (1950s–60s) to transitional and constitutional Spain's *nuevo cine con niño*, that give rise to the two *cines con niño*. There are, naturally, at least two minds about the persistence of the two Spains. A Spanish cultural history textbook from 2010 declares the end of the two Spains thanks to economic development and the establishment of a stable democracy:

> El desarrollo económico y social de los años sesenta y setenta, el crecimiento de la clase media y la voluntad de reconciliación hicieron posible el final de la división histórica de las *dos Españas* y fueron base fundamental para el establecimiento de una democracia estable. (Muñoz and Marcos 2010: 135; italics in the original)

> [The social and economic development of the sixties and seventies, the growth of the middle class and the will to reconcile made possible the end of the historic division of the two Spains and were the fundamental basis for the establishment of a stable democracy.]

This second, and latest, edition of *España ayer y hoy* concludes at the beginning of the economic crisis of 2008 and does not mention the 2007 Law of Historical Memory nor the heated debate that surrounded it. Such omissions belie the text's celebratory tone regarding a strengthening economy and democracy founded on the basis of Francoist impunity and in the absence of truth commissions for human rights violations during the dictatorship. As Jo Labanyi has shown:

> [A]ttempts toward the end of the Franco dictatorship to deal cinematically with this violent heritage were followed by a ten-year gap, until the appearance in the mid-1980s of a number of novels and films representing the civil war and their escalation since the late 1990s to create a memory boom, which has resulted in the publication of a large number of testimonies. (Labanyi 2007: 89)

The films of Carlos Saura, Víctor Erice, and Manuel Gutiérrez Aragón in the 1970s and 1980s anticipate the memory boom since the 1990s. By

2007, proponents of the Law of Historical Memory no longer espoused a reconciliatory stance. Furthermore, scholars trace the root causes for the 15 May 2011 popular movement known as the 'Indignados', which emerged in March 2011 in reaction to the severe economic crisis and converged upon Madrid's Puerta del sol, to economic policies from the transition: 'Social peace was engineered by means of rising real wages that outstripped both inflation and productivity, while levels of state and private borrowing also increased . . . The burden of transition was placed largely upon the workforce' (Charnock et al. 2012: 6). The economic crisis followed by the disbarment in 2012 of former judge Baltasar Garzón for work related to his investigation of the crimes of Francoism (Graham 2012: 129; Hogan 2016a: 68) suggest that Spain's democracy remains a work in progress.

The origin of the two Spains dates back to tensions arising between the forces of tradition and modernity in Spain from the nineteenth century. Another Spanish cultural history textbook credits social tensions, anarchist terrorism, regionalism and Spain's defeat in Cuba in the nineteenth century for generating the two Spains of the Civil War; 'Todo produce una polarización cada vez mayor de la población (las "dos Españas") que dará lugar, casi inevitablemente, a la Guerra Civil de 1936' (It all produces an increasing polarisation in the population (the 'two Spains') that will give rise, almost inevitably, to the Civil War of 1936) (Pereira-Muro 2003: 179). Santos Juliá's history of the two Spains hesitates to determine authorship of the concept and, instead, presents it as a network of metaphorical responses to contemporary crises:

[A]quí aparecerán muchas voces entrecruzadas, para que se vea que el relato no es una ocurrencia de tal o cual intellectual, sino que es cosa común y con entidad suficiente para impregnar durante un período más o menos largo de tiempo la conciencia colectiva con metáforas y mitos en directa relación con alguna crisis, más o menos traumática, de la que pretenden dar cuenta. El pueblo en guerra por su independencia y su libertad; la anomalía y decadencia, la muerte y resurrección de España; la nación dormida, inconsciente de que un poder ajeno le impide crecer; la vieja y nueva España; el romance del pueblo en guerra contra invasores y traidores; el mito de la única España verdadera contra la Anti-España espuria y extranjera, son algunos de estos relatos que han gozado de particular vigencia. (Juliá 2004: 18)

[[H]erein appear many intersecting voices, so that it is possible to see that the account is not the occurrence of one or another intellectual, but rather something very common and with enough presence to impregnate during a more or less long period of time the collective consciousness with metaphors and myths in direct relation to some crisis, more or less traumatic, of which they wish to assess. A people in war for their independence and freedom; anomaly and decadence; the death and resurrection of Spain; a nation asleep, unaware of a power that prevents it from growing; the old and new Spain; the romance of a people at war with invaders and traitors; the myth of one true Spain against the illegitimate and foreign Anti-Spain, are some of these accounts that have enjoyed a certain validity.]

For *The Two* cines, the crisis consists of access to public discourse by the defeated children and grandchildren of Franco. Philosopher and essayist José Ortega y Gasset and poet Antonio Machado, whom Juliá counts among many apologists of the two Spains (Juliá 2004: 149), respond to civil conflict that gave rise to the Civil War in 1936. Cultural historian Rafael Abella, in fact, paraphrases Machado's Proverb LIII of *Campos de Castilla* (1910) when he describes the Civil War:

> En la cruenta lucha que durante tres años años habían sostenido las dos Españas, a una de ellas, la vencida, se le había helado el corazón. Toda España era ya zona nacional. Ante ella se ofrecía una nueva vida colectiva que no podía fundirse en una idea común porque España había quedado dividida en afectos y desafectos, en vencedores y vencidos. (Abella 1996: 15)

> [As a result of the bloody fight between the two Spains during three years, the heart of defeated Spain had frozen. All of Spain was now the National zone. Faced with a new collective life in which common ground could not be achieved, Spain had been divided into the affected and disaffected, into the victors and the defeated.]

Machado's likeness and poetry appear in a film of the *nuevo cine con niño*, *La lengua de las mariposas* (Cuerda 1999). The two Spains are perhaps the two biggest collective stars of the *nuevo cine con niño*. As Ann Davies observes in her article on *El espinazo del diablo* (Del Toro 2001):

> When talking of the Spanish Civil War it is a commonplace now to note that the conflict was rooted in the notion of the *dos Españas*, radically opposed notions of Spanish identity aligned along a left/right political axis; and while the realities were often more complex, this binary struggle over Spanish identity can nonetheless be perceived in many films set in the Spanish Civil War. Indeed, many of the films of the past twenty-five years that deal with the Civil War can be read as attempts to recuperate the 'lost half' of Spanish identity that became of necessity submerged with Franco's defeat of Republican forces and the repression that ensued afterwards. (Davies 2006: 136; italics in the original)

The Two cines stands on the shoulders of research on historical memory in Spanish cultural studies to propose an intervention that foregrounds the discourse, dialogism, and biopolitics of the child protagonist. By identifying and theorising the *nuevo cine con niño* as a regenrification of the *cine con niño*, *The Two* cines illuminates common strategies of deployment and appropriation of the child protagonist in the public sphere. Sarah Wright's *The Child in Spanish Cinema* from 2013 is the first monograph to date on the child protagonist and argues that he or she serves as prosthetic memory that facilitates the audience's connection with the past.

The Two cines reframes the study of contemporary Spain, pulling the focus from either of the alternating monologues of Francoism and Republican memory to dialogism and the exploration of the ideological cal intersections of the two Spains over the child. So often, the child protagonist, a conversant in this dialogue, disables the spectator's critical apparatus and enables pathos, which is true to a certain extent for genre films in general that

> can exploit the automatic conventions of response for the purposes of pulling the rug out from under their viewers. The very relaxing of the critical intelligence of the audience, the relief that we need not make decisions – aesthetic, moral, meta-physical – about the film, allows the genre film to use our expectations against themselves, and, in the process, reveals to us expectations and assumptions that we may never have thought we had. (Braudy 1999: 617)

If we entertain the idea that we may be relieved of passing judgement on the quality of *nuevo cine con niño* films, although this is not Colubi's example, I suspect that these features are designed to redirect our powers of moral evaluation with regards to the child protagonist, the child's behaviour, and adults' behaviour towards the child. I propose reading the *nuevo cine con niño*'s dialogism with the *cine con niño* as a calculated effort to talk back to its Francoist precursor and re-assert the Second Republic's right to a voice.

Although narrative strategies coincide, each of the two Spains and corresponding two *cines* espouse their own opposing ideologies. It may go without saying that ideology does not belong only to the domain of fascism. Terry Eagleton's study of ideology whittles down, from sixteen to six, definitions that edify our understanding of coincidences and divergences in the ideologies of the *cines con niño*. Both cinemas amount to collective and symbolic self-expressions that promote and legitimise, most formally through Francoist censorship in the *cine con niño*, the interests of either Francoist or constitutional Spain in the face of opposing agendas (Eagleton 2007: 29). The two *cines* part ways with respect to each cinema's position vis-à-vis the ruling group and the extent to which it distorts the truth (30). *The Two* cines argues that the *cine con niño*, although momentarily offbeat here and there, is ultimately in lock-step with Francoist ideas; this has been censorship's express intention. The absence of transitional justice suggests that films exhibiting the crimes of Francoism do not correspond with the interests of the Spanish ruling class. In fact, Garzón's disbarment was another casualty of the bipartisan pact of silence:

> The backlash against him is not only classically rightist, however, since it derives
> from an unspoken assumption held across virtually the entire post-Franco political
> class that has a common interest, almost irrespective of 'ideology', in not exposing
> itself, or the state apparatus, to the uncertain political consequences of exorcizing the
> violence of the recent past. (Graham 2012: 129)

Nuevo cine con niño films do not emanate from the political class and indeed question the ideology behind the pact of silence. The Law of Historical Memory recognised the illegitimacy of Francoist courts and facilitated the opening of mass graves and removal of Francoist monuments but it did not overturn the 1977 amnesty and, therefore, it 'was met with muted applause on the left, and by indignant disbelief on the right' (Golob 2008: 136). The *nuevo cine con niño* responds in the language of genre to this injustice by reimagining similar characters and situations with new tragic or historically inaccurate restorative resolutions, or both at once as in *El laberinto del fauno* (Del Toro 2006).

Rick Altman's genre functions are a useful point of departure for our analysis of the mechanisms of the two *cines* and requires some disambiguation on account of the multiple definitions of 'ideology' to which Eagleton alludes. For Altman, there are two main schools of thought in genre studies: the ideological, arising from Marxism, and the ritual, arising from structuralism. The ideological genre function follows Louis Althusser and defines its ideological nature entirely on the state origin of the cinema. Francoist *cine con niño* subject to censorship, rather than the *nuevo cine con niño*, would clearly satisfy the ideological genre function. However, counter-hegemonic subtexts occasionally squeak by, as we would expect from performances in the ventriloquial vein, and even the expression of state must be adapted to a Spanish cultural context.

The presence or absence of unity, an aspect that Altman links to the ritual function, dovetails with the politics of Francoist and constitutional Spain. Altman compares the genre functions:

> Whereas ritual critics interpret narrative situations and structural relations as offer-
> ing *imaginative* solutions to a society's real problems, ideological critics see the same
> situations and structures as luring audiences into accepting *deceptive* non-solutions,
> while all the time serving governmental or industry purposes. Here too, genres have
> a particular role and importance, for it is through generic conventions that audiences
> are lured into false assumptions of societal unity and future happiness. (Altman
> 1999: 27; italics in the original)

Happy reunion as a common resolution in the *cine con niño*, exemplifying Franco's Spain as *Una, grande, libre* (One, great, free), contrasts with exclusionary disunion or undesirable reunion achieved through too great a sacrifice in *nuevo cine con niño* conclusions. *Cine con niño* films often deceptively project, thus, a unified contemporary society while *nuevo cine con niño* features focus on past injustices that characters remedy with success or failure. Often, characteristics of both genre functions, such as unity or lack thereof, are apparent in both child-starred genres.

The fact that *nuevo cine con niño* films are not subject to state censorship and are often produced by their own directors within or beyond Spain (Almodóvar, Armendáriz, Del Toro) disqualifies them from Altman's narrow ideological function definition. Their proposals of alternatives to Francoist repression and audience response, however, do squarely situate them within Altman's ritual function:

> [T]he narrative patterns of generic texts grow out of existing societal practices, imaginatively overcoming contradictions within those very practices. From this point of view, audiences have a very special investment in genres, because genres constitute the audience's own method of assuring its unity and envisioning its future. (Altman 1999: 27)

Here the child protagonist, on point as a universal symbol of the future, and his or her fate are prescriptive for the nation's future. In the face of state policies and rulings that repeatedly uphold the 1977 amnesty, the *nuevo cine con niño* offers up its counter-argument. Leo Braudy's observation with regards to genre in Hollywood filmmaking is also true of the *cines con niño*: 'a genre will remain vital, as the western has, and the musical has not, so long as its conventions still express themes and conflicts that preoccupy its audience' (1999: 616). Production and spectator numbers indicate that childhood under Francoism continues to preoccupy Spanish audiences.

The critical mass of the *nuevo cine con niño* genre-in-the-making (Bakhtin 1981: 11) appeared from 1997 to 2010 when thirteen films, practically a film a year, dealing with childhood during the dictatorship were released. This filmography includes Oscar nominees (*Secretos del corazón* (*Secrets of the Heart*) (Armendáriz 1997), Pedro Almodóvar) and the Academy Awardee *El laberinto del fauno* (*Pan's Labyrinth*) (Del Toro 2006). More than ten million filmgoers in Spain viewed the most prominent *nuevo cine con niño* films from *Secretos del corazón* to *Pa negre* (*Black Bread*) (Villaronga 2010); this combined total spectatorship, barring possible overlap, exceeds the current box-office record and equates to more than a fifth of Spain's present population, providing evidence for an audience-driven cinema. Most heritage films of the *nuevo cine con niño* reify the two Spains despite historical realities, as Ann Davies also notes, that are more than two dimensional. Our purpose is to analyse filmic representation, which indeed falls along the lines of binary, rather than conduct a historical study of twentieth and twenty-first century Spain in all of its complexity.[5]

The two most common complaints lodged against the *nuevo cine con niño* films (recall Colubi) are their dualistic simplicity and their repetition. The binary, in fact, and repetition, intertext, and dialogism are indicators of genre. The dualism of the two *cines con niño* and two Spains is replicated in genre studies and represents another defining characteristic of genre formations. Dualism extends beyond the two genre functions to binaries within the films themselves. Altman explains: 'Constantly opposing cultural values to counter-cultural values, genre films regularly depend on dual protagonists and *dualistic* structures (producing what I have called dual-focus texts)' (1999: 24; emphasis in the original). *The Two* cines translates Altman's observation of genre to the Spanish cinematic context, thus the dualism of the child-starred cinemas is none other than that of the two Spains. Across the *cines con niño* this conflict is evident, and it is also the root of tension within films of the *nuevo cine con niño*. The latter cinema demonstrates dialogism, a defining characteristic of genre, both within the more recent productions and also reaching back to the *cine con niño*:

> Both intratextually and intertextually, the genre film uses the same material over and over again. A common complaint levelled against genre films, 'If you've seen one you've seen 'em all', correctly describes their *repetitive* nature. The same fundamental conflicts are resolved over and over again in similar fashion – the same shoot-out, the same sneak attack, the same love scene culminating in the same duet. Each film varies the details but leaves the basic pattern undisturbed, to the point where shots used in one film are often recycled in another. (Altman 1999: 25; italics in the original)

The Two cines focuses on the *nuevo cine con niño*'s relationship to the *cine con niño*, how it manipulates intertext and how it regenrifies its Francoist precursor. Therefore, our examination of the *cine con niño* will allow us to better understand the *nuevo cine con niño*. The new child-starred cinema rewrites the *cine con niño* from the perspective of the losing band of the Spanish Civil War; accordingly: 'Rewriting film history is one of the fundamental rhetorical strategies accompanying regenrification' (Altman 1999: 80). Guillermo del Toro's *nuevo cine con niño* films also re-write Spanish history with Republican rather than Francoist victories. The *nuevo cine con niño* remixes the same ingredients in different proportions for the tastes of a different audience.

Dialogism, Ventriloquism and Biopolitics
of the *cines con niño*

Altman's film genre study makes reference to Mikhail Bakhtin's work on the novel as process whereby Altman's genrification corresponds to Bakhtin's 'genre of becoming' or 'genre-in-the-making' (Altman 1999: 140; Bakhtin 1981: 7, 11). Bakhtin's dialogism, synonymous with Altman's intertextual repetition, brings us back to our metaphor of ventriloquism as an expression of biopolitics and the appropriation of the child or child protagonist. While ventriloquism is present in the relationships among the characters of the *cine con niño*, it functions more abstractly on the level of genre in the *nuevo cine con niño*. Both child-starred cinemas, the more recent group in particular, exhibit double-voiced discourse in a number of ways, for instance, by speaking to the past (the Spanish Civil War, Francoism, *cine con niño*) and to the present (impunity). Bakhtin defines the dialogical imagination in the following terms:

> Every moment of the story has a conscious relationship with this normal language and its belief system, is in fact set against them, and set against them *dialogically*: one point of view opposed to another, one evaluation opposed to another, one accent opposed to another (i.e., they are not contrasted as two abstractly linguistic phenomena). This interaction, this dialogic tension between two languages and two belief systems, permits authorial intentions to be realized in such a way that we can acutely sense their presence at every point in the work. (Bakhtin 1981: 314; italics in the original)

Dualism is also evident in Bakhtin's theorisation of the novel. Nevertheless, heteroglossia comes into play to complicate this binary during moments of counter-hegemonic discourse in the *cine con niño*, when the child dummy talks back in embedded ventriloquism for instance, in the re-signification of *cine con niño* intertexts in the *nuevo cine con niño*, and when tales from the periphery of the Spanish state, the regional cultures of the Basque Country and Catalonia and even the binational co-productions of Guillermo del Toro, call into question centralist mandates and turn the narrative features of the *cines con niño* on their heads. Bakhtin defines the concept:

> Heteroglossia, once incorporated into the novel (whatever the forms for its incorporation), is *another's speech in another's language*, serving to express authorial intentions but in a refracted way. Such speech constitutes a special type of *double-voiced discourse*. It serves two speakers at the same time and expresses simultaneously two different intentions: the direct intention of the character who is speaking, and the refracted intention of the author. In such discourse, there are two voices, two

meanings, and two expressions. And all the while these two voices are dialogically interrelated, they – as it were – know about each other (just as two exchanges in a dialogue know of each other and are structured in this mutual knowledge of each other); it is as if they actually hold a conversation with each other. Double-voiced discourse is always internally dialogized. Examples of this would be comic, ironic or parodic discourse, the refracting discourse of a narrator, refracting discourse in the language of a character and finally the discourse of a whole incorporated genre – all these discourses are double-voiced and internally dialogized. (Bakhtin 1981: 321; italics in the original)

Although Bakhtin only names it once in *The Dialogic Imagination*, ventriloquism (expropriation and appropriation) (1981: 289, 293) is the subtext of dialogism and double-voiced discourse throughout his study:

The author does not speak in a given language (from which he distances himself to a greater or lesser degree), but he speaks, as it were, through language, a language that has somehow more or less materialized, become objectivized, that he merely ventriloquates. (Bakhtin 1981: 299)

In the regenrification of the *cine con niño*, the *nuevo cine con niño* ventriloquates, it incorporates in order to voice doubly, the structural characteristics of its predecessor. For us, ventriloquating is macro and refers to regenrification across texts while ventriloquising is micro and refers to relationships among characters within a text.

It is necessary to add nuance within our deployment of the ventriloquism here before developing this metaphor for biopolitics further in content chapters. I propose subcategories of ventriloquism in order to best describe the power dynamics apparent in and across the child-starred cinemas. Appropriative ventriloquism is the classic form exemplified in 'Franco en Salamanca II' through the imposition of authoritative discourse on the child dummy who has no recourse to question authority. As Bakhtin puts it:

It is not a free appropriation and assimilation of the word itself that authoritative discourse seeks to elicit from us; rather, it demands our unconditional allegiance. Therefore authoritative discourse permits no play with the context framing it, no play with its borders, no gradual and flexible transitions, no spontaneously creative stylizing variants on it. (Bakhtin 1981: 343)

Thus, appropriative ventriloquism cannot be double-voiced (Bakhtin 1981: 344). Here the dummy is the quintessential docile body 'that may be subjected, used, transformed and improved' (Foucault 1979: 136). It is instrumental in a greater biopolitics, defined by Giorgio Agamben, who follows Michel Foucault, as 'the growing inclusion of man's natural life in the mechanisms and calculations of power' (Agamben 1998: 119). It also describes, as we will examine in Chapter One, the expropriations and indoctrinations of as many as 30,000 children under Franco (Duva and Junquera 2011: 12). The Auxilio Social state orphanage system enacted the regime's discourse on childhood: 'la infancia pasó a formar parte de ese sector de lo que podía y debía integrarse en el Nuevo Estado, aunque fuera, eso sí, con los ajustes necesarios' (childhood became a sector that could be and had to be integrated into the New State, although, this is for sure, with the necessary adjustments) (Cenarro Lagunas 2006: 150). The Francoist state reformed the docile bodies of Republican children through abuse (Cenarro Lagunas 2006).

However, within the *cines con niño* the child dummy often undermines his or her ventriloquist. Carnivalesque ventriloquism, therefore, describes a reversal of power in which the dummy talks back to the ventriloquist. I borrow 'carnivalesque' from Bakhtin's discussion of François Rabelais's works to express a permissible and temporary inversion of roles (1984). Carnival and the novel, for Bakhtin, are a 'means for displaying otherness' (Holquist 2002: 86). The child of the *cines con niño* embodies Francoism's others and it is through carnivalesque resistance that they assert their voices and express counter-hegemonic discourse. Finally, prosopopoeial ventriloquism, which draws upon theorisations by Karen Lury (2010) and Jacques Derrida, consists of the child dummy's ability to give voice to a marginalised third party, most often relating to those silenced and reduced to bare life by Francoist repression. The appropriation at the heart of ventriloquism takes the more abstract form of the adoption of characteristics of the *cine con niño* in the *nuevo cine con niño*. *The Two* cines argues that the *nuevo cine con niño* enacts a political appropriation and re-accentuation of the *cine con niño*.

Chapter Summaries

Chapters One to Six of *The Two* cines analyse the child protagonist, the *cine con niño*, and their appropriations. Chapter One revisits Manuel Gutiérrez Aragón's 1982 film, *Demonios en el jardín*, and revises Marsha Kinder's taxonomy of the New Spanish Cinema in light of more recent headlines of the stolen children of Francoism to offer a historical overview of the regime's use of children and to contend that the feature's situation in the 1940s and 1950s and release in the early 1980s encompasses the ideological politics of the initial stage of child appropriations and the monetary development of its later stages. In Chapter Two I examine appropriative and carnivalesque ventriloquism within economic and sexual scenarios.

This chapter investigates the dialogism of the commercial exploitation of Joselito's 'golden voice' in the *cine con niño*'s child musical film *The Little Nightingale* (Del Amo 1956) and the sexual exploitation of the child singer in the *nuevo cine con niño*'s *Bad Education* (Almodóvar 2004). Chapter Three further elaborates ventriloquism as, first, an expression of Francoist anxiety of subaltern rebellion by children and colonial subjects and, second, as a tool for the transmission of traditional gender roles. Marisol's third film, *Tómbola* (Lucía 1962), is a retelling of Aesop's 'The Boy Who Cried Wolf' with a sinister subtext that reveals the ideological function of the *cine con niño*, Francoism's political use of children and incorporation of child stars and the infantilisation of its African (Equatorial Guinea) territories. Chapter Four conducts a case study of the debut films of Marisol in *Un rayo de luz* (Lucía 1960) and Clara Lago in *El viaje de Carol* (Uribe 2002) to demonstrate the appropriation of the *cine con niño* in the cultural production of constitutional Spain. Although these features share a literary intertext, each film offers exceptional insight into the utilisation of the child protagonist during the twentieth and twenty-first centuries for differing genre functions and opposing ideals of family, nation, class and gender. Chapter Five, by contrast to previous chapters, considers the enabling properties of prosopopoeial ventriloquism that are apparent in the *cines con niño*'s films in the Gothic mode: *Marcelino pan y vino*, *El espíritu de la colmena* (Erice 1973), *Urte ilunak* (Lazkano 1992), *Secretos del corazón* (Armendáriz 1997), *El espinazo del diablo* (Del Toro 2001) and *El orfanato* (Bayona 2007).

The shift from Chapter Five to Chapter Six is one from micro to macro: character to genre. Chapter Six focuses entirely on the ritual function of the *nuevo cine con niño*. I further trace the forty-year time span of the *nuevo cine con niño* from the transition to democracy (1973–) through the memory boom (1990s–today). I examine dialogism and the ritual function in a selection of three intricately linked films: *El espíritu de la colmena* (Erice 1973) from the early transition to democracy, *Secretos del corazón* (Armendáriz 1997) released during José María Aznar's conservative administration (1996–2004), and *El laberinto del fauno* (Del Toro 2006) corresponding to José Luis Zapatero's socialist government (2004–11). I am able to reveal the *nuevo cine con niño* as a genre-in-the-making with the imaginative alternatives to Francoism and its *cine con niño* that their respective historical contexts allow. Chapter Seven reveals how heteroglossia in Basque and Catalan-language *nuevo cine con niño* films *Urte ilunak* (*The Dark Years*) (Lazkano 1992) and *Pa negre* (Villaronga 2010) challenges the norms and normativity of both Francoism and the *cines con niño*. The figure of the ghostly gay child (Stockton 2009), the haunting of a child's non-normative sexuality, in *Pa negre* is key to understanding how the first Catalan-language feature to win a Best Film Goya is the exception that queers the representational rules of cinema's retrospection on post-war childhood.

Chapter Eight investigates transatlantic dialogism with recent Latin American cinema, focusing on the coming-of-age and the political mobilisation of the child protagonist. This chapter extends the comparative impetus of the genre study from the interactions of genre and nation in Spain to those of the child-starred genre and two Latin American nations under military dictatorship (Chile, Argentina) to reveal the aesthetics and dualistic narrative strategies of the political symbolism of the child protagonist's coming-of-age during conflict. Chapter Eight further demonstrates the efficacy of approaching the child-starred cinemas through genre convention and dialogism. In this case, however, the analysis of Latin American films considers genrification within broader Spanish-language film, beyond national cinematic contexts, and transatlantic dialogism. The dualism of the two Spains appears in other national contexts (two Chiles, two Argentinas) as not only an indication of conflict but also as a defining characteristic of child-starred genre film.

The Two cines con niño concludes with a close reading of the spoof film *Spanish Movie* (Ruiz Caldera 2009) in which I provide a synthesis of the ventriloquism, dialogism, and biopolitics of Francoism as depicted in the *cines con niño*. *Spanish Movie* (Ruiz Caldera 2009) is, like its character named 'Ambrosio', an irreverent and entertaining salad of intertextual references and stock characters for Spanish cinema freaks. Ruiz Caldera's film illustrates many of the elements that form the new child-starred cinema, including Joselito's appearance that distracts from the disappearance of the co-protagonist's son. The conclusion examines how *Spanish Movie* speaks to national cinema, the relationship between genre and nation, the intertextuality of genre cinema, and its function. *Spanish Movie* calls attention to the repetitiveness of genre films and national cinema for comedic effect while new child-starred cinema features like *El laberinto del fauno* regenrify Spanish child-starred cinema's political conventions by routinely reversing them. In fact, this chapter explores *Spanish Movie*'s grotesque Gothic child. I argue throughout this book that genre is a process in which the new *cine con niño* participates by reinterpreting Francoist customs, thereby regenrifying the *cine con niño* for the other of the two Spains. *The Two* cines examines how each Spain or each national faction speaks through the child protagonist.

Notes

1. All translations in the Introduction are mine.
2. The *cine con niño* is the first child-starred genre formation though it is not comprised of the first child-starred films in Spain. Early Spanish cinema had its own Mary Pickford, Alexia Ventura, and Jackie Coogan, Alfredo Hurtado 'Pitusín' (Wright 2013: 4). The Second Republic also had its ensemble cast of activist child characters in a propaganda film, *Nosotros somos así* (Valentín R. González 1936), who intervene as the moral arbiters of one child's father involved in a labor dispute. They hold political meetings to fight for bread with chocolate to assuage their hunger and for more recess and less study. One girl even embodies 'La pasionaria' Dolores Ibárruri, leader of the Communist Party. See Wright (2013: 4–11) for child stars before the *cine con niño*.
3. They identify the following genres in contemporary Spanish cinema: comedies (popular, subgeneric, *comedia madrileña*, post-modern comedy, international copro, generational rebellion, *esperpento* tradition, *La España eterna*), the thriller (*cine negro*, literary adaptations, crime/action, retro/period, youth culture with delinquency and drugs, psychological, erotic/sexual), the musical, and the fantasy/science-fiction/horror/adventure film (Jordan and Morgan-Tamosunas 1998).
4. 'El gran ciclo comercial de los años 50 y primeros 60 fue el llamado "cine con niño", en función del protagonismo asumido por más o menos repelentes niñitos, progresivamente dados al canto. Su origen se remontaría a ciertas derivaciones neorrealistas, atribuibles a modelos como *Sciuscià*, *Ladri di biciclette*, *Proibito rubare*, etc. y perceptibles en películas como *Día tras día* (1951) o *Segundo López, aventurero urbano* (1952); de su cruce con otros ciclos como el religioso y el musical folclórico, saldrían títulos de tanta resonancia como *Marcelino, pan y vino* (1954) de Vajda o *El pequeño ruiseñor* (1956) de Antonio del Amo, respectivamente. Tras las huellas de Pablito Calvo y Joselito, sus correspondientes "niños prodigio", surgirían otros muchos emuladores que no lograrían superar a sus modelos y que explotarían el filón hasta el agotamiento, momento en que una serie de niñas no menos repelentes les sucedieron, con Marisol y Rocío Dúrcal a la cabeza' (The great commercial series of the 1950s and early 1960s was the so-called 'cine con niño', in relation to its main characters played by more or less repellant little children, progressively inclined to sing. Its origin would harken back to certain neorealist derivations, attributable to models like *Sciuscià*, *Ladri di biciclette*, *Proibito rubare*, etc. and perceivable in films like *Día tras día* (1951) or *Segundo López, aventurero urbano* (1952); and its crossing with other series like the religious and folkloric musical, renowned titles like *Marcelino, pan y vino* (1954) by Vajda or *El pequeño ruiseñor* (1956) by Antonio del Amo, respectively. Following in the footsteps of Pablito Calvo and Joselito, their corresponding 'child prodigies', would come many other imitators and they would not be able to overtake their models and they would thoroughly exploit the trend, reaching the moment in which a series of girls

no less repellent would follow, with Marisol and Rocío Dúrcal in the lead) (Gubern et al. 1995: 275).

5. See Casanova (2016) for historical studies recommendations: 'Beyond the testimony literature of those people who endured Franco's violence, future generations will know history mainly through conventional history books and whatever documents, photographic and audiovisual material we are able to preserve and bequeath to them. This will involve the preservation of archives and state support for historical scholarship, as well as a civic environment which protects and promotes the free exchange of information and open debate. These are the requirements for excavating and recording the history of those parts of the recent past which are still to be opened up. Remembrance and opinion; commemoration and heritage; these are something else' (Casanova 2016: 219).

The Black Market and the Stolen Children of Franco in *Demonios en el jardín*

'Cuando en el 2002 estrenamos *Los niños perdidos del franquismo*, la sociedad española se estremeció al ver que el robo de niños en el contexto de la dictadura argentina y que habíamos llorado cómodamente sentados en el sofá de nuestras casas también se había producido en España.' (Armengou 2011: 123)

[When we premiered *Franco's Forgotten Children* in 2002, Spanish society shuddered when it saw that the stolen children of Argentina's dictatorship for whom it had cried from the comfort of its home sofas had also occurred in Spain.][1]

Introduction

Chapter One conducts a close reading of *Demonios en el jardín* (*Demons in the Garden*) (Gutiérrez Aragón 1982) and, to a lesser degree, incorporates the documentaries *Los niños de Rusia* (*The Children of Russia*) (Camino 2001) and *Els nens perduts del franquisme* (*Franco's Forgotten Children*) (Armengou, Belis and Vinyes 2002), in order to illuminate the historical context of the stolen children of Franco and set the stage for the broader biopolitics of Francoism. *Demonios en el jardín* depicts the two Spains through a family split between the victorious, his conservative grandmother, and the vanquished, his single mother. The black marketeer grandmother's quashed efforts to reunite the family offer an alternative to Francoism by rejecting its genre strategy of promoting unity.

Marsha Kinder's 1983 essay, 'The Children of Franco in the New Spanish Cinema', identifies a trend in films from 1973 to 1980 by directors – José Luis Borau (1929–2012), Víctor Erice (1940–), Carlos Saura (1932–), Jaime de Armiñán (1927–), Jaime Chávarri (1943–), and Manuel Gutiérrez Aragón (1940–) – who were children during Francisco Franco's regime (1939–75) and whose features depict sensitive, precocious, and even murderous children and stunted, childlike adults. Including Gutiérrez Aragón's *La camada negra* (*Black Litter*) (1977), Kinder draws a parallel between the filmmakers of the New Spanish Cinema and their cinematic progeny:

> They were led to see themselves as emotionally and politically stunted children who were no longer young; who, because of the imposed role as 'silent witness' to a tragic war that had divided country, family and self, had never been innocent, and who, because of the oppressive domination of the previous generation, were obsessed with the past and might never be ready to take responsibility for changing the future. (1983: 57–8)

By contrast to *Black Litter*, a biting satire of a home-grown right-wing terrorist clan, *Demonios en el jardín* depicts the politically rooted power split in a family whose conservative side owns a grocery store in 1940s and 1950s Torre del Valle (Zamora). At the center of the conflict is the sickly seven-year-old boy Juanito (Álvaro Sánchez Prieto), whose manipulative traits do not correspond with Kinder's observations of the silent, murderous, or helpless and victimised child. The current chapter revisits Gutiérrez Aragón's 1982 film and Kinder's taxonomy of the New Spanish Cinema in light of recent headlines of the stolen children of Francoism to propose that the child protagonist of *Demonios en el jardín* symbolises a stolen child of Franco.

Although *Demonios en el jardín*'s depiction of an infirm boy whose grandmother owns a food store may make it one of Gutiérrez Aragón's more autobiographical films (Heredero 1998: 81, 83; Deveny 1999: 131), this study does not take a biographical approach to the feature but rather a socio-historic analysis that considers the symbolism of the custody battle over Juanito in context. *Demonios en el jardín* is a family saga surrounding Juanito's care. Juanito is the son of Ángela (Ángela Molina), Doña Gloria's (Encarna Paso) niece charge and the orphan of a Republican father. The boy's grandmother, Doña Gloria, conducts business with black-market foodstuffs at her shop called El Jardín. His father Juan (Imanol Arias) is Doña Gloria's younger son, a Falangist, and title demon. Rather than assume paternal responsibility for his son, Juan leaves for Madrid to serve Franco as a waiter while Ángela raises Juanito in her father's remote country house. Juanito does not have a relationship with his grandmother until he becomes ill, which prompts Doña Gloria's intervention and catalyses the battle between his Francoist grandmother and 'rojilla' (red) single mother over the physical and moral well-being of the boy.

Scholarship on *Demonios en el jardín* has focused on paternal and fraternal figures in the film or on the family as national allegory rather than centred on the child and his tutelage. Edmond Cros perceptively compares *Demonios en el jardín* and *La historia oficial* (*The Official Story*) (Luis Puenzo 1985) but does not examine the ties between the stolen children of Argentina's so-called Dirty War and Franco's dictatorship. Cros evaluates the severity of political repression and familial separation in each feature:

> également, dans les deux films, le destin d'un enfant arraché dans des conditions sans doute différentes à sa famille (*Historia oficial*) ou à sa mère (*Demonios en el jardín*) mais où se trouvent impliquées cependant diverses modalités de la répression politique, plus brutales dans le cas du film argentin, plus sournoises dans celui du texte espagnol. (Cros 1994: 331)

> [Similarly in both films, the destiny of the child snatched from her family (*Historia oficial*) or his mother (*Demonios en el jardín*) occurs under different conditions no doubt but diverse modalities of political repression are implied in both cases, more brutal in the Argentine film, more sly in the Spanish text.]

The critical lacuna regarding child appropriation in *Demonios en el jardín* has a historical explanation. Studies of *Demonios en el jardín* (Hopewell 1986; Cros 1994; Willem 1996; Deveny 1999) were published during the second half of the 1980s and the second half of the 1990s but the system of stolen children was not exposed until 2002, excepting a singular *Interviú* article from 1981, with *Franco's Forgotten Children*.

This documentary introduced the history to the Spanish public, as Montse Armengou informs in the current chapter's epigraph, while also informing Hispanists and jurists. Ricard Vinyes's work formed the basis of Baltasar Garzón's report *Sumario 53 /2008 E* on human rights abuses during the dictatorship. *Franco's Forgotten Children* has also had an impact in literature, inspiring Benjamín Prado's 2006 novel *Mala gente que camina* (Souto 2013: 225). A 2013 Telecinco mini-series *Niños robados* (*Stolen Children*) with Blanca Portillo as Sister María Gómez Valbuena serves as further evidence of the increasing diffusion and visibility of Spain's history of stolen children. Similar to the Madres y Abuelas de la Plaza de Mayo (Mothers and Grandmothers of the Plaza de Mayo) in Argentina, organisations like SOS Bebés robados (SOS Stolen Children) and founders Mar Soriano of Plataforma afectados clínicas de toda España causa niños robados (Platform for Those Affected by the Stolen Children Cases in all of Spain) and Antonio Barroso of Asociación nacional de afectados por adopciones irregulares (National Association for Those Affected by Irregular Adoptions) support stolen children in Spain, like themselves, and their families. Similar to the child trafficking that extended through Europe and reached America (Soriano 2011; Torrús 2017), work in opposition on behalf of the victims crosses borders.

A few significant firsts took place, built on the activism of these Spanish groups and that of the Argentine Mothers and Grandmothers, in 2016 and 2017. In November 2016, the government of Canarias approved the first law specific to the cases of stolen children that followed the same measures as those utilised by the Argentine Mothers and Grandmothers and established a special commission and police unit for these cases (Anonymous 2016: n.p.). The local government of Gran Canaria has been the first to apologise for its role in the stolen children affair (ibid.). In December 2016, Madrid's courts ruled that there is no statute of limitations on stolen children (Carrera 2016: n.p.). This determination is particularly significant because the greatest number of reports of abductions, almost three times the figures from Barcelona and Cádiz in 2011, were filed in Madrid (Anonymous 2011: n.p.). It also allows for the first case, against Dr Eduardo Vela, to be heard, beginning in January 2017 (Pozas 2017: n.p.). While the injustices of child appropriations during Argentina's Dirty War were well known for decades in Spain, Armengou highlights in her historical work and in this chapter's epigraph that similar cases in Spain are only more recently coming to light and undergoing adjudication in Spain.

Situating *Demonios en el jardín* within broader Spanish film history (1955–) allows variations on a pervasive appropriation narrative to emerge: from adoption in *Marcelino pan y vino* (*The Miracle of Marcelino*) (Vajda 1955), to kidnapping, ventriloquism and vocal exploitation in Marisol's (Pepa Flores) and Joselito's (José Jiménez Fernández) *cine con niño*, to the more recent documentaries of child exiles turned political pawns of two governments in *Los niños de Rusia*, stolen children in *Franco's Forgotten Children* and finally to resolutions of the historical fiction films *El laberinto del fauno* (*Pan's Labyrinth*) (Del Toro 2006) and *Pa negre* (*Black Bread*) (Villaronga 2010), to name a few. Nevertheless, of these titles, the symbolic treatment of the custody battle for Juanito in *Demonios en el jardín* most closely resembles, on the micro-scale, one mechanism of appropriation studied by Montse Armengou, Ricard Belis and Ricard Vinyes and reported by Natalia Junquera, Jesús Duva and María José Esteso Poves. The analysis that follows will contextualise the appropriation of Juanito by Doña Gloria within a biopolitical theoretical framework including the practice of child appropriations from the 1940s through the 1980s.

The Biopolitics of the Stolen Children of Franco

Franco's regime stripped children, in particular those of Republicans, of their rights and reduced them to bare life as a first step to ensure its reproduction and continuity. The separation from their families during the

Civil War and the criminalisation of Republicanism facilitated children's disfranchisement in the ensuing dictatorship. During the war, in 1937, the Republic safeguarded children domestically by establishing 170 colonies, in Levante, Aragón, Cuenca, Albacete, and Catalonia, that housed 16,953 children (Alted Vigil 1996: 213). Beyond Spain's borders, during the same year, tens of thousands of child exiles reached host families in Great Britain, France, Belgium, Denmark, Holland, and Switzerland (Alted Vigil 1996: 215). The USSR received an expedition of 3,000 Basque children that was second in numbers only to that of the 4,000 Basque children who travelled to Great Britain (Alted Vigil 1996: 215–16). Another near 500 refugees found accommodation in specialised boarding schools in Morelia, Mexico (ibid.). Repatriation of exiled youth and appropriation of those children who remained in Spain would be high priorities for the consolidation of Franco's power during the immediate post-war.

Following the war, the New Spain subjected children to, per Giorgio Agamben's definition of biopolitics, 'the growing inclusion of man's natural life in the mechanisms and calculations of power' (1998: 119). Child appropriations offer the clearest example of the inclusion of the child's natural life in the calculations of Franco's power. According to Vinyes and Garzón, as many as 30,000 children were stolen during the dictatorship (Duva and Junquera 2011: 12). Appropriations developed in two to three stages. During the initial stage, ideology drove the appropriations in which the state exercised tutelage over children born to incarcerated Republican mothers and the repatriated child exiles in accordance with Francoism rather than with the politics of their parents. Doctor Antonio Vallejo Nágera's (1889–1960) racial eugenics informed the imprisonment, conceived as a quarantine to obstruct the spread of 'cancerous' leftist ideas, of Republican militants and their families. The doctor advocated for the 'regeneración de la raza' (racial regeneration) by means of sanitising the environment: 'el mejoramiento de la raza está supeditado al saneamiento del medio ambiente' (the improvement of the race was dependent on the healing of the environment) (Vallejo Nágera 1938: 14). The extrication of children from their Republican mothers aimed presumably at re-locating the young to an environment that the regime deemed healthier.

More than 1,000 children were under state custody during the immediate post-war; by 1943, 1,042 minors were under the supervision of religious schools and public institutions (Armengou et al. 2002: 59). The Ministerio de la Justicia, by 30 March 1940 law in effect through 1944, took charge of the 'destacamento hospicio' (orphanage detachment), or forced deportation and separation of children at the age of three from their prisoner mothers (Armengou et al. 2002: 56–7). The deported children were one population that inhabited the brutal Auxilio Social state orphanage system, which Vinyes refers to as 'campos de concentración de niños' (concentration camps for children) in his documentary. Another fate befell children of Republican mothers during the first post-war stage of appropriations whereby they were given to married couples judged more appropriate for their upbringing (65). The Ministerio de la Gobernación's decree from November 1940 outlined the characteristics of suitable parents: "'personas irreprochables desde el triple punto de vista religioso, ético y nacional'" (people who are irreproachable from the religious, ethic, and national points of view) (63). Some children were adopted expressly to work as servants in Francoist families (Cenarro Lagunas 2006: 156). These irregular adoptions transferred custody from political opponents to (and by) supporters of the regime without the consent of the biological parents.

Franco addressed the child exiles through newsreel and then abducted them by virtue of repatriation and renaming. In 1937, during the youth exodus, Franco spoke to the children of the world, and indirectly to the exiles, through the 'Franco en Salamanca II' newsreel. His twelve-year-old daughter Carmencita, shown seated beside Franco on her mother's lap, prays for the well-being of children around the world and particularly for those in the hands of the enemies of her fatherland (Figure 1.1). The

Figure 1.1 Dictator Francisco Franco as ventriloquist with daughter-dummy Carmencita Franco Polo on her mother Carmen Polo's lap. © De Filmoteca Española.

performance entails Franco asking his daughter to address the children of the world. It begins when Franco, with feigned nonchalance, turns to his daughter and prompts her to speak: 'Oye nena, ¿quieres decirles algo a los niños del mundo?' (Hey sweetheart, do you want to tell the children of the world something?). Carmencita, poorly simulating spontaneity, enquires: 'Bueno, no, pero ¿qué les digo?' (Well, no, but what should I say?). The dictator gives his daughter carte blanche in her address of the children of the world: '¡Lo que quieras!' (Whatever you want!) If Franco is taken at his word, he grants Carmencita freedom of speech. However, poor acting skills on the part of father and daughter reveal a contradiction. Franco apparently scripts Carmencita's speech, which supplicates by virtue of rehearsed dialogue:

> Pido a Dios que todos los niños del mundo no conozcan los sufrimientos y las tristezas que tienen los niños que aún están en poder de los enemigos de mi patria, a los que yo envío un beso fraternal. Y . . . ¡Viva España! (1996: 450)

> [I pray to God that all the children of the world do not experience suffering and sadness as do children still under the power of my fatherland's enemies, to whom I send a fraternal kiss. And . . . Long live Spain!]

Carmencita's words are laden with her father's rhetoric while Franco mouths the words that Carmencita speaks. The Francoist ideological genre function (Altman 1999), upon which I touched in the Introduction, reinforced obedience and unity, two concepts that the post-Franco film *Demonios en el jardín* will directly challenge. As we will see, Gutiérrez Aragón's 1982 film, a year that some scholars date as the end of the transition to democracy with the election of the Socialist party, represents the interests of constitutional Spain.

Ventriloquism is the art of illusion, redirection and, most importantly, speaking for and through an often child-like other. As 'Franco en Salamanca II' so masterfully demonstrates, Francoist ventriloquism consists of the imposition of state discourse on the child's body, thereby neutralising the potential insubordination and making it appear as if the child acts independently. Thus, an authority figure camouflages the reproduction of state ideology and power structures by commandeering and usurping the body of another. The transgression of another's body and seizure of his or her voice signifies denial of the other's subjectivity. In theoretical terms, the ventriloquist's manipulative and parasitic relationship with the dummy converts his charge into a docile body. Michel Foucault's definition of the docile body highlights the objectification of the body as an item of utility: 'A body is docile that may be subjected, used, transformed and improved' (1979: 136). As it pertains to the analysis at hand, a docile body is one prepared for and engaged in ventriloquism.

Remarkably, in this recording Francisco Franco reveals himself to be the author of Carmencita's rehearsed words as he mouths the speech she delivers. Echoes in the newsreel of ventriloquism, which dramatises the symbolic appropriation of a child's voice and body, exemplify and foreshadow the appropriations that his regime would commence just a couple of years later. According to ventriloquism scholar Steven Connor: 'Ventriloquism is one of the most pervasive metaphors by which issues of identity, ownership and power have been articulated within a culture of performance' (2001: 75). The biopolitics of Francoism are clearly expressed through the performance art of ventriloquism, whose tension resides in the power struggle between the ventriloquist and his resistant dummy. We will call the Francoist and thus domineering and disabling variant seen in 'Franco en Salamanca II': appropriative ventriloquism. Its converse, to be seen in *Demonios en el jardín*, we will refer to as: carnivalesque ventriloquism. This dynamic involves the obstinate dummy talking back to his ventriloquist in opposition to appropriation.

As early as 1937, official internal communications of Franco's Burgos government, convinced that children were exported to serve as propaganda for the Republic, began designing a plan to bring the exiles back (Armengou et al. 2002: 71). An article from *Fotos* on 29 July 1939 celebrates and credits the effort: 'Los niños que los rojos arrancaron de sus casas después de pasar privaciones y hambre en tierra extranjera, Auxilio Social los devuelve a sus hogares' (The children whom the reds yanked from their homes after suffering privations and hunger in a foreign land, Auxilio Social returns them to their homes) (Otero 2004: 129). Other histories tell of greater obstacles. The Delegación extraordinaria de repatriación de menores (Extraordinary Delegation for the Repatriation of Minors), as of 1942, worked to repatriate these children but a year later the government found that neither biological nor host parents would consent to the operation (Armengou et al. 2002: 73–4). Similarly, the governments of Mexico and the USSR refused to recognise Franco's regime and therefore denied repatriation. Very few child exiles left those countries; 34 of 3,291 returned in 1956 after Joseph Stalin's death and only 61 of 430 departed from Mexico (Alted Vigil 1996: 219). A special directive attended to the children who returned successfully. The 4 December 1941 law allowed for name changes, rendering returning children untraceable for their remaining families (Armengou et al. 2002: 63). In other cases, children were used as bait to capture their political opponent parents (Cenarro Lagunas 2006: 152).

The situation of *Demonios en el jardín*, a film set in the 1940s and

1950s and released in the early 1980s, encompasses the ideological politics of the initial stage of the appropriations and the monetary development of the later stages. Child appropriations, active through the late 1980s, transformed into a business of newborn trafficking for sale to adoptive parents. From the 1950s to the 1980s, the setting of the thefts changed from the prisons (stage one) to the clinics and then the hospitals (stages two and three of the appropriations). The machinery in place – with the same intermediaries of the state, church, and doctors – became a profitable business in which children were taken from their single mothers at the hospital and sold, for from 50,000 to a million pesetas (Duva and Junquera 2011: 22), to Francoist families. Although Juanito's appropriation remains within the family, *Demonios en el jardín* shares key characters and strategies with this history of the coercion of single mothers and their stolen children.

Contextualised within the economics of the extra-diegetic and diegetic black markets, Juanito's appropriation in *Demonios en el jardín* reveals that the victims of speculation – disadvantaged consumers of *estraperlo* and families robbed of their children – originated from the same socio-economic and political sector. José Martí Gómez's social history of early Francoism, *La España del estraperlo, 1936–1952*, relates the prevalence of the black market, tracing it back to the first year of the Civil War, and the government's practice of looking the other way:

> El gobierno, consciente de que existe un mercado clandestino, hace pública una declaración formal del estilo de las que viene repitiendo desde 1939 de forma incansable sin que al aparecer sirvan para nada: 'El gobierno va a mostrarse implacable con la odiosa y repugnante figura del especulador sin conciencia.' Aparece por primera vez, reconocida oficialmente, la palabra de moda desde 1936: estraperlo. (1995: 174)

> [The government, aware of the existence of a clandestine market, makes public a formal declaration in the style of those that it has been tirelessly repeating to no avail since 1939: 'The government will demonstrate its mercilessness with the odious and repugnant figure of the speculator without a conscious.' The word that had been popular since 1936 – blackmarketeering – it recognised officially for the first time.]

However, historians Manuel González Portilla and José Urrutikoetxea Lizarraga further show that the regime was not only aware but also complicit with the black market, thus Francoism's inflammatory language quoted above also describes its own actions. González Portilla and Urrutikoetzea Lizarraga document that the regime's economic policies ran in parallel to the black market – equating the high prices of the official and unofficial markets from 1950 to 1952 – and famished and impoverished the vanquished. These historians describe the period as: 'años de una "venganza social" aceptada y alentada a nivel político, que las fuerzas socio-económicas e ideológicas vencedoras en el conflicto civil ejercen contra los asalariados y las clases populares' (years of an accepted and politically promoted 'social retribution' that defeating socio-economic and ideological forces from the civil conflict exerted against low-wage workers and the popular classes) (González Portillo and Urrutikoetxea Lizarraga 2012: 242). Economic policies also sought to persecute the defeated in many ways. The regime worked to disintegrate the families of the vanquished by stealing their children, in order to invest in Francoism's future by indoctrinating the young, and impoverishing the defeated. Black-market foodstuffs reached their highest prices in 1942 and more than half of agricultural production (bread, oil, rice, sugar, beans, lentils, garbanzos and potatoes) was sold as *estraperlo* (ibid.: 245, 244, 238). Doña Gloria sells these staples in El Jardín where Juanito is on display surrounded by these black-market goods as he too figures into the clandestine market and the mechanisms of Franco's power.

El estraperlo de los niños: Juanito in *Demonios en el jardín*

The cast of characters and their setting provide the basis for my symbolic reading of Juanito as a stolen child Franco and, more specifically, as *estraperlo*. I will conduct close readings of sequences that correspond to three stages (initiation, appropriation, and consolidation) of Juanito's shifting custody. The participants, location, and circumstances of the inception of Doña Gloria's appropriation of Juanito display the hallmarks of the stolen children of Francoism. An illness, pulmonary in Juanito's fictional case rather than a supposed lethal otitis in the historical cases, precipitates Doña Gloria's intervention. Characters conspire to take over custody of Juanito, indulge him at El Jardín, facilitate his introduction to his father and Franco, and finally attempt to consolidate the family through Ángela's and Juan's sham marriage.

Initiation of the plot takes place outside church after mass where Doña Gloria receives recommendations from a doctor regarding Juanito's care. The scene assembles the trinity of Spanish child appropriators: religious (the church), medical (doctor), and economic (black marketeer). The doctor (Eduardo MacGregor) advises: 'No creo que el niño tenga nada malo pero es un niño delicado, se cría mal, descalzo, cogiendo frío. Creo que es conveniente que lo vea un especialista' (I do not think that there is anything wrong with the child but he is delicate, poorly raised, barefoot and catching cold. I think that it would be convenient for a specialist to see him). He negatively evaluates Ángela's care of her son and insinuates that Doña Gloria's wealth puts her in a better position to attend to Juanito. Recalling the criteria for appropriators – *religioso, ético, nacional* – and the three pillars of Francoism – God, fatherland, family – Doña Gloria proves an ideal custodian for Juanito. The matriarch remarks to her daughter-in-law Ana (Ana Belén), who has an affair with Juan and does not have children with her husband: 'Dios me va a castigar por no ocuparme de ese niño' (God will punish me for not taking responsibility for that child). Reportedly, Doña Gloria's relationship to the church motivates her involvement with Juanito. Nevertheless, her charitable impulse does not go further than her grandson, since we see her ignore the gypsy children who sing and beg around her during these conversations. Access to resources becomes the crux of the black marketeer's argument; she is announced as 'la reina del estraperlo' (queen of the black market) upon her arrival at Ángela's house, in the following sequence.

At Ángela's house, Doña Gloria persuades her niece to allow her to care for the ailing child by means of reason and, what will become, an exchange of goods. Doña Gloria hands over the food and clothes that she has brought Ángela as she argues her case about the wardrobe and education at her disposal for Juanito: 'Nosotros llevaríamos a Juanito a un buen colegio y recibiría la educación que le corresponde. Bien calzado, vestido. Es un niño delicado como su padre' (We would take Juanito to a good school and he would receive the education to which he is entitled. He would be well dressed. He is a delicate boy like his father). She further reveals her interest as matriarch and implies how poorly suited Ángela is to be Juanito's mother as she rummages through Ángela's dusty furniture and Juanito's notebook:

> Mi nuera Ana no puede tener hijos. Dios da niños a quien no los necesita y a otros se los niega. Tienes la casa muy limpia. Mire, lo que más admiro en la mujer es la limpieza. Y educas muy bien al niño. No pienses que queremos quitarte a tu hijo. Sólo queremos lo mejor para él y para ti que eres tan buena.

> [My daughter-in-law Ana cannot have children. God gives children to those who do not need them and refuses them to others. You have a very clean house. Look, what I most admire about a woman is cleanliness. And you are educating the boy well. Don't think that we want to take your son away from you. We just want what is best for him and for you, who are so good.]

As Doña Gloria paces through Ángela's kitchen, her dialogue similarly pivots from indirectness alluding to lack of 'legitimate' grandchildren, to a critique of Ángela's housekeeping, to praise for Ángela's education of

Juanito, and finally to a statement of disinterest and goodwill. Gutiérrez Aragón signals Doña Gloria's power over Ángela through Encarna Paso's standing posture that towers over the seated Ángela simmering with rage while she skins fish and peels potatoes. The two mothers only appear on the same level, both seated when Doña Gloria compliments Ángela's lessons to Juanito and both upright when Ángela literally and metaphorically stands up to Doña Gloria as the matriarch unconvincingly states that no one wants to take Juanito away from her.

Doña Gloria's words ('delicate') recall those of the doctor but claim her maternity ('mi hijo Juan' (my son Juan)) and draw upon Francoism's ideologues. Her allusion to cleanliness is charged with the rhetoric of Doctor Vallejo-Nágera and the values of the Sección Femenina de la Falange (Women's Section of the Phalange). Doña Gloria's sarcastic comment makes reference to Francoism's politics, as does an earlier quip regarding the imprisoned fathers of children in town: 'algo habrán hecho' (they must have done something). According to Emilio Silva, President of the Asociación para la Recuperación de la Memoria Histórica: 'el uso del término "limpieza" explicita cuál era uno de los principales objetivos de los golpistas' (the use of the term 'cleanliness' explains one of the principle objectives of the orchestrators of the coup) (Silva in Esteso Poves 2012: 17). Silva continues: 'Robar la identidad, secuestrar a niños y niñas para salvarlos, para que crezcan "limpios del marxismo", da medida de la ilimitada actividad criminal de la dictadura militar del general Franco' (Stealing identities, kidnapping boys and girls to save them, so that they can grow up 'free from Marxism', gives carte blanche for the criminal activity of General Franco's military dictatorship) (19). Doña Gloria wishes to purify Juanito of his mother's noxious influences. Her persuasion is coupled with the threat of blackmail in the following sequence by the local henchman Osorio (Rafael Díaz), who is interested in currying favour with Doña Gloria and warns Ángela, calling her 'rojilla', that someone could tip off the authorities to the storage of black-market goods at her place. Although the contraband comes from El Jardín and is not Ángela's, it could serve to land her in jail and achieve her separation from Juanito. Ángela capitulates.

During Juanito's appropriation at El Jardín, the boy can be found on display among the black-market goods. The symbolic interaction between character, Juanito, and setting, El Jardín, here carries greater weight with regards to my thesis of Juanito as *estraperlo*. The boy is better dressed and fed at the store while Doña Gloria also educates him in terms of the local politics of vanquished and victorious, indicating from behind the cash register which clients align with each camp. His uncle (Eusebio Lázaro) gives

Figure 1.2 Juanito (Álvaro Sánchez Prieto) on display at El Jardín in
Demonios en el jardín.

him a gastronomical tour of Spain. These images associate the boy with
monetary instruments and culinary merchandise. During the daytime,
Juanito rests on a mattress in the store surrounded by doting adults and
gourmet goods (Figure 1.2). The boy appears as if showcased in front of
the shelves of other products. On market day, the mattress upon which
Juanito lounges is carried out in the front of the store amidst the peddlers
and their goods. He also seems implicated in something untoward since
his bed hides the alcohol that a young store employee drinks on the sly.
The film thereby establishes a parallel between the open-air market, the
black market, and Juanito.

Juanito's biggest excursion, beyond the storefront and the local cinema's projection booth, entails his meeting both Franco and his father on
the dictator's visit to the reservoir nearby. The dictator's motorcade that
passes through town is as disappointing as the Americans' in *Bienvenido
Mister Marshall* (Berlanga 1953) and the long-awaited paternal encounter
that follows in Gutiérrez Aragón's film (Deveny 1999: 133). Hopewell
and Deveny have noted this sequence with regards to the disillusion-
ment with or demystification of the father figure (1986: 93; 1999: 133). I,
rather, wish to examine power and the place of the child in the sequence.
First, Juanito's descent into the reservoir crosses direction with a veritable
parade of *nacionales* (Phalangists, Moroccan soldiers, priest with Bible
in hand, Civil Guard) emerging from Franco's tent. A Phalangist wrests
Juanito away from his mother as she is searched. Neither the child nor

the Republican mother has a right to the privacy of their bodies. The handheld camera movement here adds trepidation and differs from the steady camera in the greater part of the feature, whose lighting renders meta-cinematic homage to the films of Juanito's and Manuel Gutiérrez Aragón's youths.

Juanito, aware of the doctor's carte blanche with regards to his family's indulging his every whim, manipulates and is manipulated. The former casts Juanito in the carnivalesque variant of ventriloquism in which the dummy is contrary and in charge. In fact, he repeatedly fakes asthma attacks in order to get his way. During the reservoir sequence, the dynamics of ventriloquism reappear. The blocking of Juanito, Juan, and Ángela indicates a power differential here as it did in Ángela's kitchen and the 'Franco en Salamanca II' recording. The echoes of appropriative ventriloquism are strongest in Juan's instruction of Juanito in this sequence. Juan manhandles his son, with aggression similar to Ángela's body search, and orders him to salute Franco with '¡Arriba España!' (Long live Spain!). Juanito refuses to greet the dictator, hidden behind the white tent, and takes off running in the opposite direction, indicating antithetical politics, towards his mother. Juanito's is not a docile body upon which to improve (Foucault 1979: 136). He does not obey his father in Gutiérrez Aragón's oppositional film as Carmencita does in Franco's propaganda. The imposition of Francoist discourse of Juan on Juanito, although failed, is indeed an indication of successful appropriative ventriloquism of Juan by fictional Franco, who in fact separates Juan from the rest of his family for his own service at the beginning of the film.

The positioning of Ángela and Juanito vis-à-vis each other contrasts the hierarchical stance of Juan. Ángela crouches down to Juanito's height in order to hug him and answer his question about the split between the vanquished and the victorious in his family:

> Juanito: ¿Por qué te llamaron eso? [Why did they call you that?]
> Ángela: ¿Qué? [Call me what?]
> Juanito: Rojilla. [Red.]
> Ángela: Cuando la guerra no éramos de lado de Franco. [During the war we were not on Franco's side.]
> Juanito: Si papá es de Franco y tu rojita, ¿yo qué soy? [If Dad is with Franco and you are red, what am I?]
> Ángela: Cuando seas mayor, decidirás. [When you're older, you'll decide.]

The staging and content of the conversation convey a message of freedom of thought and equality between the two. Whereas Juan attempts to ventriloquise Juanito to Franco's liking, Ángela espouses more egalitarian politics and philosophy of child rearing.

This behaviour indicates Ángela's growing rebellion that Doña Gloria attempts to quell by consolidating the family through Ángela's marriage to Juan—the third stage of the appropriation. In a reversal of fortunes, Doña Gloria and Ángela come face to face again at Ángela's kitchen table. The scenario echoes the earlier kitchen sequence during which Doña Gloria put into action her power play for Juanito. This time, the two women sit on the same level and Ángela, again with peeling knife in hand, asserts her maternal rights and her right of refusal. Ángela consults Ana and Juanito and generously forgives but refuses to marry Juan: 'me corto el cuello o se lo corta usted antes de casarme con ese cantamañanas' (I would rather slit my throat or rather you slit it before I would marry that good-for-nothing man). Ana has become close with Ángela, remains repulsed by her husband, and harbours animosity for her lover and thieving brother-in-law Juan.

The following sequence displays a reception that could be for Ángela and Juan's wedding, in the case that she succumbed to family pressure, but is for Juanito's Saint's day instead. Resemblance to the opening sequence's wedding scene allows for some doubt as to whether Ángela has accepted the loveless marriage ('no hace falta que dormáis juntos' (it is not necessary that you sleep together)) that Doña Gloria proposed. During the event, Ana shoots Juan in the arm when he makes advances on her. Ana's husband shoulders the blame. The ironic family photo, taken in black and white with Juan's slung arm, closes the film and reveals a telling void at the head of the family's place (Cros 1994: 186). We could speculate that the vacancy may indicate that a figure more powerful and higher-ranking than Juan, namely dictator Francisco Franco, resides at that privileged position and is responsible for the photographic family reunion as master ventriloquist.

Juanito undergoes a temporary repatriation, returned to the father's house or fatherland, in *Demonios en el jardín*. My contextualisation of the film within the biopolitics of stolen children suggests that Ángela chooses exile to the countryside at the time of her pregnancy by contrast to Cros's interpretation of her departure as an expulsion from paradise, a dubious one at that, following original sin in El Jardín (1994: 187). She prefers solitude and poverty over the cleaning duties she performed at El Jardín under Doña Gloria's tutelage. These chores recall the fate of children adopted as domestic servants. The queen of the black market then utilises Juanito as bait, as in historical cases, to recapture his Republican mother. Doña Gloria's appropriation of Juanito represents the matriarch's repatriation of the boy. The film's plot, beginning with Ana's wedding of convenience but not ending with Ángela's, defies restoration and advocates for the resistance to social pressure of the traditional family model on the characters in Franco's Spain. Juanito's approach to Franco and his father at the reservoir is staged as a descent rather than an ascent. In the early years of the transition, *Demonios en el jardín* violates Francoism's ideological genre function and the reunion of the ritual function to offer an alternative and oppositional outcome in a carnivalesque inversion of Francoism.

The Child as Contraband in the Garden

Manuel Gutiérrez Aragón ironicises the traditional family structures that served as backbone to Francoism. The director reinterprets the language of Francoism regarding *demonios familiares* that Manuel Vázquez Montalbán defined as:

> Denominación ambigua frecuentemente empleada por Franco en sus discursos para referirse unas veces a los defectos de un supuesto carácter unitario español: falta de solidaridad, anarquía, individualismo; otras a tradicionales diablos históricos: el enciclopedismo, la masonería, el separatismo, el comunismo. (1977: 28)

> [An ambiguous name frequently used by Franco in his speeches to refer sometimes to defects in the supposedly unitary Spanish character: to lack of solidarity, anarchism, individualism; and other times to traditional historic demons: encyclopaedic doctrine, masonry, separatism, communism.]

The demons are not the vanquished, but rather the victors in *Demonios en el jardín*. Gutiérrez Aragón exposes the manipulation of Juan and of the store stocked with black-market goods. The film indicts Francoists as the vilified demons and black marketeers, despite official language to the contrary.

On the film's symbolic level, Juanito becomes another black-market good that his grandmother acquires and stores at her shop. Although a paternal grandmother appropriates Juanito with the coerced participation of his mother, the parties implicated in diegetic and historic appropriations remain largely the same: the Francoist and the doctor. Neither innocent nor murderous but rather manipulated and manipulating, Juanito's characterisation expands upon Marsha Kinder's classification of the 'children of Franco'. By virtue of Juanito's appropriation, *Demonios en el jardín* dramatises the history of the stolen children of Franco. Gutiérrez Aragón's film highlights the disunion of the two Spains, reveals the deceptiveness of the Francoist ideological genre function, and depicts the dignity of unwavering Republican convictions.

Note

1. All translations in Chapter One are mine.

CHAPTER TWO

The Appropriative and Carnivalesque Ventriloquism of Altar Boys from Joselito in *El pequeño ruiseñor* to Ignacio in *La mala educación*

Introduction

Spanish star director and Academy award-winning filmmaker Pedro Almodóvar makes his contribution to the *nuevo cine con niño* with *La mala educación* (*Bad Education*) (2004). Dialogism abounds across *La mala educación*, most importantly with the *cine con niño*'s *El pequeño ruiseñor* (*The Little Nightingale*) (Lucía 1956), and with Almodóvar's greater oeuvre, *¿Qué he hecho yo para merecer esto!* (*What Have I Done to Deserve This!* (1984) and *La ley del deseo* (*Law of Desire*) (1987). Spanish cinema, Sara Montiel's *Mi último tango* (*My Last Tango*) (Amadori 1960), and Spanish theatrical arts, Federico García Lorca's *Retablillo de Don Cristóbal* (*The Little Puppet Show of Don Cristóbal*) (1931), also infuse Almodóvar's film. My analysis will examine the unexplored dialogism of popular cinema and theatre that is implicit and explicit in *La mala educación*. I argue that symbolism within and across *El pequeño ruiseñor*, *Mi último tango*, and *Retablillo de Don Cristóbal* converges upon the carnivalesque, puppetry, and violence. These interactions indicate the ventriloquism and the respective commercial or sexual exploitation of the altar boys Joselito (José Jiménez Fernández) and Ignacio Rodríguez (Ignacio Pérez). Following Mikhail Bakhtin's theories, I will examine how Almodóvar re-accentuates the monetary exploitation of Joselito's golden voice by the town's sexton Mr Martín (Mariano Azaña) in Lucía's film as the sexual appropriation of Ignacio's voice and docile body by Father Manolo (Daniel Giménez Cacho).

The action of *La mala educación* occurs at a boys' Catholic boarding school in 1964, in Valencia in 1977, and in Madrid and Galicia in the early 1980s. The feature is a labyrinthine film-within-a-film, whereby *La mala educación* encompasses 'The Visit' and both stories are seasoned with multiple impersonations and acts of ventriloquism. Juan (Gael García Bernal) kills his brother Ignacio (Francisco Boira), a transsexual junkie who had been sexually abused in primary school, out of self-interest and of his shame of Ignacio's difference. Mr Berenguer (Lluís Homar), formerly Father Manolo (Daniel Giménez Cacho), exchanges gifts for sexual favours with Juan and aids him in killing Ignacio, who is blackmailing Mr Berenguer in 1977 for money to complete his sex change. Ignacio threatens to publish 'The Visit', his tale of the sexual abuse he suffered at Father Manolo's hands. Meanwhile, Juan passes for his brother to pitch 'The Visit' to filmmaker Enrique Goded (Fele Martínez), who was Ignacio's first love at school. Juan prefers to go by his stage name of Ángel and plays the part of Ignacio in Enrique's film. Enrique belatedly investigates and discovers Juan's ruse and crime.

La mala educación is unique within Almodóvar's oeuvre on account of its spotlight on child characters and setting during Francoism. Queer characters have been commonplace, queer children to a lesser degree, throughout Almodóvar's oeuvre since its inception during the youth counter-cultural movement of the *Movida* in the 1980s. Ignacio Rodríguez is the offspring of two characters, Tina (Carmen Maura) and Miguel (Miguel Ángel Herranz), in Almodóvar's filmography from the 1980s. Transgendered Tina visits the chapel of her school in *Law of Desire* to see the priest who abused her as a child to confess to him that he was one of only two men she has loved in her life. Tina is not interested in profit and revenge like Ignacio is in 'The Visit'. Ignacio's relationship to his abuser is negotiated like young Miguel's with the dentist in *What Have I Done to Deserve This?* Miguel agrees to the sexual relationship with the older man on his own terms: in exchange for consumer goods (a video player, a hi-fi stereo) and access to arts education (painting materials and schooling). Ignacio accepts the abuse on the condition that Father Manolo not expel his love Enrique, however, Father Manolo does not honour the agreement. Jorge Pérez acknowledges the agency of Almodóvar's children: '*La mala educación* radically refashions the familiar representation of childhood and of child sexuality, since Almodóvar re-sexualizes those bodies and bestows on them an agency to express and negotiate their affects' (2011: 146). It is certain that Almodóvar does not problematise sexual consent from minors, although *La mala educación* does present the abuse as such and privileges the desire that the two boys feel for each other over that possessed by Father Manolo for Ignacio. I will focus on Ignacio's childhood in 1964 in my discussion of ventriloquism and sexual appropriation in Franco's Spain. The child leads the flashback sequences and serves as a device whose abuse triggers the narrative strategies of horror and film noir.

La mala educación engages with its time and the abuse of power in

Spain's past. It was released just days after the 2004 election of President José Luis Rodríguez Zapatero of the socialist party (PSOE), who would legalise same-sex marriage in 2005 and pass the Law of Historical Memory in 2007. Almodóvar's feature is not the only recent film to denounce sexual misconduct within the sphere of Francoist National Catholic childhood education; José Luis Cuerda's *Los girasoles ciegos* (*The Blind Sunflowers*) (2008) (adapted from Alberto Méndez's 2004 novel by the same name) depicts a seminary student teacher's sexual assault of a young pupil's mother. Pepe Rodríguez's detailed world history of clerical sexual abuse preceded Massachusetts' Attorney General Thomas F. Reilly's staggering report of child abuse in Boston's churches by nine months. According to Rodríguez, 19 per cent of Spaniards have been sexually abused (2003: 44–5). Of that percentage, 9 per cent of Spanish boys and girls, totalling more than 300,000, have been abused by priests (44–6).

A close linkage between vocal talent and abuse emerge from Almodóvar's biography and in my analysis of child singers Joselito and Ignacio Rodríguez. Almodóvar was born in Ciudad Real (Castille-La Mancha, Spain) in 1949 and studied at school in Cáceres, Extremadura (Pavlović et al. 2009: 178).[1] Like Ignacio Rodríguez, he, too, was a soloist with a 'white voice' (*voz blanca*) who was abused alongside many other boys at school (MacKenzie 2004: 159; Torres 2004: 11–12). Similar to Ignacio, Almodóvar first wrote a story of Catholic school sexual abuse in the 1970s and required another ten years to re-work the story into a script (Fuentes 2009: 432; Burdeau and Frodon 2004: 24). Almodóvar's *Volver* (*To Return*) (2006) features former child singer Raimunda (Penélope Cruz) who had been raped and impregnated by her father before the action of the film. In early interviews, Almodóvar in fact jokes that he, too, was a *niño prodigio*: 'They discovered I had an outstanding voice that could reach something like eight octaves, and they turned me into a soloist. That's how my career as a religious singer was started' (Torres 2004: 11). Performance and the recorded voice, which often lend themselves to lip-syncing and dubbing in his films, were a part of Almodóvar's early schooling. Lynn Hirschberg of *The New York Times Magazine* writes: 'When he was a child, the priests recorded his singing and played the tapes at the door of the church to draw in parishioners' (2004: n.p.). In *La mala educación*, Spanish screen siren Sara Montiel's (1928–2013) voice is borrowed for lip-syncing by transvestite performers.

Like other retrospective films of the *nuevo cine con niño*, *Bad Education*'s double-voiced discourse addresses the past and present. Its setting in 1964 with a basis on personal experience coincides with the boom of historical memory since the 1990s. This trend in cultural production includes a number of nostalgic and parodic blends of Francoist schooling like Andrés Sopeña Monsalve's book *El florido pénsil* from 1994, adapted to the screen in 2002, and Antena Tres's reality television shows *Curso del 63* from 2009 and *Curso del 73* from 2012. Although the 1950s see the height of National Catholicism in Spain and its expression in *El pequeño ruiseñor*, Ignacio's youth in *La mala educación* the following decade displays the ongoing power of the Church. The 1960s was a decade of change and modernisation: 'Spaniards experienced the conflicting ideologies of Francoist traditionalism, with its reactionary exaltation of Catholic, patriarchal and Nationalist values and global capitalism, with its cults of the acquisition of wealth, material possessions and the free circulation of goods beyond national borders' (Faulkner 2006: 3). It was also a period of gradual abandonment of the Church (6). The film contrasts the Church's hold on state politics between late Francoism and the transition to democracy: 'The Visit's' Ignacio blackmails Father Manolo with this shifting political landscape in mind: 'La gente ha cambiado. Estamos en el '77. Esta sociedad valora más mi libertad que su hipocresía' ('People have changed. This is 1977. This society puts my freedom above your hypocrisy']).[2]

Indications of these changes appear in *La mala educación* through Ignacio's professed loss of faith and the embedded and imitated erotic performances of Sara Montiel. Ignacio and Enrique view Montiel's *Esa mujer* (*That Woman*) (Mario Camus 1969) at the Cine Olympo while Almodóvar's film also features additional appearances through transvestite impersonation of Montiel's characters in *Noches de Casablanca* (*Casablanca, Nest of Spies*) (Henri Decoin 1963) and *Mi último tango*. Marvin D'Lugo has observed the inspired use of Montiel as an axis of counter-hegemonic significations in *La mala educación*: 'The recycled image of Montiel, an emblematic expression of gender demarginalization in the post-Franco years, mirrors the social and political dynamics through which the broader plot intrigues of *Bad Education* take shape' (2009: 357). We will explore the context of the 1960s in more detail in the next chapter on Marisol's *Tómbola* (Lucía 1962) and focus greater attention here on the 1950s, the context of *El pequeño ruiseñor*, and director Antonio del Amo's biography in conjunction with Joselito's debut film.

The Dialogism and Ventriloquism of Altar Boys: Joselito's Golden Voice

The voice and ventriloquism are central to the dialogism of *El pequeño ruiseñor* and *La mala educación* and linked to representatives of the Church in each film. The 'boy with the voice of gold', Joselito, stands out in the child-starred genre as the performer most explicitly associated with the voice. The manipulation of altar boys through ventriloquism is implicit in Lucía's and Almodóvar's films. The pairing of appropriative and carnivalesque ventriloquism, which we have defined respectively as the ventriloquist's co-opting of the dummy's voice and body received by the dummy's back talk, underlies power relations in both films. However, as we can expect from a film subjected to Francoist censorship such as *El pequeño ruiseñor*, the resistance of carnivalesque ventriloquism is relatively reduced in comparison to *La mala educación*. Both films, nevertheless, add variations of commercial and sexual exploitation to *The Two* cines' representation of appropriative ventriloquism.

Popular cinema contemporary to *El pequeño ruiseñor* shares the characteristics of ventriloquism in an ecclesiastic setting: *Cerca de la ciudad* (*Close to the City*) (Lucía 1952) features a parish father who attracts local poor children with his ventriloquism act, and in another film directed by Luis Lucía, *Tómbola* (1962), the local parish priest helps Marisol (Pepa Flores) bring the criminals back to the straight and narrow. He is very impressed by Joe Carter's (Rafael Alonso) ventriloquism: '¡Me tienes que enseñar el truco por si me quedo sin monaguillo!' (You have to teach me that trick in case I need an altar boy!). The priest's joke is another instance of counter-hegemonic discourse in the film as it undermines the vocation expected of an altar boy and alludes to both the famous priest-ventriloquist P. W. Ciuró, whom we will discuss in Chapter Three, and to other ventriloquised altar boys in the *cine con niño*, like Joselito in the current chapter. Hypnosis, in which a teacher's mesmerising stare commandeers a pupil's recitation of a history lesson, is linked to education in *¡A mí no me mire usted!* (*Don't Look at Me!*) (Sáenz de Heredia 1941) and expresses the same spirit of appropriation for inculcation as in the ventriloquism examples.

In Del Amo's film, Joselito inherited his vocal talent from his father, a gypsy with whom his mother eloped to her father's great chagrin. At the opening of *El pequeño ruiseñor*, Joselito lives with his grandfather in a small Castilian town. The prodigal daughter, Fuensanta (Lina Canalejas) or 'holy font', returns to make amends with her father and son. Fuensanta's resemblance to the Bible's most notable repentant sinner is made evident when Joselito meets her, remarking that she reminds him of 'the Mary Magdalene of the sacristy' (la Magadalena de la sacristía). Joselito serves as altar boy of both the Church and the sexton, who capitalises on his singing talent for baptism and wedding performances. The Church, in the form of Don Jesús (Mario Berriatúa) and his higher-ranking uncle Don Fernando (Aníbal Vela), mediates the reconciliation of Joselito's grandfather and mother. The boy's presence, since he is another man's son, proves inconvenient to Fuensanta's rekindled and redeeming courtship with the suitor whom she slighted for Joselito's father. Consequently, Fuensanta complies with Don Fernando's recommendation that Joselito be sent to a Catholic boarding school in Guadalupe (Cáceres, Extremadura). Family reunification is complete after the characters surmount a number of obstacles: the sinful mother repents and marries Gonzalo (Luis Induni); Joselito flees internment with the permission of the Virgin Mary; and the boy is subsequently trampled by a stampede of bulls, but the voluntary transfusion of his stepfather's blood saves him and makes Joselito's blood his own. In the happy ending, the sexton rejoices that Joselito is again available for vocal performances. Great pains are taken by the main characters to comply with the Francoist ritual genre function: bloodshed, perhaps recalling that of the Civil War, is necessary to reunite the (national) family.

The Little Nightingale's ecclesiastic context situates it squarely within National Catholicism, which lasted into the late 1950s (Smith 1996: 249) and fused the cult of the child in Christianity and in Francoism. Ladislao Vajda's *Marcelino, pan y vino* (*The Miracle of Marcelino*), a worldwide success one year prior to Joselito's debut, provides the foundational reference for the *cine con niño*, National Catholic films, and the fetishisation of the child within Francoism's National Catholicism. I would like to note certain biographical parallels between Del Amo and Vajda, leaving further discussion of *Marcelino, pan y vino* for Chapters Five and Six.

The 1950s were not only known for National Catholicism but also known as the hinge decade between the famine of the 1940s and the greater economic well-being of the 1960s (Pavlović et al. 2009: 81). The end of rationing in 1952 augured creature comforts to follow, including the first television series in 1956 and the first mass-produced automobile in 1957. These signs of industrial modernity are absent in our film from 1956, however, the capitalist spirit is embodied in Joselito's stage manager. The performance of flamenco songs in *El pequeño ruiseñor* reveals the underlying economic relations between Joselito and the sexton. Flamenco historically arose, as musicologists Cristina Cruces Roldán and William Washabaugh have shown, in response to the intersection of clashing social classes (wealthy landowners versus impoverished day-labourers and gypsies) in Andalusia (2012: 28). Yet, Tatjana Pavlović has critically discussed the absence of class struggle in these flamenco-scored films (2011: 122); Joselito is charitable in his second, third, and sixth film, taking altruistic initiative to help others with the profits of his golden voice. I argue, rather, that Joselito's first film contrasts with his later features on this subject and establishes, in no uncertain terms, the protagonist's show business exploitation.

Joselito's role in his debut film and the biography of his respective director-creator Antonio del Amo (1911–91) display an unexamined tension in the film between the celebration of National Catholic values and the exposure of the boy's vocal exploitation by an agent of these values. Del Amo made ostensibly Francoist films in the Joselito series but began as a communist filmmaker, while Ladislao Vajda (1906–65) made the quintessential National Catholic film but was actually of Jewish ancestry (Pavlović et al. 2013: 321). Both Del Amo and Vajda were victims of discrimination: Vajda experienced religious persecution in Hungary and Italy (Camporesi 2007: 66) rather than political persecution like that Del Amo suffered for his communist filmmaking. Del Amo, like Luis Buñuel, who had given him his first camera (Seguin 1990: 181), worked on documentaries supporting the Second Republic during the Spanish Civil War (1936–9). In 1937, Del Amo wrote and directed *El camino de la victoria* (*The Path to Victory*) for the Spanish Communist Party, detailing eight conditions for winning the war, including 'control obrero sobre la producción' (workers' control over production) (Del Amo 1997: 211). Luis Buñuel's exile allowed him to continue in his provocative leftist vein. Del Amo, by contrast, was imprisoned for twenty days in Valencia, released and recaptured by Phalangists (Seguin 1990: 182), and even condemned to death at the end of the war (Gubern 2001: 12).

Like Fuensanta's storyline, Antonio del Amo's biography is a narrative of repentance. Interviews on the subject of the Joselito films with their self-identifying 'director maldito' (cursed director) (Abajo de Pablos 1998: 41) read like remorseful confessions for his alignment with the ideology of the regime. For instance, Del Amo disclosed to film historian Román Gubern: 'He cometido muchos errores de los que se llaman "de estómago," para sacar adelante a la familia, y no hay nada que yo odié más que lo que me he visto obligado a hacer' (I have committed many errors due to hunger, in order to support my family, and there is nothing that I hated more than what I have been obligated to do) (2001: 12). Similarly, Del Amo justified, to another interviewer, his work with Joselito according to economic necessity: 'Si claudiqué en nueve o diez películas, lo hice a sabiendas de que estaba trabajando como una prostituta; es decir, por dinero' (If I surrendered for nine or ten films, I did it knowing that I was working like a prostitute; that is to say, for money) (Abajo de Pablos 1998: 41). Del Amo ostensibly regretted his National Catholic filmmaking in the early Joselito series and expanded on his cinema work as instructor at official film schools and author of books on the seventh art.

Joselito has also expressed remorse, although on a different account: that of his cinematic exploitation. Spain's child musical stars were, by definition, show-business commodities. José Jiménez Fernández's biography tells the sad and clichéd tale of a child star fallen from grace. He rose to fame and wealth from poverty as the youngest of seven children born in 1943 to a humble family from Jaén (Heredero 1993: 231). Jiménez Fernández began singing in neighbouring towns and was discovered while performing on the radio by Antonio Guzmán Merino, his future screenwriter (ibid.). The boy star, like his female counterpart Marisol the following decade, laments his exploitation as child singer: 'Tenía una voz excepcional a una edad prematura y me convertí en una máquina de ganar millones' (I had an exceptional voice at an early age and I became a money-making machine) (232).[3] The former child star's personal denouement entailed his arrest and imprisonment in 1991 for narcotics. Joselito would re-appear decades later in reality television shows and the spoof film *Spanish Movie* (Ruiz Caldera 2009), to which we will return in the conclusion of *The Two* cines.

It is remarkable that *El pequeño ruiseñor* does not conceal Joselito's economic utilisation. The opening soundtrack of the film is comprised of religious music followed by church bells and Joselito's voice emanating from the bell tower. In the filmic space of *El pequeño ruiseñor*, the boy's voice is associated with the church while Mr Martín's mercantile relationship with Joselito, taking place in restaurant receptions following the celebration of sacraments, exposes the boy's alienated labour. In the first show, for a baptism, the film illustrates how the sexton takes the lion's share of profits while he obligates Joselito to sing. In the second performance, for a wedding, a song request alluding to Fuensanta's former transgressions publicly humiliates Joselito and earns reprimands for Mr Martín. The dynamic between Joselito and Mr Martín in these performances is similar to the power struggle between the appropriative ventriloquist and his dummy or, more specifically, the capitalist's parasitic use of labour whereby the singer's vocalisations are permissible when they earn the sexton, his ventriloquist, money and not when they call into question the exploitation. That is, Joselito's voice is permitted for appropriative ventriloquism but chastised for carnivalesque ventriloquism.

Joselito's first song, 'La estrella y el monaguillo' (The Star and the Altar Boy) tells of a 'pobre monaguillo' (poor altar boy) who dreams of reaching the star with whom he is in love (Figure 2.1). During his performance, Joselito is cast as this boy with the more age-appropriate modification that he desires sweets, which are out of his reach, rather than a true love. Joselito earns two meagre kilos in treats while Mr Martín fills his proverbial coffer with goodies and money. The sexton twice orders Joselito to sing while, to the boy's dismay, he grabs handfuls of sweets. Editing of the

Figure 2.1 Joselito (José Jiménez Fernández) sings 'La estrella y el monaguillo' with the sexton's (Mariano Azaña) direction in *El pequeño ruiseñor*.

boy's performance reveals Joselito's point-of-view shot on a big close-up of a delectable plate of candied peanuts with a medium close-up of the sexton teasingly waving—as if dangling a carrot in front of a horse's nose—a handful of the candied nuts at Joselito. Between performances, Joselito has the opportunity to sample other sweets but Mr Martín instructs the performer to sing and prevents the boy from helping himself by removing Joselito's hand from the platter.

Joselito is aware, although probably not in these terms, that Mr Martín is subjecting him to capitalistic operation. The boy protests: '¿De todo el dinero que se ha recogido, a mí qué me toca?' (Of all the money that was collected, what is my part?). Mr Martín pulls rank and argues, ventrilo-quising popular wisdom: 'Te toca callar. ¿Qué es esto? Interrogar a los superiores. Además, ¿tú no has oído, ignorante monago, que los dineros del sacristán cantando se vienen y cantando se van?' (Your part is to be quiet. What is this? Interrogating your superiors. Moreover, haven't you heard, ignorant altar boy, that the sexton's money comes and goes singing?). This instance of resistance follows ventriloquism's playbook. When the dummy talks back, the ventriloquist insists on silence and often supports his authority with the word play found in popular wisdom. But, Joselito simply smiles and shakes his head in amused resignation despite the injustice. Following another performance, Mr Martín's exploitation becomes even more apparent when he wrests a cash tip out of Joselito's hands.

The second performance to examine reveals Joselito's humiliation and utilisation through labour. In fact, on-screen audience members present for the performance of 'La campanera' (The Bell Ringer's Daughter) are mildly critical of the little nightingale's alienated and humiliated labour. Mean-spirited guests at the wedding reception request the song to irritate Gonzalo, who is also attending. Even Mr Martín finds the petition to be in poor taste and tries to ignore it. Unbeknownst to Joselito, the boy becomes complicit in the defamation of his mother with the song that repeats the rumours about her, the bell ringer's daughter. The lyrics describe Fuensanta as both the subject of a rumour mill and as God's chosen one:

> [D]ile que pare esa noria/ que va rodando,/ pregonando lo que quiere/ que por saberla tu historia,/ le están buscando cómo y cuándo dónde quiere/ ¡Ay! Campanera/ aunque la gente no crea/ tú eres la mejor de las mujeres porque/ te hizo Dios su pregonera

> [[T]ell them to stop the ferris wheel/that turns,/ proclaiming what it wants/ that in order to know your story,/ they are looking however, whenever and wherever they want/ Oh! Bell ringer's daughter/ even though people don't believe it/ you are the best of women because/ God made you his town crier]

The lyrics continue the chain of vocal surrogacy between the crowd to Joselito as they proclaim that God elects Fuensanta his town crier to communicate on his behalf. The resonance of bells, rumours, and the voice harmonise in the song. The biblical intertext remits to the film's National Catholic context.

El pequeño ruiseñor incorporates and attributes the criticism of its implicit spectators to its on-screen audience and may in fact beg the comparison to Del Amo's early filmmaking. The client who requests the slanderous song criticises Mr Martín: 'Lo que no se hace es vivir a coste de un chiquillo' (What one doesn't do is live at the expense of a child). Don Fernando, also attending the spectacle, scolds the sexton for capitalising on Joselito's voice: 'que no se comercie con su voz' (one should not trade on his voice). Client and clergy chastise Mr Martín for his fetishised commodification of Joselito's singing voice but clients persist in their utilisation of Joselito. It is remarkable that a critique that rings of communist tenets would come from a member of the Franco's church. Del Amo ventriloquises Don Fernando in order to express his own counter-hegemonic message. Ultimately, the critique of the commercial exploitation of child stars is safely attributed to the comedic character of Mr Martín, a self-serving member of the Church, and malicious clients. Mr Martín's jubilation due to Joselito's recovery at the end of the film allows for the sexton's show business to continue and, similarly, for the continuation of the Del Amo–Guzmán Merino–Joselito franchise.

The cult of the child, in Christianity and Franco's National Catholicism, and the commodification of the child's voice coincide in the figure of the boy with the voice of gold, Joselito. The little nightingale is doubly commodified as child musical star and Mr Martín's headliner in *El pequeño ruiseñor*. Lyrics and performances of Joselito's songs reveal the commercial exploitation and alienated labour of the boy by the sexton and suggest a concealed leftist critique that allows us to read against the grain of the film and of the politically persecuted director's reinvention. The pairing of the *niño prodigio*'s fetishised golden voice and the National Catholic cult of the child foreshadows the greater degree of collaboration between Spain's Church and economics in subsequent technocratic reforms that Luis Buñuel would unequivocally lampoon five years later in *Viridiana* (1961) and that would form the backdrop of Marisol's modernity in *Tómbola*.

The Dialogism and Ventriloquism of Altar Boys: Ignacio's White Voice

Appropriative ventriloquism is well matched with the carnivalesque in *La mala educación*, which portrays an eternal game of substitutions, dominations, and subjugations among its protagonists. Carnivalesque ventriloquism turns the tables on the appropriative ventriloquism that is predominant in *The Little Nightingale*. The lyrics and directions of the two songs that Ignacio Rodríguez sings in *La mala educación*, actually dubbed by boy singer Pedro José Sánchez Martínez (Vernon 2009: 60), bring to mind Joselito's performances and relationship to church representatives. In *La mala educación*, Father Manolo is Ignacio's school director, literature teacher, and lyricist. Adult Ignacio's return to school in 'The Visit', played by Juan dressed as Ignacio's fictitious sister Zahara, sets this tone of resistance to power and gender norms in the feature. In fact, Almodóvar explores the duality of ventriloquism by appropriating and re-signifying recitations and lyrics for and against domination through the body of the transvestite or transsexual performer and impersonator. The cross-dressed performance of Sara Montiel's feminine sexuality and the grotesque of García Lorca's puppet play inform Almodóvar's carnivalesque return to the Salesian Fathers Catholic school.

Ignacio's visit to Father Manolo puts into motion the plot of revenge with carnivalesque resistance and word play. The aggrieved party's return consists of his going back to school and Almodóvar's return to *Law of Desire*. Adult Ignacio/Zahara's encounter with Father Manolo recalls adult Tina's with a twist. Tina sings the ecclesiastic lyrics to her former priest lover's piano accompaniment and then expresses her affection for him. Nevertheless, Ignacio/Zahara turns the Eucharistic liturgy around on Father Manolo. While Father Manolo confesses his sins in the celebration of the Eucharist, Ignacio/Zahara ventriloquates and revises these words to accuse the paedophile: 'Por tu culpa' ('Through your fault'). Almodóvar details this and another moment of appropriation in relation to Catholic ritual in his film:

> Il y a une utilisation de la liturgie dans le récit . . . Il y a aussi une scène où l'enfant chante pendant la messe. C'est un moment de splendeur que l'enfant s'approprie pour transmettre un message à l'autre enfant qui le regarde. (Burdeau and Frodon 2004: 27)

> [There is a use of the liturgy in the story . . . There is also a scene where the child sings during mass. It is a moment of splendour that the child appropriates in order to transmit a message to the other child who watches him.]

With nowhere to go, the boys communicate through the language available to them.

Besides liturgy and ecclesiastic song, *La mala educación* appropriates film culture and popular music as well. Ignacio sings 'Moon River', with re-written lyrics from 1961's *Breakfast at Tiffany's* (Blake Edwards), and 'Jardinero' (Gardener), with new lyrics set to the music of 'Torna a Sorrento' (Return to Sorrento), for Father Manolo. The direction of 'Gardener', suitably overlaid on a song telling of a lover's nostalgic plea for return, recalls Joselito's 'The Star and the Altar Boy'. Father Manolo likely composes new lyrics to both songs – although we are only told that he composed 'Gardener' – that in fact suggest the sexual relationship between himself and Ignacio.

Young Ignacio's voice-over narrates 'The Visit' as Father Manolo reads the story and the audience views the flashback. Ignacio sings 'Moon River' during an excursion to a river for students on the honour roll. His song to Father Manolo's guitar playing is the prelude to an act of abuse that the audience does not see, viewing instead the carefree swimming of Ignacio's classmates that is idealised in slow motion. Ignacio sings wistfully as he looks over his shoulder to the childhood activities that we imagine he would prefer. The sexual imagery of murky water in the song contrasts with the crystalline purity in which Ignacio's peers play. Erotic overtones of the song foreshadow the abuse:

> Moon River no te olvidaré,/ yo no me dejaré llevar/ por el agua/ agua turbia/ del río de la luna/ que suena al pasar/ río y luna/ dime dónde está mi Dios, el bien y el mal/ yo quiero saber/ qué se esconde en la oscuridad/ y tú lo encontrarás

['Moon River always on my mind/ I won't be swept away/ by the water, the muddy water/ of that Moon River/ As it flows along/ River and moon/ Tell me where to find/ my God and good and ill/ Tell me/ I'm longing to know/ What is hidden/ in the dark/ And you'll find it']

The lyrics tell that a dark undercurrent is sweeping Ignacio away as the aggressor, Father Manolo, approaches him. They represent Father Manolo's sexual advance in fluid terms. The appropriative ventriloquism in which Father Manolo scripts Ignacio's song grooms the boy for the abuse.

This instance of appropriative ventriloquism within an educational context, dovetails with traditional theories of pedagogy that conceive of the pupil as a passive receptacle for learning. Naomi Segal's study of pedagogy and pederasty further illuminates the potentially sexualised element of passive instruction. First, she describes the assumptions regarding children: 'as either innocent vessels or potential delinquents' (1998: 24). Father Manolo's pedagogical doctrine and actions objectify Ignacio, perversely, through sexual abuse. Segal enumerates the many metaphorical models of instruction in physical terms; she explores provocative analogies including hydraulics or fluid transfer and even bank deposits and she ties a hydraulic system of male desire to pederasty in the schools. In traditional pedagogy, the teacher is the subject and the student is the obedient object or receptacle. Segal finds that the teacher-pederast mirrors this structure in his sexual abuse of a pupil:

> Nothing resembles the filling and depositing process, in which something containable is made to flow into an available container, with results both unpredictable and unexamined, so much as the act of penile penetration ending in orgasm . . . In this scheme the teacher must be a physically mature male. (1998: 6)

Segal, thus, draws a parallel between the transfer of bodily fluids and knowledge. I connect Segal's theorisations to ventriloquism and pederasty by virtue of the empty container or vessel. Both intercourse and ventriloquism operate on the basis of transfer and characterise Father Manolo's relationship with Ignacio.

The sexual violence provokes Ignacio's indignation and injury. Ignacio shouts 'No!', falls and splits open his head. Almodóvar digitally represents not the abuse of Ignacio Rodríguez but rather its effects: Ignacio's face is split vertically in two by a stream of blood (Figure 2.2). This symbol of fracture or fragmentation is apparent in many instances of the film: first from the torn posters in the opening credits mimicking those pasted to the external wall of the theatre, the DVD cover of García Bernal's face split

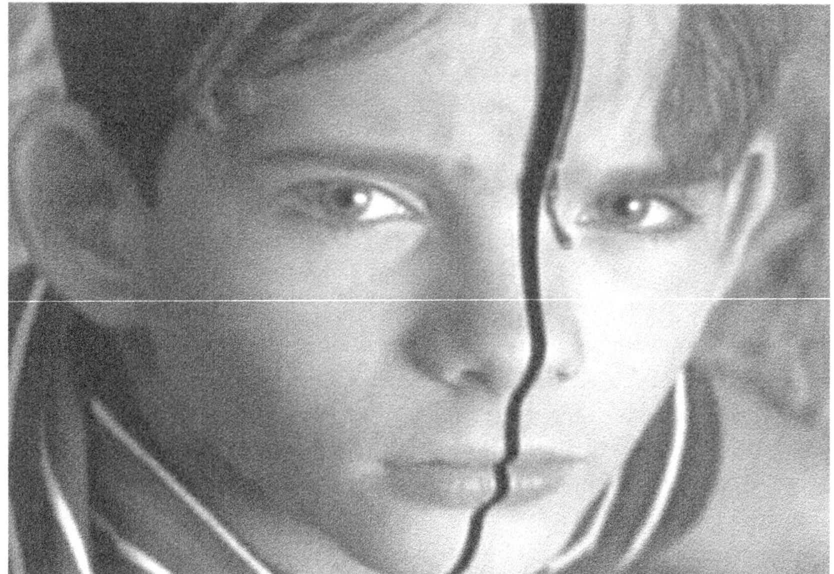

Figure 2.2 The abuse fractures Ignacio (Ignacio Pérez) in *La mala educación*.

between Zahara and Ángel, and in the décor of the sets and tiled mosaics outside Ignacio's and Juan's Valencian apartment building. Ignacio, as the song tells, does not forget 'Moon River', nor the sexual abuse that shattered his youth.

The natural imagery of Ignacio's next song remits to the garden of childhood with an ironic perversion of innocence or garden of Eden with a foretold loss of innocence. The song's fall from grace may also prefigure the 'falling' or lowering of Ignacio's voice in maturation. Ignacio performs 'Gardener' for Father Manolo's birthday. The school's director re-writes the lyrics to 'Torna a Sorrento' and requests that Ignacio sing for him. Father José (Francisco Maestre) leads Ignacio down a long hallway and then positions Ignacio on his mark to perform for all of the priests seated on the opposite side of an elongated table, as if in homage to Leonardo da Vinci's 'Last Supper' or in mise-en-abyme with *Viridiana*'s blasphemous rendition of the painting. The song evokes the perversion of an Edenic garden, like the tainted riverside locus amoenus:

> Jardinero, jardinero/ noche y día entre tus flores/ encendiendo sus colores/con la llama de tu amor/ Mas poniendo en cada cáliz/ la sonrisa de tu anhelo/ con los ojos en el cielo/ donde tienes tu ilusión/ y tus flores, jardinero/ de corolas encendidas/ que al unirse agradecidas/ te embalsan con su olor/ sé que tu labor/ cultivando las flores/ que a tus amores/confió el Señor

['Gardener, gardener/ night and day among your flowers/ Setting fire to their colours/ with the flame of your love./ And you place in every calyx/ the smile of your yearning/ With your eyes turned up to heaven/ where all of your hopes reside/ And your flowers, gardener/ with their carollas burning brightly/ join together in gratitude/ and embalm you with their scent/ Continue with your labour/ cultivating all the flowers/ entrusted to your love/ by the Lord']

The sexual nature of these lyrics, recalling the hydraulics of desire, is evident in the feminisation of Father Manolo's pupils as flowers, whose chalices the priest fills. The shot-reverse shot between Father Manolo and Ignacio that adopts the priest's point of view in this sequence and also the slow-motion during 'Moon River' sexualise the boys for their spectators (Pérez 2011: 149; Vernon 2009: 63). The children are eroticised recipients of the director's inculcation. Father Manolo's students, as he sees it, are receptacles of his supposed care and knowledge. His victims and spectators know that they are bodies that the priest sexually abuses.

Ignacio is the only child singer of the *nuevo cine con niño* and his performance is the best reflection of Joselito, child star from the 1950s. As we have seen, a sexton exploits Joselito for his singing talents in *El pequeño ruiseñor*. The sequence in which Joselito interprets 'The Star and the Altar Boy' is very similar to Ignacio's 'Gardener'. In both cases, a representative of the clergy directs the child's performance during a meal. Neither boy has much opportunity to eat and instead performs for diners. Father José interrupts Ignacio's lunch so that the boy may sing for the priests during their meal. As if a ventriloquist or puppeteer, Father José stands next to his dummy, Ignacio, with his hand on his shoulder, and then indicates that he will watch Ignacio's performance closely (Figure 2.3). Father José stands with a cane in his right hand and Ignacio appears as if he is another extension of Father José's body at his left hand. The image may also recall the most famous boy puppet, Pinocchio (Figure 2.3). On stage right, Father José's gestures conduct Ignacio with similar gestures to the sexton, who marks the rhythm of Joselito's song (Figure 2.4). Father José is not the only appropriative ventriloquist in this act because Ignacio performs Father Manolo's lyrics for the school director's birthday.

It is worth contrasting the settings of the boys' Catholic boarding schools in Cáceres.[4] Vocal direction is strict for Ignacio, in favour of solo song, and for Joselito, against his flamenco solos. The school choir director remarks that Joselito's Flamenco music is not 'religioso pero tiene alma' (religious but has soul) and 'se llama saeta porque se clava' (it's called an arrow because it pierces). The musical director, in fact, harmonises Flamenco with ecclesiastical music by tracing a genealogy: 'todo cante flamenco viene del gregoriano' (all Flamenco song comes from Gregorian chant).

Figure 2.3 Father José (Francisco Maestre) introduces child singer Ignacio Rodríguez in *La mala educación.*

Figure 2.4 Father José directs Ignacio in *La mala educación.*

Joselito's choral performance of 'Ubi Caritas', shot from a heavenly high angle, shows how lost and homesick the young Flamenco vocalist is even at front and centre of the chorus. Customary law from the Middle Ages documents the conduct of the child singer: 'the boys' physical discipline in the choir is only one aspect of their liturgical decorum as prescribed by the customaries. Children were assigned extensive liturgical duties that required considerable skill, practice, and stamina' (Boynton 1998: 199). Joselito's flamenco styles clashes with the greater structure of church music.

The little nightingale is prohibited to sing out of turn, or out of place. While completing a chore of collecting water from the cloister's fountain,

Joselito's song, 'El pregón de las campanas' (Town Crier of the Bells), draws a crowd of monks from out of the recesses of the monastery. Joselito drops the ceramic water jugs he's filled almost as if in a delayed reaction to a glass-shattering high C. If we consider Segal's analogies, the accident may also connote Joselito's faultiness as a recipient of Catholic teaching and prefigure his 'rebellious' escape. This song draws a parallel between himself, the towncrier of the bells, and his mother, the bell ringer's daughter. The director of the monastery protests: 'Te parece bonito? ¿Cantar así como si estuvieras en la calle?' (Do you think this is appropriate? Singing as if you were in the street?). This complaint designates the monastery as a place of controlled and surveyed vocalisation.

As we would expect from Almodóvar's anticlerical film, church representatives are higher-ranking and more despicable in *La mala educación* compared to *El pequeño ruiseñor*. Yet, Ignacio is, to a certain degree, successful in evading complete control. As I mentioned earlier, Ignacio at times uses liturgy and ecclesiastic music for his own ends. The boy's choral performance of 'Kyrie Eleison', filmed from front, centre, and above, becomes a vehicle for connection with Enrique. Like Joselito's, Ignacio's positioning is part of a system of control and surveillance that reaches back to the Middle Ages: 'Most customaries contain extensive prescriptions governing where and how children should be positioned both inside and outside the abbey church, and regulating the timing of their movements through the monastery' (197). The boys' chorus sings from the balcony, which Almodóvar captures in low angle to bestow greater importance on the boy lovers than on a higher power. To a certain extent, Ignacio bucks the system, which historically assigned 'children to a particular location in the choir . . . to facilitate the adults' observation of them' (198). Indeed, Ignacio's staging facilitates Enrique's observation of him more so than Father Manolo's, who officiates with his back to the congregation in pre-Vatican II custom. The choreography of Ignacio's movements in time with those of his classmates can also be seen in sequences of physical education. The traumatic split between the boys upon Enrique's expulsion disrupts Ignacio's choreography. Cinematic storytelling with a high angle and iris indicate the power and surveillance of the school's direction. Ignacio's proverbial deal with the devil has been broken.

Both *El pequeño ruiseñor* and *La mala educación* expose the ideological and ritual functions of the Francoist *cine con niño*. After a brush with death by bull stampede, Joselito reunites his family thanks to a blood transfusion from his stepfather and resumes his church show-business career. According to Altman and the ritual genre function: 'it is through generic conventions that audiences are lured into false assumptions of societal unity and future happiness' (1999: 27). Unity achieved through sacrifice and reconciliation promise a happy home life for the characters of the *cine con niño* film and comply with the Francoist ideological genre function. *La mala educación*'s pessimistic plot first offers an imaginative alternative to the Francoist legacy, in observance of another aspect of the ritual genre function, through the former child victim's blackmail scheme. But, the carnivalesque inversions of victim and aggressor lead to the demise of both. Adult junkie Ignacio Rodríguez turns the tables on his former literature teacher and abuser two years after Franco's death, holding him literally accountable for the abuse. Ignacio's monetary revenge is foiled when he overdoses with drugs supplied by his would-be victim. Financial dealings in both films, whether they are the representation of capitalistic exploitation of child labour by a director who made films for the Spanish Communist Party or a character's attempt to turn a profit on his childhood sexual abuse, aim at undermining Francoist power structures. Their portrayals of antagonism towards representatives of National Catholic Spain provide examples of carnivalesque opposition to Francoism.

From Puppets to Pupils

Resonances of puppetry are not coincidental in *La mala educación* but rather form part of *Bad Education*'s dialogism across genre. They create meaning through intertextuality with a Billy Club puppet play (from the *Títeres de cachiporra*) by Federico García Lorca and suggest the curtailed autonomy of children under Franco. In fact, Juan/Ángel's acting portfolio includes performances with the Bumblebee amateur theatre group (*Teatro del abejorro*) of Lorca's *The Little Puppet Show of Saint Cristóbal* and Mark Twain's *The Diaries of Adam and Eve* from 1897 and 1905. In certain ways, Lorca's and Twain's works foreshadow Ignacio's song: either through the puppetry of Lorca or the allusion to the Garden of Eden in Twain. Since Lorca's title character is in fact 'Don' Cristóbal, not 'San' Cristóbal, it is possible that Almodóvar alludes in this revision to his ecclesiastic re-location of the theatrical work. In accordance with Bakhtin's theorisation, *La mala educación* re-accentuates Lorca's puppet play: 'The historical life of classic works is in fact the uninterrupted process of their social and ideological re-accentuation' (1981: 421). The intertext from Lorca highlights the grotesque and carnivalesque modes in puppetry that underlie the sexual abuse of child Ignacio and the gender bending of adult Ignacio's desired sex change and drag performances. This is not the first time that Almodóvar's cinema has engaged in intertextuality with Lorca; *All About*

My Mother showcases a performance of *Yerma* (1933–4) on the common subject of maternity.

García Lorca's puppet play from 1931 draws from the grotesque violence of Pulcinella, who first appeared in the Neapolitan *Commedia dell'arte* in 1620 (Grantham 2001: 208, Rudlin 2002: 139). Pulcinella, who inspires the puppet Don Cristóbal, is a 'juvenile delinquent in a man's body' who takes what he wants 'by sheer force and brutality' (Grantham 2001: 208–10). In Lorca's play, Don Cristóbal is a billy club-wielding older doctor who bargains with Rosita's mother in order to wed the younger woman. Cristóbal beats and kills his patients rather than cures them and uses violence as his primary bargaining tool with Rosita's mother. The work displays the grotesque's emphasis on the lower stratum of the body, exaggerated fertility, and carnivalesque inversion (Bakhtin 1984: 19, 23, 11). Cristóbal is an unruly, vulgar, and drunk puppet whose third utterance in the play offers urination, which is also typical of Pulcinella (Rudlin 2002: 142), as an excuse for tardiness to the stage (García Lorca 1963: 1,022). The primacy of the lower stratum over the upper and the inversion of traditional roles align with the carnivalesque: Cristóbal is a doctor who kills his patient for the money stowed in his buttocks (1,027) and who responds to 'Buenos días' (Good day) with 'Buenas noches' (Good night) (1,024). Rosita's sexual maturity is likened to the ripeness of fruit: 'tiene dos pechitos/ como dos naranjitas' (1,029) (she already has two little breasts/ like two little oranges). Her sexuality and fertility are hyperbolic; Rosita cheats on a sleeping Cristóbal with numerous lovers and has a litter of four children as if she were an animal (1,041–2). For this, Cristóbal beats her mother to death.

Sarah Wright sees a trickster function as central to Lorca's marginal and minor works like his puppet plays. The trickster, like Pulcinella and Cristóbal, is a character who mocks order and deceives (Wright 2000: 3). In *The Little Puppet Show of Don Cristóbal*: 'The *prologuista* is a trickster-figure, no more than a digression, a showy distraction, symbolic of the ambiguous space on the threshold between presence and absence, creating then blurring the delineation of a gap between the world of appearance and illusion and the external reality' (16). The puppet play indeed begins with a prologue in which the Poet and Director clash as they each attempt to assert their authority over the following play and its audience. The Director's first line chastises the Poet: 'Haga usted el favor de callarse. El prólogo termina donde se dice: "Voy a planchar los trajes de la compañía"' (Do us a favor and be quiet. The prologue ends where it says: 'I am going to iron the company's suits') (García Lorca 1963: 1,020). Their dynamic recalls the squabbles regarding speech between a ventriloquist, here the Director, and his dummy, here the Poet. In turn, the Poet exerts influence over the audience and Cristóbal over the play's characters. The Poet greets: 'Hombres y mujeres, atención; niño, cállate' (Gentlemen and ladies, attention; child, be quiet) (1,019). Wright explores how the prologue extends into the play and the dialogical duel between the Poet and the Director:

> The *prologuista* is no longer a generic poet/director figure, but has split into the arguing personae of the Poeta and Director. The audience is witness to a discussion regarding the play's characters. The Director's solution is to round up the characters by brute force and cart them off, thereby bringing an end to the dramatic action. But it is less than clear as to where authority resides regarding the content of the play. The notion of a dialogue with different narratorial positions is beginning to emerge very clearly. (Wright 2000: 32)

The Director's response is also typical of ventriloquism wherein a frustrated ventriloquist boxes up the back-talking dummy. Don Cristóbal exerts his force on Rosita's mother so that her speech surrenders power to him: 'Di: Tengo miedo . . . Diga: ¡ya me ha domado don Cristóbal! . . . Como domaré a tu hija' (Say: I'm scared . . . Say: Don Cristóbal has tamed me! . . . Like I will tame your daughter) (García Lorca 1963: 1,033). Authority and domination are at stake in this play, which serves beautifully as intertext in *La mala educación*. The threatening potential of Father José's cane reminds us of Don Cristóbal's billy club.

The hostile relationship among the Director, the Poet, and Cristóbal offers parallels with the ventriloquial struggle for power and authority between the film director and Juan/Ángel and between the school director and Ignacio in *La mala educación*. The act of reading 'The Visit' links the two directors. Child Ignacio's face in big close-up splits open like curtains (Figure 2.5) to transition to Father Manolo's face half lit in the same shot size. The image cuts to the corresponding page of 'The Visit' followed by another hard cut to Enrique's face with the same visual characteristics. This editing, shot size, and lighting draw a parallel between the two directors. How is it, then, that Enrique abuses Juan? The carnivalesque informs the switching and inversion of roles between the director and actor; at times Enrique takes advantage of Juan and at others Juan uses Enrique. The film contains other parallels, carrying the 'Moon River' bathing sequence to Enrique's swimming pool at Avenida del Agua, 11.

The audience witnesses intercourse between adults Enrique and Juan in lieu of the scene of abuse in 'Moon River'. Enrique is aware of their deceptive two-step and plays the role of predatory crocodile before and as he auditions Juan/Ángel through sex for the role of Zahara: 'Juan me permitió que le penetrara con frecuencia, pero sólo físicamente' ('He allowed me to penetrate him frequently but only physically'). The film director's sexual exploitation of his actor recalls Father Manolo's sexual utilisation of Ignacio. Young Ignacio resists Father Manolo within his ability, by rejecting the religion he represents: 'Pienso que acabo de perder la fe en este momento. Al ya no tener fe, ya no creo en Dios ni en el Infierno. Si no creo en el Infierno, ya no tengo miedo y sin miedo soy capaz de cualquier cosa' ('I think I've just lost my faith at this moment . . . so I no longer believe in God or hell. As I don't believe in hell I'm not afraid . . . and without fear I'm capable of anything'). The digital facial fracture at the moment of abuse prefigures adult Ignacio's break with his abused male body for makeover as a woman.[5]

The fissure in Ignacio's identity is mirrored in the multiple embodiments associated with him, including Juan's impersonation of him and his film character's drag performance of Sara Montiel. Almodóvar's trickster expands on qualities found in *The Little Puppet Show of Don Cristóbal* since he is also 'the protagonist in a plot involving switches in gender, shape-shifting or the mischievous intermingling of the sacred and the profane, performing miracles or violating taboos' (Wright 2000: 3). A relative lack of sexual taboos, forms of sacrilege that include responding 'We'll see' ('A ver') rather than 'Amen' and stealing 'divine' ('divino') church silver for drug money, drug sniffing, transvestism, and transsexualism characterise Almodóvar's tricksters and play into his expression of the grotesque. Almodóvar transforms the grotesque violence of Don Cristóbal and his purchase of the 'sexually ripe' Rosita for marriage with a nod to the commercial exploitation of Joselito and the sexual violence upon soloist Ignacio in *La mala educación*.

Let us turn to the drag performances of Sara Montiel that relate to Zahara. Enrique is thoroughly disconcerted and impressed by Juan/Ángel's acting chops when he confirms, through a trip to Juan's and Ignacio's hometown in Galicia, that Juan has been impersonating his deceased brother. He is now convinced that Juan/Ángel is capable of shape shifting into any role, including that of Zahara. In 1964, the boys watch Montiel's *Esa mujer* on a date at the Cine Olympo. In 1977, Zahara, played by Ángel in Enrique's film, lip-syncs to Montiel's 'Quizás, quizás, quizás' (Perhaps, Perhaps, Perhaps) from *Noches de Casablanca* (*Casablanca, Nest of Spies*) and, in 1980, Juan/Ángel studies the best Montiel impersonator's rendition of 'Maniquí parisien' (Parisian Mannequin) from *Mi último tango*.

The incredibly rich dialogism with *Mi último tango* consolidates puppetry, ventriloquism, and impersonation. In Amadori's film, Montiel plays Marta Andreu, a poor theatrical chambermaid whose vocal talent is unappreciated. However, when the headliner Luisa Marival (Luisa de Córdoba) loses her voice on stage, Marta throws her voice from off stage in order to restore the illusion of Marta's beleaguered performance. The montage, composed of crosscuts between the two songstresses, gives preference to the playful rendition by the true star of the film. The song tells of a flirtatious fashion mannequin who travels to Madrid from Paris. Marta's blond braids infantilise her even as she performs womanly wiles. She is a trickster and her looks deceive. As Marta performs the song in Luisa's place, she pulls off another ruse; although we see Marta hanging up garments from behind a changing screen, she does not in fact undress. In another, albeit accidental, deception, Marta is mistaken for Luisa on an ocean-liner journeying to Argentina. When Luisa is unable to travel, Marta continues to masquerade as Luisa in the diva's glamorous costume. The impersonator wears this style wardrobe in *La mala educación*, rather than the maid's uniform and braids in which Sara Montiel performs the song in *Mi último tango*, to more closely emulate Montiel's star persona (Figure 2.5).

La mala educación indeed displays a fetishisation of Montiel's voice, as Marvin D'Lugo and Marsha Kinder observe: 'The emphasis on Montiel's recorded voice further underscores the power of what Marsha Kinder identifies as an "audio fetish," itself part of the broader historical fetishization of the singer' (D'Lugo 2009: 373). A narrow focus on the carry-over from Montiel to *La mala educación*, however, elides the fetishisation of the voices of altar boys Ignacio Rodríguez and Joselito, whose exploitation is more apparent and explored to a greater extent. Fetishisation of Ignacio is, in fact, not simply vocal but also sexual. Kathleen Vernon

Figure 2.5 A Sara Montiel (Sandra) impersonation in *La mala educación*.

underscores the 'mismatch between voice and body that renders Juan's identity suspect' (2009: 65). She further questions the drag performance: 'If the goal of a successful female impersonator is to make the spectator aware of the coexistence of contradictory identities, and ultimately of the performative nature of gender roles while simultaneously embracing the illusion, then Zahara can be said to fall short' (ibid.). I would re-accentuate Vernon's observations here. In fact, I suggest that the performance points to ventriloquism, a form that revels in the abyss between the success and failure of deception. Vernon further writes: 'his performance achieves the obverse of the cinematic and musical fantasies of the unified subject and utopian fusion of self and other, giving form instead to their dystopic double' (ibid.). In my interpretation, the dystopic double and the split identity are hallmarks of ventriloquism.

The song's singing mannequin and marionettes elsewhere in Almodóvar's film, namely the larger-than-life giants and big heads ('gigantes y cabezotas'), also remit to puppetry and the carnivalesque (Figure 2.6). In fact, the giants and big heads that Mr Berenguer and Juan observe in a Valencian museum as they plot Ignacio's murder are figures of medieval origin that are paraded for Corpus Christi, a day that celebrates the body during Holy Week (Pelauzy 1978: 187). Often, they carry billy clubs like the *títeres de cachiporra*. This religious reference, the observation of the Eucharist by Father Manolo and group physical training and soccer match point to the emphasis on the body and even its transubstantiation in *La mala educación*. Transformation and impersonation in body and voice inform ventriloquism, which we can also understand as an adult's vocal impersonation of a child.

Figure 2.6 Juan (Gael García Bernal) and Mr Berenguer (Lluís Homar) plot at a Valencian carnival museum in *La mala educación*.

Conclusion

The dialogism of *La mala educación* masterfully melds the ventriloquism of the child singer from popular cinema and the violence of puppetry from popular theatre for a re-accentuation of both. Almodóvar creates his original film with inspiration from the grotesque and the carnivalesque challenging of authority in García Lorca's *The Little Puppet Show of Don Cristóbal* that sexualises his child protagonist. *El pequeño ruiseñor* casts doubt on the propriety of Joselito's vocal performances, a counter-hegemonic undercurrent that recalls Del Amo's earlier politics, to suggest the economic fetishisation of the child singer. Almodóvar re-accentuates the ventriloquism of Joselito as a sexual appropriation of Ignacio Rodríguez. The fetishisation of the voices of these altar boys for profit or pleasure unveils the political economy and biopolitics of National Catholicism.

La mala educación is an example of the *nuevo cine con niño*'s damning revision of its Francoist precursor, which we will continue to explore throughout *The Two* cines. Ventriloquism of the child dummy in Del Amo's and Almodóvar's features utilises the child's voice and body for the ventriloquist's economic or sexual benefit. In both cases, the directors base their critique of Francoism on this exploitation. *The Little Nightingale*'s conclusion restores order and complies with Francoism's ideological genre function. *La mala educación* peels away the layers of social convention during and after Franco as it makes over Juan-as-Ángel-as-Zahara. But Almodóvar's film also utilises the child as a means to an end: Ignacio's childhood abuse is both Juan's ticket to a movie career and it gives rise to a tortuous film noir tale. Appropriative ventriloquism takes on another shape in Chapter Three's *Tómbola*, a Francoist film that identifies its ideology and embodies its teachings through the character of a ventriloquist kidnapper.

Notes

1. Almodóvar moved to Madrid at the end of the 1970s, taught himself filmmaking, and made his first feature film, *Pepi, Luci, Bom y otras chicas del montón* (*Pepi, Luci, Bom and Other Girls on the Heap*) in 1980 (Pavlović et al. 2009: 178). Almodóvar received an Academy Award for Best Foreign Language Film in 2000 for *Todo sobre mi madre* (*All About My Mother*) (1999).
2. All translations in Chapter Two are mine except those provided in the English subtitles to *Bad Education*, which I denote with quotation marks around the text inside the brackets.

3. However, Joselito's statements during the same years have also been contradictory; he added nuance elsewhere: 'Yo no soy el clásico niño explotado' (I am not the typical exploited child) (Moix 1993: 276). The context of his remarks, from the years of his arrest for drug dealing, could challenge Joselito's credibility.
4. Almodóvar based the school on his own experience in Cáceres and planned to film in the region but logistics prevented him from doing so (Anonymous 2003: n.p.).
5. Isolina Ballesteros is right to point out Almodóvar's tragic and punitive treatment of Ignacio: 'by linking Ignacio's sex change to drug addiction and death, Almodóvar appears to punish Ignacio for his/her transgression even as he denounces the repressive climate in which s/he had to live' (2009: 94). She notes: 'Even though Almodóvar has always championed the performativity, instability, and ambiguity of identity, there are signs, even from very early in his career, that the transformation of identity is not as free from contradictions and consequences as many imagine. The imitations and impersonations activated in performance may help characters endure traumas, perhaps even cure them, but they may also support duplicity and (self-) deception' (Ballesteros 2009: 95). Performativity is indeed complex in Almodóvar and I train my focus on it as a manifestation of the grotesque, the carnivalesque, and the identity crisis latent in ventriloquism.

CHAPTER THREE

Ventriloquism, Kidnapping and the Carnivalesque in Marisol's *Tómbola*[1]

'Y quería hacer de mí el modelo de niña inocente, conformista y buena, para que fuera la referencia de todos los niños de nuestra generación, tan traumatizada y despersonalizada, que tenían que ser los continuadores del fascismo'

(Pepa Flores cited in Morales 1979: 27)

[And he wanted to make me into the model of an innocent girl, conformist and good, so that I would be a reference for all the children of our generation, as traumatised and depersonalised as the continuers of fascism had to be.][2]

Introduction

The success of the biggest child star of the 1960s, Marisol (Pepa Flores), followed that of her male counterparts of the 1950s, Pablito Calvo and Joselito. Marisol's stardom continued the *cine con niño* genre of child-starred films through the 1960s in the company of fellow child actresses Ana Belén, Rocío Durcal, and twins Pili and Mili. Chapter Three further elaborates ventriloquism as an expression of Francoist anxiety of subaltern rebellion by children and colonial subjects and as a tool for the transmission of traditional gender roles. In fact, both a 1960 guide for women under Franco, by the Sección Femenina de la Falange, and a 1963 manual for ventriloquists are instructive in Marisol's gendered and biopolitical re-education. Ventriloquism, which appears in symbolic form through the interactions of characters and films throughout *The Two* cines, is incarnated in the character of the ventriloquist Joe Carter (Rafael Alonso) in *Tómbola*. But his ventriloquism extends beyond his dummy Marisol. The child protagonist's paternalism towards her best friend, who is likely from Spanish Guinea, supports an allegorical analysis of the biopolitics of Spanish colonialism in Africa. María Belén's character (Joëlle Rivero) invokes the colonial relationship between Spain and Africa, and thus the outcome of territorial appropriation. The 'musa blanca' (white muse's) sidekick María Belén is, effectively, the dummy's dummy. *Tómbola* chillingly reveals the Francoist ideological genre function and children as Franco's colonised subjects.

I continue to trace the counter-hegemonic nature of the *viejo cine español*'s child-starred films. Thereby, I focus on the slippage between its distillation of Francoist values and their perversity in the film's fable of the taming and domestication of a wayward girl. As I demonstrated in Chapter Two, the *viejo cine español* allows for such resistant readings. Rob Stone's chapter on the cinema of childhood similarly asserts that Marisol's films: 'let slip an occasionally subversive attitude in the way her characters often triumphed over adults in admittedly hackneyed plots' (2002: 86). The hegemonic and counter-hegemonic veins of *Tómbola* (Luis Lucía 1962) involve whether Marisol's alertness and corresponding speech are rewarded or punished. The internal contradictions of *Tómbola*'s plot reveal the failure of Francoist instruction such that Marisol must be re-educated by virtue of kidnapping by a ventriloquist. Marisol is the ventriloquist's dummy: a body that the ventriloquist's voice animates as an instrument for the reproduction of ideology. Her lessons are indicative of the Francoist ideological genre function and the conclusive reunion of all characters, most notably the repentant and redeemed, features the ritual genre function of the *cine con niño*. As such, the singing star's vocality is key to her roles and this chapter's case study of Pepa Flores. I further the dialogue on Marisol's filmography and iconography by offering Francoist and oppositional readings of the star-text of the public persona and the private actress's biography, their fusions and fractures, apparent in Marisol's oft-overlooked third film.

Pepa Flores's biography is a story of transformation from rags to riches and from the underage actress of Francoism's *viejo cine español* to the politically subversive cross-over adult performer in limited work with directors of the *nuevo cine español*. Young Pepa Flores made ten films under the stage name of Marisol from 1960 to 1969. Born to a family of modest means in Málaga in 1948, Flores was discovered thanks to her televised appearance in the Noticiario-Documental of Coros y Danzas de la Sección Femenina (News-Documentary of Choirs and Dances of the Women's Section of the Phalange) at the age of eleven in 1959 (Barreiro 1999: 29, 33, 36). The daughter of producer Manuel Goyanes saw Flores on this programme and raved to her father about the girl's talent (38). The next year, Marisol was created under Luis Lucía's direction in her first film, *Un rayo de luz* (*A Ray of Light*), which we will discuss in the next chapter beside a more contemporary *nuevo cine con niño* film. The following year she starred in *Ha llegado un ángel* (*An Angel Has Appeared*). Once discovered by Goyanes, Pepa Flores moved from Málaga to Madrid to live with her producer's family under the constant surveillance, censorship, and control of her producer. Thirty-one-year-old Pepa Flores denounces her exploitation as Francoist darling at the hands of Goyanes in the epigraph of the current chapter. Flores and film scholars alike understand Marisol, Francisco Franco's favourite actress, as the embodiment of the Francoist ideals of service to country and family. In her own skin and in her body of work, the performer lived the political, economic, and cinematic changes that Spain underwent in the 1960s and the country's transition in the aftermath of Franco's death in 1975.

The performer's name change from her childhood moniker Marisol back to her given name Pepa Flores, in fact, marks her maturation, her personal politicisation away from Francoism (Fidel Castro was a witness at her wedding to Antonio Gades in Cuba) and her deviation from the *viejo cine español*. She then worked with Juan Antonio Bardem, Mario Camus and Carlos Saura in *La corrupción de Chris Miller* (*Behind the Shutters*) (1973), *Los días del pasado* (*The Days of the Past*) (1978), and *Bodas de Sangre* (*Blood Wedding*) (1981). It is my contention that *Tómbola* is the most revealing of the biopolitics of the exemplary child during 1960s Francoism. An allegorical reading of *Tómbola* and the biography of Pepa Flores illustrates the high cost that the *niña prodigio* paid while playing her most important role: model Francoist child.

Marisol's first two films – *Un rayo de luz* (Lucía 1960) and *Ha llegado un ángel* (Lucía 1961) – are her most commonly studied features. Núria Triana-Toribio, Román Gubern, Rob Stone, Peter Evans, and Miguel A. Pérez Gómez contribute the few critical studies that focus on Marisol's filmography and iconography in the Francoist and the popular *viejo cine español* (Luis Lucía and Fernando Palacios, among others) remains less studied than the artistic and oppositional *nuevo cine español*. According to Triana-Toribio, Marisol's features were: 'the *Don Quijote* of the child-star musical as a national genre' (2003: 95). Marisol's relationship with María Belén, who observes the similarity, is reminiscent of Don Quixote's with Sancho Panza. Carlos F. Heredero similarly contextualises Marisol's features within the *cine con niño* and views them as a means of updating Joselito's films (1993: 234). For Heredero, Marisol's movies develop alongside but in contrast to the *nuevo cine español*: 'dando lugar así a un contrapunto infantiloide, musical y sentimental que discurre en estrecho paralelismo con el cauce renovador transitado por el antagonista y minoritario "nuevo cine español"' (providing an infantile, musical, and sentimental counterpoint that closely parallels the innovative and antagonistic minority 'New Spanish Cinema') (ibid.). Only Miguel A. Pérez Gómez concentrates on Marisol's fascinatingly contradictory and dreadfully sinister children's film, *Tómbola*. Pérez Gómez judges *Tómbola* to be Marisol's most important film, 'por ser la película que marcó una época, la que forjó el mito de la cantante-actriz malagueña, y la que mejor representa el carisma de la misma' (since it is the film that defined an era, the one that solidified the myth of the singer-actress from Málaga) (2010: 146). This chapter is interested in the popularity of the film to the extent that this demonstrates its emblematic function for late Francoism. I expand on existing scholarship by focusing on *Tómbola* and conducting a symbolic reading of Pepa Flores's life and work manifest in Marisol's third film.

The 1960s were the years of rapid economic development, including tourism, a change in censorship laws, as well as student and worker protests. In 1962, Manuel Fraga Iribarne became Minister of Information and Tourism to work on political reform (such as the right to association) and a relatively, within the Francoist limits of the time, more liberal press law that was passed in 1966. However, after growing activism against the regime in about 1967, Fraga was forced to resign in 1969 (Pavlović et al. 2009: 104–5). Triana-Toribio summarises Marisol's successful hybridity in the changing Spain of the 1960s: 'Marisol came to embody a new discourse of Spanishness celebrated by the regime. Hers was a Spanishness cosmetically and aesthetically closer to Europe, but which still contained the anti-democratic and National-Catholic creed that legitimated the regime' (2003: 87). The year after *Tómbola* was released, Spain implemented the First Economic Development Plan in collaboration with the World Bank (Pavlović et al. 2009: 104). From 1958 to 1964, the tourism industry grew exponentially; from hosting a few million visitors a year to about fourteen million (ibid.). Although the 1960s were a decade of improved economic well-being, the penultimate decade of the dictatorship consisted in 'a new "packaging" of old values' (Triana-Toribio 2003: 87). The new ventriloquial package was Marisol, who embodied a modern image of Spain that welcomed tourism and commerce. As Román Gubern notes, Marisol was a commercial product in her own right and a veritable market phenomenon: 'Marisol se convirtió en una adelantada de las estrategias del merchandising, con muñecas, discos, cuentos, cromos, etc.' (Marisol became a precocious success in merchandising strategies, with dolls, records, stories, trading cards, etc.) (2001: 13). The marketing of Marisol, her characters' protests, and the curtailing of these outbursts situate her squarely within Spain's 1960s.

Marisol served Francoist ideological and mercantile purposes. Producer Manuel Goyanes and director Luis Lucía fashioned Marisol as the icon for 1960s Spain by controlling her body and voice. The outstretched arm of Goyanes in a photo from Pepa Flores's *Interviú* article (Morales 1979: 26), similar to Franco and the ventriloquist gracing the cover of P. W. Ciuró's manual for ventriloquism, demonstrates his reach and purview over his charge, Pepa Flores. Goyanes and Lucía fashioned the young girl as the icon for 1960s Spain, renaming her 'Marisol' to signify Spain as a new European sea-and-sun destination, by controlling her body and voice and stripping Flores of her identity.

Tómbola is an episodic frame narrative of a tale that questions speech like its intertext: Aesop's *The Boy Who Cried Wolf*. In Lucía's remake of the fable, Marisol plays the trickster of Aesop's title. The film structurally ventriloquates the fable in order to transmit its message of proper conduct; re-writing parables was a common strategy in Francoist education. María Elena Soliño advises that 'we should understand the use of fairy tales as part of the wider fascist educational system established by Franco's government' (2002: 49). Marisol, orphaned by both her parents, lives with her wealthy uncle (Guillermo Marín), an insurance man, and attends an all-girls school with her best friend María Belén (Joëlle Rivero), the dark-skinned daughter of an African ambassador. Marisol and María Belén are involved in kidnappings in both episodes of the film. As is the case with Aesop's protagonist, Marisol dissembles about or exaggerates a supposed emergency – by inventing the abduction of María Belén during a horseback riding excursion with classmates – only to find herself subsequently in greater danger.

Later, while on another field trip, Marisol observes the robbery of a painting from the Prado Museum. She alerts her uncle, whose company insures 'La madonna de las rosas' (The Madonna of the Roses), a role model for girls in the 1930s (Jabois 2015: n.p.), but he dismisses her testimony and Marisol is left with the only recourse of reporting the theft on the television and investigating on her own. Marisol subsequently receives a call from one of the robbers, a ventriloquist who lures her into the thieves' den with his dummy, Marieta, in order to protect himself and his fellow criminals by silencing her. Marisol convinces the thieves, who jointly play the role of the wolf in Lucía's remake of Aesop's fable, to return the painting, and justice is served when they are captured in their act of contrition. Marisol warmly receives her new friends to the film's title tune when they are released from jail.

The Ventriloquist Backdrop to *Tómbola*

Tómbola recalls the ventriloquist act starring the Generalísimo himself in 'Franco en Salamanca II' (Franco in Salamanca II), the 1937 newsreel discussed in Chapter One. We recall that the blocking of the recording, in which the ventriloquist (Franco) stands while his dummy (Carmencita) is seated to his side, reveals a structure very similar to the staging of ventriloquism performances since the turn of the century that can be seen on film, in *Sanz y el secreto de su arte* (*Sanz and the Secret of His Art*) (Francisco Sanz and Maximiliano Thous 1918), and can be read in print, as on the cover of P. W. Ciuró's 1963 manual for ventriloquism. Among the early film's cast of sixteen 'actores mecánicos' (mechanical actors) or ventriloquist's dolls, *Sanz y el secreto de su arte* portrays three characters of interest to our ventriloquial elucidation of *Tómbola*: two child dolls, Juanito and Pepito, and one unnamed adult Afro-Cuban dummy. Ciuró's manual also features a Pepito with similar characteristics to Sanz's doll and evidences Franco's appreciation for ventriloquism. The impertinence of the child dummies, including the violence exerted on them in both texts, and of the former colonial subject in *Sanz* are pertinent to *Tómbola*'s representation of children and colonial subjects.

Sanz y el secreto de su arte is part-performance and part-documentary of Francisco Sanz and the behind-the-scenes mechanism of his ventriloquism. Sanz (Valencia 1895–1939) travelled widely as a ventriloquist and, a friend of playwright Jacinto Benavente, was well-known in artistic circles (Rey Reguillo 2004: 227). The Filmoteca de la Generalitat de Valencia's restauration in 1997 of *Sanz* offers privileged access to the historical design of ventriloquism performance and to the construction of the dummies themselves. Child dummies Juanito and Pepito lay the groundwork for ventriloquist performances to come by P. W. Ciuró and *Tómbola*'s fictional Joe Carter. Juanito represents the misbehaved, out-of-control, and loose-lipped child who does not do as he is told but rather tells what his parents do. He represents the danger of tattle-telling or revealing information that embarrasses adults.

Juanito has been punished (he kneels with his arms extended as if on a crucifix) for having tortured a cat with his brother. He is a monstrous child who does what he pleases and his appetite (for chocolate and sardines) has nearly no limits. The information that Juanito divulges suggests that his father is having an affair with their maid. However, there is no need to fear Juanito, *Sanz* assures, because the film visually deconstructs his mechanical underbelly for the spectator's benefit. Sanz demonstrates how Juanito is entirely predictable and under the control, verb choice is significant, of his adult-ventriloquist: 'Todos sus movimientos obedecen a resortes, combinados con los pistones, de la muñeca izquierda' (All of his movements obey springs, combined with pistons, in his left wrist). A prejudicial joke likening children and women reveals both groups to be sources of threat due to their independence: 'Lleva, en vez de corazón, un perfecto mecanismo, ¡Qué bien, si con las mujeres pudiera hacerse lo mismo!' (He has, in place of a heart, a perfect mechanism, How wonderful! If only one could do the same with women). Marisol in *Tómbola* embodies both groups.

Sanz's Pepito is the 'digno émulo de Juanito, dice todo lo que sabe, y a veces más de lo que ha aprendido' (a deserving emulation of Juanito, he says everything he knows and sometimes more than he has learned). Pepito is *pícaro*. He uses clever word play to evade Sanz's questions about his academic performance. The child dummy boasts: 'Este año ha faltado muy poco para que me dieran el primer premio . . . Muy poquito . . . Se lo dieron al que estaba a mi lado' (This year I was really close to receiving the first prize . . . Really close . . . They gave it to the classmate beside me). His ironically mangled conjugations ('sabo' instead of 'Sé' (I know)) also expose his lack of diligence. Pepito defines history, skirting, and glossing over a very similar question put to Marisol at the beginning of *Tómbola*, as: 'La sucesión de los sucesos que sucedieron y los que vayan sucediendo sucesivamente' (It is the succession of the events that occurred and those that would occur successively). Sanz is not amused and threatens Pepito with violence: 'Como no sepas mejor la Doctrina, te encierro en un cajón' (If you do not learn your Christian Doctrine, I will lock you up). The menace incites violence between the two: 'Temiendo ser encajonado, Pepito se l[í]a a bofetadas con el Maestro' (Afraid of being locked up, Pepito and Maestro Sanz come to blows). But 'master teacher' Sanz has the upper hand and is thus able to box Pepito away. The menacing autonomy of both child automatons in *Sanz* is negated at the conclusion of each segment; either by exposing Juanito's mechanical puppet strings or by imprisoning or even symbolically interring Pepito.

The so-called 'disaster' of 1898 in which Spain lost Cuba, Puerto Rico, and the Philippines took place during Sanz's early childhood and is the likely backdrop to the carnivalesque but still humiliating depiction of the Afro-Latino character. This character is unnamed in the film but bears resemblance to 'Negro Panchito' found elsewhere in Sanz's repertoire (Izquierdo Anrubia n.d.: 15; Ramos Altamira 2010: 152). Very few details are provided to allow for a tentative identification. The film, in fact, is incomplete and, naturally, Valencia's Filmoteca has only been able to restore available material (Rey Reguillo 2004: 231). The character's skin colour, speech patterns, and reading material are the only indicators. He appears on stage with the film's breakout star Don Liborio, who identifies him as a coalman. The coalman reads the newspaper entitled *Nuevo Mundo* and responds to Liborio's repeated taunting in this way: 'Estando yo aquí, no tolero que se permita Vd. nada. Retírese, si no quiere morir de dos tiritos en la cabeza. Na má ¡Eeeee . . . so é!' (My presence here will not tolerate that you take any liberties. Withdraw if you do not want to die by two gunshots to the head. Just like that. That's it!). His language recalls that of Afro-Cuban casino rueda dance and, thereby as well, the dancer who appears alongside Liborio in other Sanz performances (Izquierdo Anrubia n.d.: 15).[3] Furthermore, the coalman's employment is probably a form of professional blackface, likening the colour of soot to the man's skin tone, an allusion that repeats in *Tómbola*. Elsewhere in Sanz, Liborio refers to the coalman in oxymoronic fashion as 'Blanca Flor de Chimenea' (White Chimeney Flower), making the contrast between Spanish whiteness and the blackness of the African diaspora more evident (Izquierdo Anrubia n.d.: 15). In carnivalesque fashion and despite his disadvantage in social status, the coalman is more cultured and dignified than Liborio, who takes the other man's hat from his head and picks his own nose. Liborio's 'esclavo de cerillas' (matches slave) is a Spaniard, an actual human rather than a doll, who lights his cigarette. The 'Nuevo Mundo' may be a reference to the Americas and to the change in Spain's world order post-1898 and carnivalesque inversion of Spain as (former) imperial power.

The ventriloquist author P. W. Ciuró was a Catalonian priest, ventriloquist, and magician, twenty years Sanz's junior. His manual from 1963 makes reference to Sanz's gallery of dummies and attests to ventriloquism's popular comeback during Franco's regime: 'La ventriloquía, además de ser un medio encantador de entretenimiento se ha puesto de moda en nuestros días' (Ventriloquism, in addition to being a form of entertainment has become fashionable today) (Ciuró 1963: 22, n.p.). Ciuró documents that, on the twentieth anniversary of the coup and Nationalist triumph, the 'Jefe de Estado', Francisco Franco, honoured the ventriloquist, Balder, for his productions (ibid.). The guide reproduces Francoist rhetoric in its recent history of the art form when it enumerates other famous ventriloquists from before 'nuestra guerra de liberación' (our war of liberation) (ibid.), more objectively known as the Spanish Civil War (1936–9). The ventriloquist speaks from the perspective of the Nationalists, that Franco's forces liberated Spain from the, democratically elected, Second Republic by virtue of the 18 July 1936 mainland coup d'état and victory in 1939.

The speech and obedience-related power struggle between Marisol and her captors is typical of the performance in which the ventriloquist and dummy compete for word and attention. Ciuró's manual, in fact, publishes a script for a dialogue between a ventriloquist, named Mr Flox, and a 'niño travieso, casi descarado' (naughty, almost shameless boy) (120), called Pepito. Pepito is Marisol's homologue since she boasts similar identifying characteristics in *Tómbola* and recalls Sanz's dummy by the same name. Ciuró's dialogue presents word play and, like *Tómbola*, a cheeky child who is scolded and ultimately subdued. Pepito's interruptions begin during Mr Flox's first address of their audience. The child dummy interjects to assert his rights and voice in the performance. As Mr Flox speaks to the ladies and gentlemen, Pepito objects: '¿Y para los niños nada?' (And what about the children?) (ibid.). The impudent child dummy insists on stealing the spotlight and word from Mr Flox. Pepito questions: '¿No tengo derecho de hablar yo también aquí?' (Don't I have a right to speak here too?) (ibid.). Mr Flox answers Pepito that he is not allowed to speak out of turn: 'Solamente cuando te pregunte' (Only when you're asked). The ventriloquist directs Pepito's speech.

Mr Flox's affirmations on the subject of proper conduct are most relevant to *Tómbola*. The ventriloquist explains to Pepito how to be a model child: 'Tú serías un chico modelo si fueras puntual a la escuela, aplicado, estudioso . . . etcétera, etcétera' (You would be a model child if you were punctual to school, diligent, studious, etcetera, etcetera) (121). Mr Flox's instructions on exemplary behaviour, coupled with his admonishments of Pepito's inopportune speech, paint a portrait of juvenile good conduct. Yet Pepito is not a well-behaved boy, as the contrary-to-fact construction denotes, and the ventriloquist does not treat him as such.

The squabbles between ventriloquist and dummy escalate when Flox and Pepito compete directly for the attentions of *señoritas* in the audience. Pepito boasts that the young ladies think that he is more handsome than Mr Flox, illustrating that the child is a threat to the ventriloquist. Flox subsequently calls Pepito a little rascal or swindler ('granujilla') (Ciuró 1963: 122) and locks the boy up in his suitcase. The audience hears Pepito's muffled cries, '¡Socorro!' (Help!), as Mr Flox carries the valise off stage (123). The scripted audience receives the violence towards Pepito with applause. As in the case with Marisol, misbehaviour, both vocal and otherwise, represent a point of contention between the ventriloquist and dummy. Ventriloquists, and other adults, in the 1918 and 1962 films and 1963 dialogue react in similar ways to the child-dummy's outspokenness; Marisol and both Pepitos are captured and muffled.

What is at stake, or lost, in ventriloquism is the subjectivity of the dummy, although the act relies on the dummy's struggle to regain it. Marisol becomes the 'dign[a] émul[a]' of Sanz's Juanito and Pepito. The female gendering of the dummy, having been male in Sanz and Ciuró, in *Tómbola* is achieved in accordance with the Sección Femenina's manual as Marisol proves herself to be an outstanding student of traditional womanhood.

Ventriloquising Marisol

The kidnappings that propel *Tómbola*'s plot, like ventriloquism, involve the appropriation of a child character's body and voice. The child abduction storylines of the film expose its biopolitical machinations and, in so doing, reveal the sinister exploitation of children by the regime through kidnapping for successful indoctrination. The re-education of Marisol is, like her all-girls schooling, gendered and related to her caretaking abilities and speech. Marisol's defiance of authority stems from her verbosity and back talk to adults who respond by coopting or silencing her speech. The ventriloquism of Marisol in *Tómbola* involves a two-stage campaign to quell the girl's incessant yet well-meaning disobedience and to perfect her docility.

Initial sequences of the film demonstrate that Marisol is too rambunctious for her family and school to handle and recalls Juanito's inattention to classroom lessons. For instance, Marisol rebelliously enters the main door of the school singing 'La Marseillaise', with the accompaniment of her classmates, in order to cheekily demonstrate to the school's director that even the French Revolution has its music. The first verse of the French national anthem, 'Allons enfants de la Patrie' (Onward the Children of the Fatherland), casts Marisol similarly as the leader of the Spanish fatherland's youth. The animated schoolgirl continues her dramatised and long-winded rendition of the French Revolution, complete with sound effects, to her history teacher's dismay given that he had only asked the year in which the revolution began. The instructor disapproves of Marisol's verbosity and the sequence demonstrates the star's tendency to get carried away with her narrations. The girl's next response to her teacher, nevertheless, slyly neutralises her popular subversion by roughly dating the French Revolution between the two historical events that Franco's regime most celebrated: 'entre Cristóbal Colón, hasta el Movimiento Nacional' (between Christopher Columbus, up to the National Movement). Of course, Marisol's overwrought story of Marie Antoinette's guillotining also serves as a cautionary tale for overindulgent girls. Opening sequences showcase Marisol's vocality (including song, sound, and narrative ability) and establish it as both entertaining, to her classmates and audience, and unacceptable to authority figures like her teachers.

In the first stage of the offensive to rein in Marisol, the young protagonist displays her problematic docility when she is tested, and fails, in a leadership role during the school's horseback riding excursion. Yet, Marisol's friend is separated from the others during the field trip and the protagonist's imagination gets the best of her when she spins the tale that a hunter in the vicinity has taken María Belén captive. Lucía's film is careful to extinguish any potential critique of Franco's Spain by underscoring the girls' safety. To this end, it so happens that the military is practicing manoeuvres in the same recreational field and enthusiastically lends a hand in searching for the missing girl. An impromptu military campaign in fact aids Marisol and shows the importance and efficiency of patriotic service.

It is significant that Marisol be, like the infantry, vigilant but not thoughtful. Marisol affirms: 'Yo no pienso nada. Vigilo, observo y tomo nota' (I do not think anything. I am vigilant, I observe and I take note). Pérez Gómez is right to contextualise Marisol's declaration within the regime's instruction for children: 'Se trata de representar la imagen de una sociedad al servicio de una causa, siendo esa causa la España del movimiento nacional-catolicista, la idea del niño vigilante y portador de valores' (It consists of representing the image of a society at the service of a cause, the cause being the Spain of the National Catholic movement, the idea of the vigilant and value-bearing child) (2010: 152). Marisol articulates her usefulness as a docile body for Francoism, yet the girl's vigilance is punished in the Aesopian intertext to counter-hegemonic effect. Marisol's suspicion and hyper-alertness are to blame for the international incident that she creates; she pushes Francoist didacticism to its breaking point. The episode of María Belén's separation, and imagined kidnapping, remarkably proves that Marisol's observance of Nationalist instruction backfires.

While Marisol's dummy-like embodiment of Nationalist ideals is implicit in the film's first anecdote, the ventriloquial subtext of the film is first made explicit by the introduction of the character, Joe Carter 'ventrílocuo tragicómico' (tragicomic ventriloquist), and his deception of Marisol in the second stage of the campaign to re-educate the unruly star. The anecdote of the art theft, comprising the remainder of the film, again proves that alertness, outspokenness, and robbery are punishable offences. The painting that unites Marisol and the thieves serves as the axis of the second episode of the film and as a symbol of ideal femininity. The 'Madonna de las rosas' depicts the motherhood of the Virgin Mary as she is portrayed embracing baby Jesus. The painting's theft becomes a catalyst for Marisol's feminine education and the gendering of her rehabilitation.

The disappearance of the work of art allows Marisol to reveal her maternal and nursing talents in addition to her singing and dancing artistry. The 1960 manual of the Sección Femenina outlines the objectives of the women's organisation and *Tómbola*'s characterisation of Marisol on the basis of: domestic, child-care, and maternal teachings, regional song and dance and religious and patriotic concerns (cited in Otero 2004: 94). Marisol's character in her 1962 film, thus, incorporates the subjects that the Sección Femenina had deemed essential to a woman's education two years earlier. Women's social service centered on caretaking and: 'women's rights as defined primarily by their childbearing and/or nurturing capacities' (Ofer 2009: 3). These motherly qualities alone can be gleaned from the Franco family newsreel from 1937, which portrays a voiceless Carmen whose sole role is to buttress her daughter seated on her lap. Carmen Polo's value, reduced to maternal utility, is second to her daughter's.

At the thieves' safe house in *Tómbola*, Marisol transforms, and she is effectively domesticated. Her education in an all-girls private school, which teaches her how to cook and change diapers, prepares her for this function. Blond Marisol assumes the role of nurse when the three greedy robbers are bedridden after injuring one another in an armed skirmish, invoking echoes of *Goldilocks and the Three Bears*. Thereby, the men provide Marisol the opportunity to practice her school lessons of first aid, which she pretends are 'el único sobresaliente de [su] vida' (the only outstanding grade of her life). While Marisol teaches the criminals a lesson in honesty, the thieves permit Marisol to realise her potential as a 'niña buena' (good girl) despite her protests.

The thieves represent the wolves who threaten the shepherdess, rather than her sheep. Yet, the antagonistic criminals and the film's young protagonist have more in common than the spectator might initially expect since they all transgress in their own right. Giorgio Agamben's understanding of modern political life can help explain the collusion between Marisol and the wolfish thieves and provides the link between Foucauldian biopolitics and my theorisation of Francoist ventriloquism in *Tómbola*. The bare life of the *homo sacer* in Agamben's discussion accurately describes Marisol while his conceptualisation of the relationships among the *homo sacer*, the sovereign, and the wolf bandit reveal much about *Tómbola*'s characterisation. The *homo sacer*'s and the wolf bandit's bare lives are a result of their lack of protection under the law. The *homo sacer* is the sacred man: '*who may be killed and yet not sacrificed*' (1998: 8; emphasis in the original). His natural life is made bare as a result of being stripped of his right to live and becoming, in a sense, a ward of the state. With respect to the *homo sacer* and the wolf bandit 'anyone was permitted to kill without committing homicide. The medieval ban also presents analogous traits: 'the bandit could be killed . . . "To ban someone is to say that anyone may harm him"' (104–5). Although the *homo sacer* and the bandit would seem very disparate, Agamben considers that in 'the bandit and the outlaw (*wargus, vargr*, the wolf, and, in the religious sense, the sacred wolf, *vargr y veum*),

German and Scandinavian antiquity give us a brother of *homo sacer* beyond the shadow of any doubt' (Rodolphe Jhering cited in Agamben 1998: 104). Marisol's misbehaviour causes her kidnapping and thus she and the bandits are collectively banished to a hide-out near the French border. Despite their transgressions, the wolfish bandits in *Tómbola* and Marisol cooperate to redeem each other and accept their bare lives.

Ceding control of her speech, and subjectivity, to grown-up authorities constitutes Marisol's bare life. Adults, whether law-abiding or law-breaking, instruct Marisol with regards to her utterances and behaviour. For instance, Marisol's uncle, who insures the painting, does not believe his niece's tale of the theft. The young informant protests that her uncle and his insurance associates: 'No me dejaron ni siquiera abrir la boca' (They didn't let me even open my mouth). The prohibition is not simply a figure of speech, but actually physical since Marisol's uncle muzzles his niece with his hand in order to silence her fabulations (Figure 3.1). The girl's guardian aims to control her speech by restraining her body. Not to be deterred, however, Marisol appears on television to notify the thieves that she would be able to recognise them in a line-up.

The ventriloquist kidnapper more artfully gains Marisol's cooperation and silence in *Tómbola*. While Marisol throws her voice via television to lure the robbers, ventriloquist Joe Carter throws his by phone in order to trap Marisol. Joe calls Marisol under the vocal guise of his fictitious

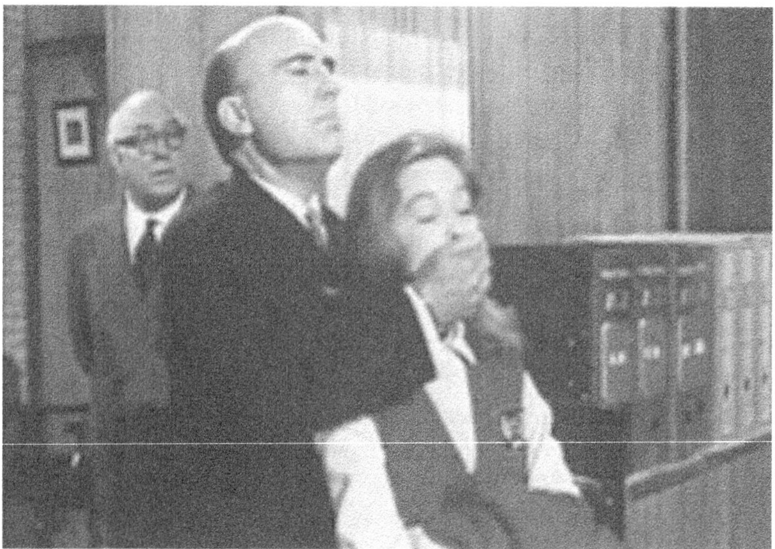

Figure 3.1 Marisol's Tío Pablo (Guillermo Marín) muzzles her in *Tómbola*.

Figure 3.2 Marisol (Pepa Flores) and Marieta, the dummy who resembles her in *Tómbola*.

daughter the 'muñeca parlante' (talking doll) Marieta from Valladolid. The dummy persuades Marisol not to turn her father in if he returns the painting. Marisol heeds her sense of charity and agrees to help Marieta while also revealing their likeness (Figure 3.2). The star tells María Belén: 'es una niña como tú y como yo, bueno, mucho mejor que tú y yo porque encima es pobre' (she is a girl like you and I, well, much better than you and I because, to top it off, she is poor). The protagonist's words establish hers and María Belén's conditions as dummies, since she asserts their similarity with Marieta. Marisol's physical and onomastic resemblance to the blonde dummy is also undeniable while her balding uncle's appearance is also curiously similar to Franco's. The girl takes the ventriloquist's bait, agreeing to go to Marieta's house alone and 'guardar un secreto' (keep a secret). Marisol surrenders her vocality and subjectivity with her voice.

Muteness is compulsory to Marisol's lesson. She promises Joe Carter's dummy that she will not tell anyone where she is going, but María Belén follows her friend and informs the police when Marisol goes missing. When the three men kidnap the witness, Marisol understands: 'me metí en la boca del lobo' (I entered the wolf's mouth). The girl's figure of speech conveys the danger of the situation and also metonymically designates speech, by virtue of the wolf's mouth, as perilous. The captive promises to remain mum, giving Marieta her 'palabra de honor que no se entera nadie' (word of honor that no one will find out). When Joe Carter reveals to Marisol that he animates Marieta's voice, the ventriloquist does so in the language of obedience: 'Yo soy una niña muy buena y siempre hago lo que me mandan las personas mayores' (I am a very good girl and I always do what grown-ups tell me to do). Marisol, Marieta's homologue, is more often outspoken and disobedient despite instructions from adults. In typical ventriloquial performance, Marieta undermines her ventriloquist when she warns Marisol not to trust the thieves. The bandits, like Joe hushing Marieta, order Marisol to be quiet.

Marisol becomes complicit in her own captivity and silencing. One of the abductee's enquiries to her captors is, first, of fundamental import to the counter-hegemonic reading that *Tómbola* invites and, second, implicates the political use of children under Franco. At first, the thieves remedy Marisol's misbehaviour with the threat of force and the mishandling of their weapons. Marisol agrees to obey – by either keeping quiet or singing – out of charity, collusion with, or fear of the gun-bearing criminals. The men abduct Marisol in order to control her vocalisation; nevertheless, Marisol convinces her captors that allowing her to sing would mask the kidnapping: '¿quién puede imaginar que va secuestrada una niña que canta?' (who could imagine that a kidnapped girl would sing?). Marisol's deceptively innocent rhetorical question exposes the commercial exploitation of the child stars of the *cine con niño* films since musical numbers help to disguise the violence of Marisol's kidnapping and ventriloquism in *Tómbola*.

Tómbola, like the performance of Mr Flox and Pepito, is a meditation on power and the child's right to speech and subjectivity. Lucía's film argues for the limitation of the child's vocalisation even in the case of informing on the theft of a national treasure. In *Tómbola*, three thieves steal two valuable national treasures: the 'Madonna de las rosas' and Marisol. The wolfish thieves teach Marisol that she should be obedient and not speak up. The criminals only allow her vocalisation when she sings to mask their second crime, her kidnapping. They ventriloquise the girl in order to diffuse her insubordination. The ventriloquists Mr Flox and Joe Carter instruct their dummies, Pepito and Marisol, that obedience makes an exemplary child. Although the film ends happily, the cautionary tale teaches that the country is only safe for the obedient. *Tómbola*'s education for young girls is as deceptively benign as a wolf in sheep's clothing.

Spanish Colonialism and María Belén:
The Dummy's Dummy

María Belén's character invokes the colonial relationship between Spain and Africa. Just as the coalman's origins are not clearly named in *Sanz y el secreto de su arte*, María Belén's are left undefined. She is the daughter of an ambassador from 'un país africano' (an African country) near the Congo. Confusion and indeterminacy are underscored when a priest whom Marisol asks for counsel cannot make heads or tails of the affair. It is likely that María Belén's character alludes to Spanish Guinea, which gained independence five years after *Tómbola*'s release. Casting, since Spanish Guinean Joëlle Rivero plays María Belén, may help specify. Furthermore, the year of the film's release, 1963, coincides with an important referendum intended to appease the United Nations, who supported Guinea's independence, and to delay the loss of Guinea as a Spanish colony by changing its status to autonomous region (Martín-Márquez 2008: 283). These geopolitical dynamics play out through Marisol's friendship with María Belén. In fact, the rewriting of the fable casts Marisol as the shepherdess who must protect her sheep, the African girl. In keeping with ventriloquism, there is also a reversal of fortunes in which María Belén serves as liaison to the police for Marisol's rescue and reunion with her family and friends, who now include her kidnappers.

Let us first take into account Spain's infantilisation of its African territories in order to better contextualise the child character of María Belén. Alberto Elena convincingly presents Spain's conception of Africans as inferior children and this representation's centrality to Spanish colonialism in Africa: 'La noción de la inferioridad del negro se constituiría, en realidad, como una de las piedras angulares del colonialismo español en los territorios de Guinea, por más que la propaganda insistiera hasta la saciedad en su naturaleza antirracista' (The notion of the inferiority of the black man would constitute, in reality, one of the cornerstones of Spanish colonialism in Guinean territories, no matter how much propaganda insisted on its own anti-racist nature) (2010: 168). Constructing the inferiority of Africans paved the way for Spanish intervention in the continent: 'la reducción del negro a una inequívoca condición de *homo infantilis* justificaba de manera evidente la (cristiana) intervención tutelar' (the reduction of the black man to the unequivocal condition of *homo infantilis* evidently justified (Christian) tutelary intervention) (169). Relegating adults to the status of children establishes a hierarchy of power that allows for paternalism and exploitation. In *Tómbola*, Marisol exhibits a tutelary role over María Belén.

The opening song, the episode of the horseback riding excursion, María Belén's hair and wardrobe, and a series of racial comments subordinate the black Spanish African character to the white Spanish character. To begin with, the girls are classmates, but Marisol is taller and appears older than María Belén. On the bus ride to school, Marisol sings 'Chiquitina' (Little One) for and referring to María Belén. The song is about a young girl who wants to grow up quickly: 'quisiera ser tan alta como la luna' (she would like to be as tall as the moon). That is, the Spanish African character is more childlike than her Spanish classmate. The opening song signals the coming-of-age narrative, in particular the passage from girl to young woman, in *Tómbola*. The protagonist later celebrates her birthday with all her friends, singing while suggestively loosening the neckties of the (older) boy band members who play the title song. Marisol sings 'Chiquitina' to María Belén from a place of relative maturity, at the same time that her appearance suggests her impending transformation in the film.

Hair styles are significant in the ageing of the characters. As the song goes: 'Chiquitina, chiquitina, le dicen los muchachos al verla pasar/ Buenos días Chiquitina/las trenzas de tu pelo ¿quién las cortará?' (Little One, Little One, the boys say to her as she passes by/Good morning Little One/who will cut your braids?). Braids and pigtails are the appropriate styles for maidens and this is how Marisol and María Belén, respectively, wear their hair during the first song. Marisol's hair dos, however, evolve over the course of the film from braids to a corn silky mane with or without a headband, to a pony tail to, while in the custody of the kidnappers, a young lady's demure head covering. María Belén's short cut only changes the colour of its bows. At other times, like during Marisol's birthday party, she appears as a black, miniature Marisol wearing the same white dress in similar fashion to the resemblance between Marisol and the braided hair of Marieta the dummy (Figure 3.3). The song offers the first allusion to gender violence in the children's film with its narration of what amounts to boys' cat calls of a young girl on the street that reference her physical maturation or loss of virginity as, metonymically, a result of cutting.

For the school's horseback riding excursion, Marisol has been charged with leading the group and keeping it together; that is, she is the shepherdess of the flock. The two girls are dressed in the same way again. Marisol's active imagination, however, causes her to worry about María Belén's safety. In the preceding scene at the gym, María Belén tells Marisol that there is quite a lot of unrest in her country: 'en mi país están pasando tantas cosas. Lo de las tribus, ¿sabes?' (so much is going on in my country. With the tribes, you know?). Apparently, the tribes are trying to topple the 'legitimate government', for which her friend's father the ambassador

Figure 3.3 María Belén (Joëlle Rivero) and Marisol in similar wardrobe while Marisol receives the phone call from Marieta during her birthday party in *Tómbola*.

works. It becomes Marisol's responsibility to protect María Belén, her sheep, from the rebel tribes by maintaining the integrity of the flock, that is, exerting power and oversight over the metonymic colony turned best friend. María Belén assures Marisol that she is not in peril because: 'aquí en España no hay ningún peligro' (here in Spain there is no danger).

Dark skin signals danger in *Tómbola*, in fact. When María Belén wanders off, Marisol is suspicious of a hunter whom they saw in half black face: 'María Belén, ¡cuidado! Que el cazador no era blanco' [María Belén, Watch out! The hunter was not white]. María Belén in fact befriends the man, a railroad employee who likes to hunt. He washes the black off half his face, contrary to Marisol's estimation: 'lo que parecía una mancha era piel' (what looked like a stain was skin). María Belén indicates that her face cannot turn black with dirt ('ponerse un asco' (become disgusting) as the hunter says) because she indicates that it is already black. María Belén's skin colour is a subject of conversation throughout the film that highlights the Spanish language's negative associations with the colours of brown and black. A military officer refers to María Belén as 'la amiga de chocolate' (the chocolate friend) that's gone missing. She herself wishes she were blonde and blue-eyed like Marisol. To which Marisol responds: 'también [tus ojos] son color del cielo, María Belén, pero de un poquito más tarde cuando ya han salido las estrellas' (your eyes are also the colour of the sky, María Belén, the starry night sky). María Belén indicates her skin tone in order to conjure up the idiom 'marrón' (a problem) regarding

Marisol's capture: 'si las cosas se ponían de un color como este' (if things were to turn this colour). Marisol warns María Belén that if she does not explain what is going on, she will become very angry ('me voy a poner negra'). Many of these cosmetic references recall that of the soot and Sanz's coalman. Coincidentally, Marieta the dummy conjures up the coal yard as well, lying that she is calling Marisol from one.[4]

In carnivalesque inversion, María Belén is not lost, Marisol has simply 'cried wolf', and María Belén must watch out for Marisol. She emerges from the shadows, tailing Marisol when the protagonist goes to the 'wolves' den'. When Marisol does not return, María Belén leads adults to Marisol's meeting place. A character insists that kidnapping, like those in the movies, only very rarely occur in Spain. Marisol, nevertheless, is able, with the help of a town priest, to convince the thieves to turn themselves in. The sinners repent, and order is restored.

Ventriloquising Pepa Flores

Carmencita Franco, Marisol, Pepito, and finally Pepa have ventriloquism in common. Marisol's on- and off-screen personas are similar with respect to Francoist biopolitics. Pepa Flores's stolen childhood resembles, in fact, the child singer abducted in *Tómbola*.[5] While the child star is domesticated in Lucía's film, her biography details the steps taken to convert Pepa Flores into a docile child of Franco's Spain. Michel Foucault's definition of the docile body highlights the objectification of the body as an item of utility (1979: 136). As it pertains to the analysis at hand, a docile body is one prepared for and engaged in ventriloquism. The biography of Pepa Flores can be read as a parable for the restrictive, and often abusive, fashioning and ventriloquism of the regime's ideal child. Perhaps for this reason, as she gained autonomy with age, Pepa Flores became less willing to participate in Marisol's embodiment and more reticent concerning her ill-starred childhood until finally retiring from public life. Pepa Flores's reluctance to speak about her youth leaves few interviews, including those published in a 2008 biography and a 1979 issue from *Interviú* magazine and her unauthorised 1999 biography by Javier Barreiro on which a 2009 TV mini-series is based. The actress's biography and television biopic reveal the making of the child star and thus the process of ventriloquising Pepa Flores.

Renewed interest in Marisol in the past decade, giving particular attention to the deconstruction of the 1960s model, speaks to contemporary Spain's retrospection and revision of its dictatorial past. Manuel Palacios's two-part television miniseries, *Marisol* (2009), participates in this effort by highlighting the exploitation of the child actress with ventriloquial connotations that are strikingly similar to Franco's 1937 newsreel. In the mini-series, the girl's suitability for ventriloquism is tested during her informal audition in the Madrid home office of Manuel Goyanes (Roberto Álvarez) for director Luis Lucía (Blai Llopis). Pepi, as she is called in the biopic, begins by uttering a very difficult tongue twister with remarkable ease. Her next task is more notable due to its indoctrinatory overtones. Luis Lucía asks the child to recite from an ultra-right-wing newspaper, *El Alcázar*. Marisol memorises and vocalises a piece of reactionary propaganda while mimicking the dictator's gestures: '¡Españoles! ¡Españoles todos! Queremos una España fraternal donde los parásitos no encuentren acomodo. Una España sin cadenas ni tiranías . . . Una España sin mandos políticos y sin preponderancias parlamentarias' (Spaniards! Spaniards! We want a fraternal Spain where the parasites are not welcome. A Spain without chains and tyrannies . . . A Spain without political mandates and without parliamentary preponderances). Pepi's hyperbolic, empty, and 'fraternal' message echoes that of Carmencita Franco from the 1937 newsreel. The 'parásitos' and 'tiranías' from the newspaper excerpt foreshadow Marisol's commercial subjugation while both the parasite and the ventriloquist derive their strength from the body of another. The girl thus serves as host for three parasites: dictator Franco, director Lucía, and producer Goyanes.

The mini-series illustrates the force involved in making the star and Pepa Flores accuses her producer and director for as much in *Interviú*. Whereas Marisol innocently questions in her 1962 film, Flores indicts her real-life captors. The producer restricted Marisol's freedom of movement, expression, and association. The former child star remembers Manuel Goyanes's treatment of her as if she had been a hostage: 'no me relacionaba con otra gente que no fueran las que me dejaran en aquella casa. Estaba como secuestrada' (I did not interact with people other than those who I met in that house. It was like I was a hostage) (Pepa Flores cited in Morales 1979: 28). Pepa Flores's condemnation of the Goyanes family for treating her as if she were 'secuestrada', first, echoes her character's enquiry from *Tómbola* and, second, belies the appearance of her idyllic childhood.

The sequester of Pepa Flores manifests in language connoting bondage that recurs in Pepa Flores's biography to denote the bare life of the actress. Corporal and sensory restriction – apparent in the repetition of *vendas* (bindings: blindfolds, gags, or bandages) – indicate her captivity and compound the negation of Flores's selfhood. The producer's control of his star's body is immediately evident in the cosmetic changes that

Flores undergoes. Flores reports: 'Se ocupaban de comprarme la ropa, los calcetines que tenía que usar, la forma del peinado y todo, todo; *a mí no me dejaban decir nada*' (They took charge of buying me clothes, the socks I had to use, my hair style and everything, everything; *they didn't let me say anything*) (cited in Morales 1979: 27; emphasis added). Flores's words echo Marisol's lines in *Tómbola*, protesting that her uncle and his associates would not allow her to speak in order to protect their business interests. In addition, Goyanes ordered that Flores's hair be dyed blonde and required Marisol to bandage her developing chest in order to extend her child-like appearance and, accordingly, her profitability with juvenile audiences (D'Lugo 1997: 240).[6] Flores remembers that she was not allowed to use a brassiere until she could no longer bear the painfulness of the *vendas* (Morales 1979: 28). Her cosmetic changes were accompanied by enforced and prerequisite muteness that denied her subjectivity.

Ventriloquism as a metaphor of the regime's sexual violence, indoctrination of children, and violation of human rights is reflected in the biography of Franco's favourite actress. The exploitation of Marisol's voice and body extended beyond the theatrical stage, film set, and cinema screen. Abuse of the minor for and by the regime is evident in a third-hand reference of her off-screen victimisation: 'Me llevaban a un chalet del Viso y allí acudía gente importante, gente del régimen, a verme desnuda, a mí y a otras niñas' (They took me to a house in El Viso and important people of the regime got together there to see me naked, me and other girls) (cited in Moix 1993: 278). Pepa Flores suffered additional assaults, as the actress reports in her defiant interview accompanied by nude photos, for the magazine *Interviú* in 1979.[7] Pepa discloses that a photographer molested her as a child:

> [N]os metía mano, y luego nos amenazaba *para que no dijéramos nada*. Más tarde, un día cualquiera, descubrimos en la cocina muchas fotos de niñas desnudas con *vendas* en los ojos. Se lo dijimos a Goyanes y se quedó como si nada'. (Flores cited in Anonymous 1996; emphasis added)

> [[H]e groped us and later he threatened us *so we would not say anything*. Later, a day like any other, we discovered many photos in the kitchen of naked girls with *blindfolds* over their eyes. We told Goyanes and he acted like nothing had happened.]

Flores's revelation is disturbing on a number of levels: first, that she was among many victims of molestation; second, that her guardian did not intervene to protect her; and third, that there was a later occasion during which she discovered such distressing evidence of other victims. Goyanes's apathetic response to Pepa's complaint may indicate that abuse was common and naturalised while it makes manifest that Goyanes was her producer and not her protector. The 'binding' restricts Marisol's chest, the sight and identification of the photographer's victims, and, I add, speech.

The child actress and personage was under strict instructions regarding her speech. While still under the guardianship of Manuel Goyanes, the producer monitored Marisol's words on and off set. The producer bound Marisol to a 'guión' (script), the equivalent of a verbal *venda*, for press junkets and tours: 'Cuando tenía yo que responder, pocas veces, me obligaba a llevar en un papel escrito o *apuntado en la mano*, lo que ellos me decían que tenía que contestar' (When I needed to answer, which was rare, they obligated me to use written notes or notes *written on my hand* of what they wanted me to respond) (Flores cited in 1979: 28; emphasis added). Marisol's body was a canvas on which lines were even engraved. Show-business people besides Goyanes exerted force and influence upon Flores. As she testifies to *Interviú*, the photographer-molester threatened her, and others, if they spoke about the molestation. Flores's interview and photos for the adult magazine liberate the woman from the trappings of Marisol. Pepa's appearance and interview in the adult magazine and film work with the oppositional directors of the *nuevo cine español* similarly reads as the calculated unwrapping of Marisol's *vendas*.

Conclusion

Pepa Flores's biography reveals the making and unmaking of a *niña prodigio*. The voice of Flores, now seventy years old, became hoarse from a childhood of vocal exploitation as Marisol. The abuse of Pepa's vocal chords is apparent in its deleterious consequences when, after her eighth film, Pepa's symbolic muteness temporarily somaticised: 'Me quedé muda, no podía hablar. Claro que de eso no se enteró nadie . . . El instrumento había roto' (I went mute, I could not talk. Of course no one found out about this . . . The instrument had broken) (cited in Aguilar and Losada 2008: 310). Marisol's docile instrumentality buckled under constant pressure but Pepa could not buck her show-business duties until she grew older. One reading of Flores's nudity in *Interviú* tells the story of the defiant exposition of the bare life Marisol lived as a fabled child star. Another interpretation retells the story of the commercial exploitation of Flores's body; she did not earn money for her cover photos of the sixteenth issue and, as Barreiro argues, they were largely responsible for establishing the success of the nascent magazine: 'Marisol tuvo un papel fundamental en el asentamiento y desarrollo de uno de los grupos de opinión todavía hoy más influyentes' (Marisol played a fundamental role in the establishment and development of one of today's most influential editorial groups) (1999: 139–40). Irony emerges in the contrast between Flores's own critical words in her interview for the magazine and the use of her images for the magazine's profit.

While it is true of *Un rayo de luz* and *Ha llegado un ángel* that Marisol schools adults, *Tómbola* exposes the violence necessary for adults to instruct Marisol. The dangers of Francoist teachings are readily apparent much earlier in *Tómbola* where they take the form of wolfish criminals who threaten the young protagonist. Marisol's re-education takes place only as a consequence of her kidnapping, and metaphorical ventriloquism, at the hands of thieves. The model child of Francoism is reduced to no more than a ventriloquist's dummy. The symbolically severe consequences for Marisol's outspokenness in 1962's *Tómbola* align perfectly with the impending (in 1968 and 1969) suspension of constitutional rights that was the dictator's response to worker activism (Pavlović et al. 2009: 104–5). Marisol does not lose her rights to voice and vote but rather, as a model for others, happily surrenders them. The Francoist ventriloquist has a long reach, however, subordinating a Spanish Guinean child dummy to Marisol. The disenfranchised child represents Spaniards and colonial subjects under Franco. Pepa Flores's third film ends triumphantly in compliance with the ideological and ritual genre functions; Marisol and the thieves are successfully corrected and all, including María Belén, are brought back into the fold.

Notes

1. An abbreviated version of this chapter first appeared in *Studies in Spanish and Latin-American Cinemas* 10.1 (2013: 101–15) as 'The Voice, Body and Ventriloquism of Marisol in *Tómbola* (Lucía 1962)'. This chapter adds a post-colonial reading of the character of María Belén.
2. All translations are mine in Chapter Three.
3. *Sanz y el secreto de su arte* was actually reviewed in this paper (Ramos Altamira 2010: 149).
4. Disguise is a recurring theme in the carnivalesque current of *Tómbola*: the hunter's blackface; Marisol asks a Spanish military officer if he may actually be a Chinese man in disguise; Marisol understands that the criminals remove their thief masks upon surrender and replace them with their true, good faces.
5. In this allegorical vein, Peter Evans's study of Marisol and *La nueva cenicienta / The New Cinderella* (George Sherman 1964) suggests that the actress's biography is a case of Münchausen syndrome by proxy abuse on account that her family allows her exploitation for their well-being (2004: 134): 'What is clearly

intended as a spectacular phenomenon of adult bravura emanating from the body of a child actually also becomes a complex site of resistance, of sexual self-consciousness and psychological aggression, the screen projection of the conscious and unconscious drives of her biological and commercial creators' (135). For Evans, Marisol is the Münchausen victim at the hands of her parents and parental surrogate, her producer Manuel Goyanes. Pepa Flores's body was indeed a complex site of juncture and conflict that negated and sacrificed the girl's subjectivity.

6. Marvin D'Lugo's biography of the star chronicles the trajectory of her career: 'the fact of Flores' physical development shortly required certain transformations of her screen persona from perky child star to amorous adolescent. The Marisol genre continued to work until the end of the 1960s, when, in order to accommodate her appearance of a young woman, she was situated in a series of progressively less wholesome narrative situations' (1997: 240).

7. The nude photos were taken by Flores's unofficial photographer César Lucas in 1970, who later submitted them to *Interviú* for publication in 1976, for a film project with French actor Alain Delon that never came to fruition (Barreiro 1999: 140). A judge in Barcelona sued Lucas in 1978, and lost in 1981, for 'un atentado a la moral y escándalo público' (a moral affront and a public scandal) (141).

CHAPTER FOUR

Adopting, Adapting and Appropriating in the *cines con niño*: *Un rayo de luz* and *El viaje de Carol*

Introduction

In the preceding chapters I have theorised the ventriloquial appropriation of the child protagonist's voice and body and the dialogism of the *cines con niño*. I turn my attention now to a particularly self-aware case of dialogism: adaptation. My focus will be on story, thus the narrative points of contact and departure rather than cinematic language, in two key films across the *cines con niño* that indicate the greater narrative appropriation of the *cine con niño* genre. Having explored in Chapter Three how Francoist cinema characterises Marisol as its ventriloquist's dummy in her third film *Tómbola* (Lucía 1962), we return to Marisol's first film in order to consider dialogism as narratological ventriloquism, or, following Bakhtin, ventriloquation. Subsequent oppositional filmmaking of constitutional Spain utilises the storytelling strategies of *Un rayo de luz* (*A Ray of Light*) (Luis Lucía 1960) for its political purposes. I argue that the *cine con niño* film *Un rayo de luz* and the *nuevo cine con niño* feature *El viaje de Carol* (*Carol's Journey*) (Imanol Uribe 2002) adapt the same nineteenth-century Anglo-American literary source text, Francis Hodgson Burnett's children's literature classic from 1885 *Little Lord Fauntleroy*, for opposing ideals of the two Spains.

The nature of the three texts that I analyse in this chapter calls for an intersectional approach that draws upon literary genre (Mikhail Bakhtin), film genre (Rick Altman), and adaptation theory (Deborah Cartmell, Julie Sanders, and Linda Hutcheon). Following Julie Sanders's terminology, I will examine the dialogism of adaptation and, in particular, the case of analogue and transposition between Marisol (Pepa Flores) and Carol (Clara Lago) in their respective feature-film debuts. These examples from the *cine con niño* and the *nuevo cine con niño* offer exceptional insight into the utilisation of the child protagonist in twentieth and twenty-first century Spain for contrary ideologies regarding family, nation, class, and gender.

Un rayo de luz and *El viaje de Carol* each participate in double-voiced discourse that addresses the national past and present. Lucía's feature, set and released in the 1960s, makes analogous mention of the conflict between the 'rebels' and the 'reds' in the Spanish Civil War during the 1930s. Uribe's feature is set during the Civil War (1936–9) but also dialogues with the prominent memory debate that led to the passing of the Law of Historical Memory five years later. It is productive to account for the variations on *Little Lord Fauntleroy* in *Un rayo de luz* and *El viaje de Carol* by looking at the films' historic and artistic contexts. Adaptation is a process of creation and reception (Hutcheon 2013: 7–8). Context informs both processes involved in Uribe's feature. The film's adaptation of the grandfather–grandchild narrative within another political milieu produces a tragic ending. *El viaje de Carol* is the only tragedy of the three.

In fact, *El viaje de Carol* is representative of many *nuevo cine con niño* films and their tragic outcomes. Most, *Butterfly* (*La lengua de las mariposas*) (Cuerda 1999), for instance, portray Francoism from the perspective of those who lost the Spanish Civil War and who have little legal recourse to right injustices from the ensuing dictatorship. *Carol* at times evokes the nostalgia of heritage films, like other Spanish productions of the 2000s that Sally Faulkner discusses (2013: 264); however, Uribe's feature at once longs for a peaceful childhood that the war ultimately disrupts and wistfully glosses over the terrible losses that cause Carol's exile with a sentimental farewell scene. We may recall that the Asociación para la Recuperación de la Memoria Histórica (the Association for the Recuperation of Historical Memory) began its work in exhumations (of the executed by *paseo* like Tomiche's father) two years prior to the release of *El viaje de Carol* and that the Law of Historical Memory, with all its limitations, was not approved until 2007 under José Luis Rodríguez Zapatero's socialist administration. Uribe produced and directed *El viaje de Carol* during the antepenultimate year of the right-wing government of Popular Party President José María Aznar, which was antagonistic towards the cause of historical memory.

While *Little Lord Fauntleroy* offers an example in binational – England and the United States – reconciliation following a divisive war, *El viaje de Carol* extricates its child protagonist, who is orphaned by her mother's death and her father's arrest, from harm and safeguards her across the Atlantic. As in Pepa Flores's filmography, a number of Clara Lago's parts in her evolving, increasingly commercially successful career have showcased the national identities in and of Spain, including her more recent smash success *Ocho apellidos vascos* (*Spanish Affair*) (Emilio Martínez Lázaro 2014) and 2015 sequel, *Ocho apellidos catalanes* (*Spanish Affair 2*)

(Emilio Martínez Lázaro). This chapter will explore how *El viaje de Carol* proffers greater visibility to the militia woman, through Carol's protagonism, and the Republic's unsung heroes, reversing the Francoist politics of *Un rayo de luz*. I argue that the adoption of the child protagonist in Uribe's approach to the Spanish Civil War is a political appropriation of the child's symbolism for Francoism.

The basic premise of a child's journey to the country of his or her parents' origin and the revelation of cultural differences therein with respect to recent national conflict is common to all three texts. Nevertheless, the kinship of *El viaje de Carol* with *Little Lord Fauntleroy* and *Un rayo de luz* has not been explored. While Peter Evans (2004: 130) and Tatjana Pavlović (2011: 127) indeed recognise *Little Lord Fauntleroy*'s intertext in *Un rayo de luz*, Sally Faulkner's studies of Spanish popular cinema compares *El viaje de Carol* to the 'highbrow' *El espíritu de la colmena* (*The Spirit of the Beehive*) (Víctor Erice 1973) rather than examine 'middlebrow' precursors and contemporary homologues in the *viejo cine español* (2013: 251–3). Faulkner is right that: 'middlebrow cinema, with its accessible treatment of serious themes, may provide a productive forum in which to explore pressing contemporary concerns' (251). However, *El viaje de Carol* is also double-voiced in its response both to the more immediate contemporary concern of historical memory and also through its predecessor, ventriloquating *Un rayo de luz*. I emphasise this mechanism.

Narrative Adoption, Adaptation, Appropriation

Embattled family members and neighbours represent the feuding two Spains in each feature even when conflict is located abroad. In *Un rayo de luz*, Marisol defeats the 'red-bearded' neighbour children, in lieu of Spanish Republicans or 'reds', and Carol's family divides along political lines whereby her nuclear family is Republican while her aunt's family is Nationalist. The dualism present throughout the *cines con niño* is, in fact, also a defining characteristic of film genre (Altman 1999: 24). Rick Altman's theorisation of genre functions also splits in two between the ideological and the ritual. I contend throughout *The Two* cines that the state-controlled and censored *cine con niño* exhibits the ideological function in alignment with Francoism while the *nuevo cine con niño* demonstrates the ritual function through the alternatives to Francoist control that it presents and its Republican origin of enunciation.

Hodgson Burnett's common intertext heightens and highlights the dialogism of the films and reveals the genrification, Rick Altman's term, of the *nuevo cine con niño* or, in Mikhail Bakhtin's terms, the *nuevo cine con niño* as a genre-in-the-making. Bakhtin reminds us: 'The social and historical voices populating language, all its words and all its forms, which provide language with its particular concrete conceptualizations, are organized in the novel into a structured stylistic system that expresses the differentiated socio-ideological position of the author amid the heteroglossia of his epoch' (1981: 300). *Un rayo de luz* and *El viaje de Carol* socially and ideologically re-accentuate, a concept deployed in our Bakhtinian analysis in Chapter Two, *Little Lord Fauntleroy* in cinema. Both films dialogise *Little Lord Fauntleroy* while *El viaje de Carol* also re-accentuates Burnett's and Lucía's texts with regards to register, translating them into the tragic plane.

A resounding and perennial success, *Little Lord Fauntleroy* has been adapted many times to the screen, beginning in 1921. Burnett's novel is set in New York City and in the fictional English village of Erlesboro during the late nineteenth century and tells the story of the charming seven-year-old boy named Cedric Errol who learns that his late father was an English aristocrat. 'Ceddie', the next Lord Fauntleroy, travels to England with his mother Dearest where they will be separated, at his curmudgeonly Earl grandfather's request, to live with his grandfather and assume his title. *Un rayo de luz* transposes *Little Lord Fauntleroy* from New York City to Spain and from England to Italy. Marisol discovers that she is the daughter of an Italian aristocrat and goes to Italy for the summer to live with her equally surly Italian General grandfather, the Conde d'Angelo (Julio Sanjuán).[1] *El viaje de Carol* adapts, transposes, and dialogises *Little Lord Fauntleroy*, *Un rayo de luz*, and their archetypes.

The child protagonist in *El viaje de Carol* is an adaptation of *Little Lord Fauntleroy* and an appropriation of a child of Franco from *Un rayo de luz*. Both Bakhtin's dialogism and the performance art of ventriloquism speak to the utilisation of others. Julie Sanders's theorisation of adaptation also considers appropriation. Sanders's conceptualisations depart from Deborah Cartmell's to discuss the means of adaptation by transposition and analogue, which are most pertinent to *A Ray of Light*'s and *Carol's Journey*'s approaches to *Little Lord Fauntleroy*. Transposition consists of adapting across genres (novel to film) and, recalling Bakhtin's heteroglossia: 'relocating . . . source texts not just generically, but in cultural, geographical and temporal terms' (Sanders 2006: 20). *El viaje de Carol* can be understood as an analogue to the others both because it follows the protagonist from New York City to a Cantabrian town with her mother in 1938 and because it does not depend on the audience's awareness of 'an explicit relationship to the source text' (22). Sanders, Hutcheon, and I understand appropriation in similar terms. Sanders focuses more on the appropriation of adaptation: 'as the notion of hostile takeover present in a term such as "appropriation" implies, adaptation can also be oppositional, even subversive. There are many opportunities for divergence as adherence, for assault as well as homage' (9). In Bakhtin's terms, as we saw in the Introduction:

> The author does not speak in a given language (from which he distances himself to a greater or lesser degree), but he speaks, as it were, *through* language, a language that has somehow more or less materialized, become objectivized, that he merely ventriloquates. (1981: 299; emphasis in the original)

Imanol Uribe's film and Ángel García Roldán's script ventriloquate *Un rayo de luz* in order to oppose and subvert its Francoist politics.

The political Manichaeism of which *El viaje de Carol* has been accused, is rooted in the dualism of genre film. Director Imanol Uribe attributes his narrative decisions to his politics. Uribe's response to the critique suggests the universality of his characters:

> Los personajes son arquetipos. Por ejemplo, en la presentación de la familia 'facha', que es la familia de la madre de Carol, hice un 'travelling' sobre sus caras y lo ambienté con los sones del 'Cara al sol', hasta descubrir el rostro de Adrián, que es Carmelo Gómez. Quiero que Alfonso (Alberto Jiménez) se parezca a Franco. Tengo una evidente voluntad maniquea. La guerra, para mí, la perdieron los buenos y la ganaron los malos. (Uribe cited in Aguirresarobe 2004: 214)

> [The characters are archetypes. For example, in the introduction of the 'fascist' family, Carol's maternal family, I used a travelling shot on their faces and I set it to the music of the 'Cara al sol', reaching Adrián's face, played by Carmelo Gómez. I want Alfonso (Alberto Jiménez) to resemble Franco. I have a clear Manichaean intention. The war, for me, was lost by the good guys and won by the bad guys.][2]

Uribe indicates that his film dialogises the archetypes that would predate Burnett's and Lucía's works and whose presence I wish to analyse in all three texts.[3] The various reincarnations of these characters reveal the politics of their respective contexts and assert their own agendas. The mothers of the children in each narrative are not accepted, if not outright rejected, for reasons of class in *Un rayo de luz* and *Little Lord Fauntleroy* or politics in *El viaje de Carol*. In all texts, the grandchild's charm earns him or her sway with and transforms the grandfather.

How and to what extent does *El viaje de Carol* dialogue with the narrative conventions of the child protagonist apparent in *Little Lord Fauntleroy* and *Un rayo de luz*? *El viaje de Carol* adopts the child protagonist within a new political landscape, which can be read as a political appropriation of the narrative conventions of *Un rayo de luz*. Hutcheon explains: 'the act of adaptation always involves both (re-)interpretation and then (re-)creation; this has been called both appropriation and salvaging, depending on your perspective. For every aggressive appropriator outed by a political opponent, there is a patient salvager' (2013: 8). Within the context of Spain's politics of memory and Uribe's aforementioned politics, it is difficult to see *El viaje de Carol* as salvaging *Un rayo de luz* and much more logical to see both texts as bartering with the national symbolism of the child protagonists from the literary source text in order to serve the opposing ideologies of Franco's Spain of the early 1960s and constitutional Spain of the early 2000s.

Adaptations are subject to differing temporal and cultural specificities at contextual and textual levels. The triptych I propose here spans the United States and England of the 1880s, Spain and Italy of the early 1960s, and Spain of 2002 and 1938. Despite the apparent disparity of dates and locales in this overview, these texts share their situation within their respective national contexts; each appeared twenty to thirty years after historic events of national importance. *Little Lord Fauntleroy* explores questions of American identity two decades after the American Civil War (1861–5) and ten years after the nation's centennial. Jerold Griswold reads *Little Lord Fauntleroy* within this context, noting its restoration of family harmony as national allegory (1996: 95). We can ask the same question of *Little Lord Fauntleroy*'s adaptation in Spanish cultural production: what follows the rebellion of the Nationalists in Spain? The law of the father, whose uprising against the Second Spanish Republic established the dictatorship, is accepted and obeyed by the Nationalist sector. *Un rayo de luz* and other films of the *cine con niño* promise the restoration of family harmony, in accordance with the ritual genre function, on Franco's terms while the *nuevo cine con niño* exposes this promise as illusory, undesirable, or impossible.

The stellar success of Marisol's debut film led the Francoist newspaper *Triunfo* to name 1960 'el año de Marisol' (the year of Marisol) (Moix 1993: 281). Child musical film *Un rayo de luz* follows the Spanish Civil War by approximately twenty years and belongs to the period of opening (*aperturismo*) in Francoism during which the country underwent cosmetic changes to appear more appealing for tourism and to Western democratic powers (Faulkner 2013: 4). In the preceding two decades, Franco needed to divorce Phalangism from Fascism and thus his brand of totalitarianism from that of former ally and Italian dictator Benito Mussolini's (Preston 1999: 175). Félix Atalaya's script plays out the triumph of Spanish over Italian culture through the Italian grandfather's new appreciation for Spanish music and the unification of the family in Spain. The main character's biographical details indicate that she was born from a Spanish-Italian union in 1950, towards the very end of the alliance between the two countries, prior to her father's sudden death in an airplane crash.

Un rayo de luz shines its spotlight on the Nationalist militant. Textually, the film explores the analogue of General Francisco Franco in the General Conde d'Angelo and makes reference to General Giuseppe Garibaldi, credited with facilitating unification in Italy in the latter part of the 1800s. The *Movimiento Nacional* and Spanish Civil War resonate in the character of the grandfather and in Marisol's own modelling of militaristic fervour. She defeats the red-headed Barbas Rojas neighbour children, of estranged relations from her family for a generation. Thus, Capitán Marisol defeats 'barbas rojas' (red beards) on film rather than 'rojos' (reds) in the Spanish Civil War and reunites her family in Spain. In this way, the film manipulates national identity through international relations.

El viaje de Carol highlights the history of women's militancy and the International Brigades for the Second Republic. It is set in Cantabria during the Spanish Civil War but was released in 2002, more than sixty years after the war and more than twenty-five years after Franco's death. A total of three films – *El embrujo de Shanghai* (*The Shanghai Spell* Fernando Trueba), *El florido pénsil* (*The Blossoming Garden* Juan José Porto), and *El viaje de Carol* – dealing with childhood during the dictatorship came out in 2002, making it the most prolific year of the genre-in-the-making I call the *nuevo cine con niño*. As a film of the *nuevo cine con niño*, it corresponds to the boom of cultural productions showcasing historical memory. Sarah Wright finds of these productions: 'The child is therefore symbolic not only of the loss of historical memory and its recuperation after a time-lag but also it is often a site of trauma in contemporary memory wars' (2013: 14). I suggest that the child protagonist is not only a locus of national conflict but also an agent. Carol's activism within the family politically engages her grandfather, who had retired from public life.

Conflict in *El viaje de Carol* indicates the confluence of politics and class. Spain does not share billing with the United States as do Ceddie's and Marisol's hometowns; New York City is off-screen with the exception of photos of Carol and her father from the Empire State Building and Coney Island. The story orients itself towards her maternal family in Spain rather than her mother Aurora's in-laws. For this reason, Carol's grandfather does not reject her, although he does keep his distance. Aurora's decision not to marry the local well-to-do conservative Adrián (Carmelo Gómez), who later weds her sister Dolores (Lucina Gil), instigates the schism in the family. Aurora, rather, marries an American who becomes a Brigadier for the Republic during the war. Her romance crosses borders while Carol's and Marisol's cross other lines.

Carol's ending is tragic but the conclusions of *Little Lord Fauntleroy* and *Un rayo de luz* are happy and restorative. Carol's mother dies of illness, her crush is shot and killed by her uncle, her father is captured by the Nationalists, and Carol returns to the States to live with her paternal grandparents. In other versions of the script like the one self-described as 'sweetened' (*endulcorada*), there are variations on these outcomes; in the sweetest version neither Robert nor Tomiche die. It is significant that Uribe's final product is the most tragic of the screenplays he entertained. I will explore how the political re-accentuation of *Un rayo de luz* resides in differences across the texts in addition to revealing dissimilarities regarding class and gender.

The themes of child, family, difference, and national identity have lent themselves to reincarnations at many times and in many places.[4] *Little Lord Fauntleroy* has been adapted numerous times to the big screen and its child protagonist, based on the author's own son Vivian (Wilson 1996: 248), has been played by a wide variety of actors. In 1914, thirteen-year-old Gerald Royston played the title role in F. Martin Thornton's film. Former child actress Mary Pickford, at the age of twenty-nine, played both the roles of Cedric and his mother Dearest in her older brother Jack Pickford's 1921 feature. John Cromwell's adaptation appeared in 1936 and starred twelve-year-old Freddie Bartholomew. In their reception, the fact that many readers, spectators, and scholars have called into question Little Lord Fauntleroy's masculinity, encourages the examination of Mary Pickford's, Pepa Flores's, and Clara Lago's performances of gender in the title role.

Families and Nations

The mended relationship between the stubborn grandfather, his grandchild, and the grandchild's mother displays and hierarchises respective national values and identities according to each text's historical context, origin, and political affiliations. In particular, class differences stemming from distinct models of government emerge in *Little Lord Fauntleroy*, *Un rayo de luz*, and *El viaje de Carol* while political disparities are more acute in the two films. In *Little Lord Fauntleroy* and *Un rayo de luz*, the grandfather's desire to appropriate his grandchild is pronounced, while Carol's grandfather values his solitude and political disengagement. *Little Lord Fauntleroy* lays the groundwork for these variations.

In *Little Lord Fauntleroy*, American characters are convinced of the superiority of their democracy to the British monarchy, and vice versa, although the story concludes with reconciliation on English soil. Ceddie's friendship with Mr Hobbs the grocer shows that the boy is 'unaware of social differences' with a particular disregard for class differences (MacLeod 1994: 80). Hobbs expressed his patriotism for America and prejudice against Britain. Burnett's novel highlights national stereotypes and perceptions through its narration and characters' dialogue. The narrator details Hobbs's patriotism:

> When they began to talk about the Fourth of July there really seemed no end to it. Mr. Hobbs had a very bad opinion of 'the British,' and he told the whole story of the Revolution, relating very wonderful and patriotic stories about the villainy of the enemy and the bravery of the Revolutionary heroes, and he even generously repeated part of the Declaration of Independence. (Burnett 1996 [1885]: 8)

For this reason, Hobbs has a particular aversion to the power structure of his young country's former colonial master. His anti-aristocratic sentiment would compel him to expel noblemen, whom he calls 'tyrants', from his store (Burnett 1996 [1885]: 9). However, the Little Lord is indeed the first aristocrat to grace Hobbs's store, thereby disconcerting the grocer and challenging his convictions.

The Earl of Dorincourt's prejudice is perhaps even more virulent. Mr Havisham, the Earl's servant, can attest to his master's attitudes:

> He had spent all his life in England, and was not accustomed to American people and American habits . . . he had known all about the old Earl's disappointment in his elder sons and all about his fierce rage at Captain Cedric's American marriage, and he knew how he still hated the gentle little widow and would not speak of her except with bitter and cruel words. (Burnett 1996 [1885]: 19)

The novel qualifies attacks such as these through association between the Earl's negative opinions and his personality, describing him as: 'the savage old grandfather [with] his gout and his tempers' (Ibid.: 54). Dorincourt paints American youth with a broad and unfavourable brush: 'A lot of impudent little beggars, those American children . . . They call it precocity and freedom. Beastly, impudent bad manners; that's what it is!' (Ibid.: 61). The Earl is averse to the hallmarks of the American discourse of independence: the freedom of a new, young nation. The aristocrat's aim is to appropriate and re-educate the American boy as an aristocrat. His sister is outraged at the undertaking: 'Fancy a child of that age being taken from his mother, and made the companion of a man like my brother! He will either be brutal to the boy or indulge him until he is a little monster' (Ibid.: 148). The Earl intends to spoil the little lord.

Cedric's nobility, by virtue of character even before he becomes a nobleman, wins over his grandfather, his grandfather's peasants, and all that surround him. The boy treats everyone with respect and dignity regardless of class, age, sex, or origin. Ceddie interacts gracefully with people of all stations: 'He knew nothing of earls and castles; he was quite ignorant of all grand and splendid things; but he was always lovable because he was simple and loving. To be so is like being born a king' (Burnett 1996 [1885]: 205). Dearest notes the extreme inequality on the Earl's estate:

> She had found idleness and poverty and ignorance where there should have been comfort and industry . . . And as she looked at the squalid, uncared for children growing up in the midst of vice and brutal indifference, she thought of her own little boy spending his days in the great, splendid castle, guarded and served like a young prince, having no wish ungratified, and knowing nothing but luxury and ease and beauty. (Burnett 1996 [1885]: 141–2)

Burnett contrasts greater social equality in New York with the ample divide between rich and poor in the village of Erlesboro.

Mr Hobbs and the Earl change their minds about each other's country; the Earl begs Dearest for forgiveness and Mr Hobbs moves his grocery store to Erlesboro. Ceddie's opinion of his grandfather is a self-fulfilling prophecy whereby the Earl becomes kinder to everyone in order to be worthy of his grandson's high esteem. Cedric gushes, surprisingly, at his grandfather's kindness, confident that Mr Hobbs would amend his negative opinion of earls if they met (Burnett 1996 [1885]: 109). The Earl transforms:

> He felt it to be almost incredible that he who had never really loved any one in his life, should find himself growing so fond of this little fellow, as without a doubt he was. At first he had only been pleased and proud of Cedric's beauty and bravery, but there was something more than pride in his feeling now. He laughed a grim, dry laugh all to himself sometimes, when he thought how he liked to have the boy near him, how he liked to hear his voice, and how in secret he really wished to be liked and thought well of by his small grandson. (Burnett 1996 [1885]: 137–8)

Cedric's charm achieves his grandfather's and Mr Hobbs's changes of heart.

Un rayo de luz follows the same narrative pattern, transposed to Spain and Italy, but concludes with the family's reunion in Spain. The Conde d'Angelo's xenophobia is as pronounced towards Marisol's mother Elena (María Mahor) as is the Earl of Dorincourt's towards Dearest. Elena, a singer, is as virtuous as Dearest; she refuses the aristocratic title while Dearest refuses the Earl's money. Both accept no more than what corresponds to their children (Burnett 1996 [1885]: 852). These mothers come from humble backgrounds that are the subject of discrimination by their aristocratic fathers-in-law. Elena's husband rehearses breaking the news of their marriage to his father: 'No tiene títulos como nosotros pero sí un gran corazón' (She doesn't have a title like us but she does have a big heart). Conde d'Angelo, like the Earl of Dorincourt, puts physical and figurative distance between the mother and child. Marisol's grandfather withholds the letters that Elena sends her daughter.

However, the 'ray of light' melts the heart of the 'Grumpy General' (General Cascarrabias). Her uncle offers a militaristic analogy for Marisol's victory: 'En la primera batalla has rendido al General' (You defeated the general in the first battle). The grandfather recognises to his granddaughter: 'De mi mal genio no tienes tú la culpa' (You are not responsible for my bad temper). He becomes so enamoured with Marisol that he breaks his word to her mother and demands that Marisol live with him permanently: 'Esa cría es todo. Es lo único que pueda alegrarme los años que me quedan' (That child is everything. She is the only thing that can gladden my final years). When Marisol's arguments for her return to Spain are rejected, she resorts to the ruse of a near-fatal accident to persuade her grandfather. Ultimately, the Conde d'Angelo leaves his estate behind to follow his granddaughter to Spain.

While still on the estate, Marisol bridges class and political gaps. Like Little Lord Fauntleroy with the Earl's servants, she is gracious towards her father's nanny Talla (Rafaela Rodríguez) and the peasants who work the estate's land. Marisol outdoes Ceddie, in fact, when she invites her playmates over for an afternoon snack and successfully negotiates that their parents' and the butler's salaries are doubled. Like Ceddie, Marisol does not make much of class differences nor does she revolutionise the estate's social structure. Marisol reconciles the feud between the Conde d'Angelo's family and Barba Roja's Continenza family through battle, to her grandfather's surprise. He does not expect his granddaughter to have inherited his military skill: 'Menos mal que eres chica y no me plantearás conflictos con Barba Roja' (Thank goodness you are a girl and you will not give me any trouble with Barba Roja). Marisol undertakes the battle in honour of her late father, whose childhood head wound from Barba Roja instigated the feud. She returns the gesture, hitting Barbarrojita (Antonio Vela), his son, on the head with her picket sword. In a sappy double victory pertinent to our analysis of gender, Marisol also wins Barbarrojita's heart.

El viaje de Carol re-locates the grandfather–granddaughter narrative to 1938 Cantabria and explores political polarisation within the maternal family. Carol and her grandfather are estranged due to the circumstances of her upbringing in the United States. Her late grandmother did not understand Aurora's decision to leave the hometown, wealthy, and conservative Adrián for Robert (Ben Temple). Aurora's sister and in-laws pressure Don Amalio (Álvaro de Luna) to take sides by imposing their Nationalist viewpoint upon him at the dinner table with condescending mention of American brigadiers. The grandfather affiliates with the Republic but does not have the backbone of Aurora's nuclear family. Carol, 'el garbanzo negro de la familia' ('the black sheep of the family'), inherits her convictions and bravery from both her parents and her rearing as a daughter of the Republic and of the Abraham Lincoln Brigades makes her significantly more modern than much of the Cantabrian town. Don Amalio's willingness to reveal his sympathies with the defeated Second Republic is the evidence of his growing affection for Carol.

Following the death of his wife the year before, Don Amalio retires to the town's health resort (*balneario*). Preferring the quiet life in his advanced age, Carol's grandfather entrusts her to her aunt, with whom she is entirely at odds, after Aurora dies. Carol goes to Don Amalio's new home to persuade him to live at the big house with her. He resists: 'Yo aquí estoy muy bien. Tengo mis amigos, mis partitas de domino, mis baños. No me pidas que me encierre en ese caserón lleno de malos recuerdos y en compañía de una niña pequeña' ('I'm happy here. I have my friends, my dominoes, my baths. And I'm supposed to live in a house full of bitter memories with a little girl for company?'). Nevertheless, Carol's stubbornness quickly convinces Don Amalio. More adversity faces them on the morning of the market when their house becomes a target of Nationalist graffiti that threatens to kill Carol's father: 'yanqui hijo puta al paredón' ('Yankee son of a bitch to the firing squad'). Don Amalio again prefers not to engage: 'Me parece, Carol, que dadas las circunstancias es mejor no hacer nada. Aparentar normalidad como si no lo hubiéramos visto' ('I think in the circumstances, it's best not to do anything, Carol, and pretend we haven't seen it'). Carol calls him a coward but eventually he comes around to painting over the vandalism himself. Despite the slur's suggestion, Carol is unwelcome due to her family's Republican politics rather than their American origin. Mustering more nerve, Don Amalio does not require Carol's pressure to protect Robert when his son-in-law comes looking for the escaped fighter at his house.

Like Marisol's friendships, Carol's cross class lines. Carol teaches her mute and illiterate servant Chana (Ana Villa) and begins a childhood romance with Tomiche (Juan José Ballesta) who comes from a humbler background. It is surprising that the Spanish-American protagonist, who has difficulty with the subjunctive, teaches Chana how to read and write like Maruja (Rosa María Sardá) does with Tomiche. Carol, however, does not negotiate a pay raise for Chana. Her relationship with Tomiche, like Marisol's with Barbarrojita, begins with a fight. Tomiche takes Carol's hat and she wrestles and knees him in the groin, learning the expression 'deshuevado' ('to kick in the knackers'), to retrieve it. Their families do not feud with each other. Again, tension resides within each family; Tomiche's father was killed and his Guardia Civil uncle abuses him. Carol does not reconcile her aunt's Francoist and mother's Republican sides. The opposite occurs, in fact, when Carol leaves her Aunt's house to live with her grandfather and then returns to New York after her father's capture.

Sissy Boy to Tomboys

Gender bending is present in all three works: from Little Lord Fauntleroy's feminine appearance to Marisol's and Carol's masculine exploits and dress. A critique of Cedric's femininity appears in the reception of the novel. The masculinity of female protagonists is politicised in favour of the Nationalists in *Un rayo de luz* and of the Republicans in *El viaje de Carol*. Marisol's militarism endears her further to her General grandfather. Carol's pants-wearing independence scandalises her aunt and the town's priest while it signifies her likeness to her modern mother and other women of the Republic.

The effeminacy of Little Lord Fauntleroy's look and dress has been both imitated and ridiculed. Cedric is a pretty boy with golden curls: 'he was so beautiful to look at that he was quite a picture' (Burnett 1996 [1885]: 5). The novel dedicates a significant amount of commentary, with illustrations, to the boy's attractiveness and attire, a velvet suit with lace collar or: 'his best summer suit of cream colored flannel, with the red scarf around his waist, and combed out . . . curly locks' (10). Beyond the page, Ceddie's fashions caught on and mothers began dressing their sons like the little lord (Wilson 1996: 235). But, Cedric's femininity remained problematic, as Anna Wilson notes:

> Little Lord Fauntleroy's insufficient masculinity has thus been addressed in a variety of ways: as a disease to be wiped out, as an inessential covering that a return to authenticity will correct, or as a period oddity that can appropriately be excised for more modern audiences. (1996: 236)

In fact, Wilson sees a 'butchification' of the title character in the film versions from 1936 and 1980, although not in Mary Pickford's 1921 portrayal of Cedric (1996: 236, 246). She understands the popularity of the novel despite its gender trouble as: 'a reassertion of sentimental power, that the suit in fact represents an attempt to inscribe feminine values in the public sphere' (236). Conversely, Carol's tomboyish qualities reassert the militia woman (*miliciana*), or female Republican soldier, and Republican politics and the child militant in the public sphere through Carol's mobilisation of her grandfather in *El viaje de Carol*.

Masculinity and femininity do not compete in Marisol's representation. She is equally talented as a flamenco singer and dancer as she is as a captain. Even more so than in the case of Little Lord Fauntleroy, Marisol's dress indicates the blending of the gender binary. First, she plays at sea-faring captain, to defeat the Barbas Rojas, with her shorts, braids, and made-up facial hair (Figure 4.1). The masculinity of the military campaign is clearly indicated in the girl's fake moustache and beard and in her brothers in arms. Sacrifice and heroism under Franco were gendered. A common textbook, the *Enciclopedia Álvarez* from 1959, outlines the two ways – serving in the home and nursing until their deaths on the battlefield – a woman can be a heroine:

> La mujer puede ser héroe de dos maneras: 1.a Cumpliendo diaria y ejemplarmente con sus obligaciones, y 2.a Entregando su vida cuando la Patria o las circunstancias así lo exijan. A la primera forma de heroísmo toda mujer puede y debe aspirar. La segunda forma de heroísmo no es tan frecuente, pero no faltan mujeres que han llegado a él. (244)

Figure 4.1 Marisol (Pepa Flores) leads the troops to the tune of 'Un paso firme' in *Un rayo de luz*.

[Women can be heroines in two ways: 1.a By exemplarily fulfilling their daily obligations and 2.a By giving their lives when the Fatherland or the circumstances require it. All women can and must aspire to the first form of heroism. The second form of heroism is not as frequent, but there is not a shortage of women who have achieved it.]

However, Marisol, child star of the 1960s, challenges traditional gender roles through the combat she wages to survive and defeat her family's enemy, adding a third model to female heroism at the onset of the following decade. Marisol's tomboyish side in *Un rayo de luz* is a stark contrast with her later role in *Tómbola*, which trains the girl-cum-young woman in female servitude. *A Ray of Light*'s protagonist does not tend the wounds of the soldiers, like she nurses the injured in *Tómbola* (1962), but rather inflicts the contusions. Marisol, presumably, can wage war on account of her military heritage. The family feud is annulled through the sanguine heredity of militaristic prowess put into action. Second, Marisol's birthday presents are respectively appropriate for a traditional boy and a traditional girl. The Conde d'Angelo gives her a dress for her in-house flamenco performances and a rifle for her outdoor exploits. Having required earlier that his granddaughter sing in Italian, the Conde d'Angelo's gift of a flamenco dress signifies his capitulation. Marisol's heterosexual femininity is further underscored by her suitor's gift of flowers. That Marisol enamours the boy whom she defeats in a traditionally masculine activity, emphasises that her femininity is not compromised in the endeavour. By contrast to the politics of Marisol's gender bending, Carol's gender role delineates the two Spains as her characterisation reasserts the *miliciana*, and the greater Republican collective, in the public spheres of her diegetic town and the extra-diegetic cinema. The film's contribution to the *nuevo cine con niño* consists of asserting the voice of the *miliciana* and Republican political engagement into contemporary public discourse on the Civil War. *El viaje de Carol* shares the task of exploring militancy, although to a lesser degree, with other contemporary films.[5] Carol is successful at engaging her grandfather, after all. Carol's tomboyish characteristics and clothes relate to the divide in the family and town; they are appreciated by her mother and Tomiche but not by her Francoist aunt. Both Carol and her mother arrive to town wearing pants (Figure 4.2). The pair contrasts with the town's women, including Carol's younger cousin Blanca (Luna McGill) and Aunt Dolores. While she lives with her aunt and uncle, Carol introduces Blanca to mischief and brings out the most reactionary side of Dolores in the process. Their unexplained absence while playing in the mountainside worries Dolores, who admonishes and punishes both of them. Dolores chastises Carol: 'tú, Carol, ya que eres la mayor puedes tener un poco

Figure 4.2 Tomboy Carol (Clara Lago) arrives in town in *El viaje de Carol.*

más de cabeza. En eso has salido a tu madre' ('you're old enough to have more sense, Carol. Just like your mother'). The comparison, which Carol appreciates, accurately identifies the protagonist as a mirror of her mother: 'Prefiero parecerme a ella que parecerme a ti' ('[I'd] rather [be] like her than you'). Neither Aurora nor Carol observes social mandates regarding femininity, propriety, and standard bourgeois values.

Dolores, thus, is intent to raise Carol according to the Francoist values by which she lives, berating the girl's waywardness: '¡Quítate esos pantalones! ¡Que pareces una miliciana!' ('Take off those trousers! You look like a militia[wo]man!'). By contrast to Carol, Blanca wears dresses and her hair in braids (more like the feminine Marisol in fact) while Carol wears her hair short with or without a cap and either pants or overalls for the most part. Blanca's reading of *Cinderella*, also an intertext for Marisol's fourth film (*La nueva cenicienta*/*The New Cinderella* (George Sherman 1964)), while grounded in their room further indicates her more traditional gender role and Dolores as Carol's evil stepmother. Of course, Dolores's tutelage sees to Carol's catechism in preparation for her first communion. Yet, Carol resists Francoist compliance through her apparel. She agrees to the sacrament on the condition that she may dress as boys do. While the other girls wear white dresses and veils, Carol is dressed in a sailor suit (Figure 4.3). Although Carol reaches the day of her communion, which was dubious after several tardy arrivals to catechism classes, the declaration of Nationalist victory interrupts her receiving the Eucharist. Carol, it appears, is too much of an outlier to be redeemed in the New Spain. It is logical, therefore, that she may not stay.

Figure 4.3 Carol dressed in a sailor suit for her first communion in *El viaje de Carol*.

Conclusion: Genre Functions in the *cines con niño*

The ideological genre function, as explored with Marisol's *Tómbola* in Chapter Three, is also assured in *Un rayo de luz* through state censorship and corroborated in the triumph of Marisol and her Spanish family. *Un rayo de luz* fuses the ideological function in its inception to the unity in its narrative from the ritual function. In accordance with Altman's ritual genre function that assures unity (1999: 27), *Un rayo de luz* transmits the regime's ideology of a unified, 'Una, grande, y libre', Spain. Decades later, Uribe is clear that his production furthers his own ideological agenda but the difference here, for Altman's genre functions, is that it is no longer state imposed. The dictatorship ended in 1975 and censorship ceased in 1977. *Carol*'s janus-faced orientation towards the past and the future in the retrospective *nuevo cine con niño* films strategically adopts the child protagonist, universal symbol for the future. The two genre functions (ritual and ideological) differ in terms of where they seat power: the state is responsible in the ideological genre films while the audience, more than ten million filmgoers, of *nuevo cine con niño* films has greater participation in ritual genre films. Altman reminds that 'it is through generic conventions that audiences are lured into false assumptions of societal unity and future happiness' (1999: 27). I argue that the *nuevo cine con niño* exhibits the ritual function of genre cinema but inverts its message on union with stories of disunion in the two Spains.

El viaje de Carol engages in the ritual function, first, in illuminating an alternative to Franco's Spain in 1938 and, second, in offering an example for contemporary historical memory. While Spain is Marisol's happy final round-trip destination, Carol's return to the United States plays more like an exile than a homecoming. Carol can have no future in a country where her mother has died, her father is held political prisoner, and the Nationalists win the war. Uribe's film models engagement with the politics of memory whereby a granddaughter's convictions and charm are capable of bringing her grandfather out of retirement to confront his house full of 'memories' and publicly display his opposition to the Nationalists. *El viaje de Carol* calls on an intergenerational alliance for the engagement of memory and recognition of the contributions of Republican Spain and for a more just future. The new *cine con niño* film envisions a dystopian future, caused by the totalitarian politics of rising Francoist Spain, for Carol's family and Republican Spain that highlights the polarisation of the two Spains and belies national unity. Thereby, *El viaje de Carol* rejects and regenrifies the *cine con niño*'s stories of reunion. Marisol's militancy occurs on behalf of the dictatorship while Carol's is on behalf of the democracy.

Notes

1. It is not the only adaptation in Marisol's filmography; let us recall from Chapter Three the appropriation of 'The Boy Who Cried Wolf' in *Tómbola*.
2. All translations in Chapter Four are mine except those provided in the subtitles of *Carol's Journey*, which I denote with quotation marks around the text inside the brackets.
3. Additional renditions of the story of the prodigal daughter, from Fuensanta's (Lina Canalejas) elopement with a gypsy and repentant return in Joselito's *El pequeño ruiseñor* (*The Little Nightingale*) (Antonio del Amo 1957) to Aurora's (María Barranco) return after marrying an American brigadier in *Carol's Journey*, can be found across the *cines con niño*.
4. The screenwriter of *Carol's Journey*, Ángel García Roldán identifies themes common to his script and *Little Lord Fauntleroy* but attributes his work another genealogy. García Roldán, born in Ávila in 1946, has lived in Ireland and England and considers his novel published in 1988, *A boca de noche* (*At nightfall*), to be a point of departure for *Carol's Journey* (García Roldán 2002: 7). In the novel, a British family with Spanish origins experiences a Spanish town's political tensions between the left and right during the Second World War, in which Spain did not actually participate, rather than the Spanish Civil War (ibid.). *Carol's Journey* inherits: 'el ánimo de contraste y la idea de viaje interior y aprendizaje' (the spirit of contrast and the idea of an interior journey and of learning) (8). The novel's boy protagonist becomes Carol and the novelist subsequently populates her town with characters from García Roldán's own childhood: his birthplace, his enemy Tomiche, his housekeeper Chana, his teacher Maruja, his grandfather Amalio, his aunt's

big house, a villa, and the aviator relative who parachuted a birthday gift to him from his airplane (ibid.). Imanol Uribe's contributions, with an eye on production logistics, transposed the Castilian town to Cantabria, played down the presence of the Civil War, and excised Carol's second journey in which she returns to the town as an elderly woman (8–11). Originally, the film's title was to be plural to include an adult Carol's return journey to discover Tomiche's killer, who was not her uncle (Uribe 2009). Uribe did not read García Roldán's novel; *El viaje de Carol*, by contrast, represents a collaborative project between the two screenwriters (ibid.). Hogan conducted an interview with Uribe in the Madrid office of Aiete Ariane Films on Avenida Alfonso XIII 62 28016 Madrid on Wednesday, 9 December 2009 at 11:15 a.m.

5. *Carol's Journey* is in the company of Pepa Flores, who played opposite Antonio Gades's *maquis* in *Los días del pasado* (*The Days of the Past*) (Mario Camus 1978); Manuel Gutiérrez Aragón's film about the legendary maquis 'El Andarín' in *El corazón del bosque* (*Heart of the Forest* 1979); women militants in *Libertarias* (*Freedomfighters*) (Vicente Aranda 1996), *Las trece rosas* (*13 Roses*) (Emilio Martínez Lázaro 2007), and *La voz dormida* (*The Sleeping Voice*) (Benito Zambrano 2011); and the pairing of child and adult militants in *El espinazo del diablo* (*The Devil's Backbone*) (Guillermo del Toro 2001) and *El laberinto del fauno* (*Pan's Labyrinth*) (Guillermo del Toro 2006).

CHAPTER FIVE

Prosopopeia and the Gothic Child from
Marcelino pan y vino to *El orfanato*

Introduction

The ventriloquism of the child protagonist that I have discussed thus far has been in the appropriative vein that negates the agency and subjectivity of the child character: from the representation of child appropriation to sexual abuse to abduction by a ventriloquist. In the current chapter, I will explore the liberating and empowering potential of another classification of ventriloquism – prosopopeia – and how it relates to the Gothic child protagonist from *Marcelino pan y vino* (*The Miracle of Marcelino*) (Vajda 1955) to *El orfanato* (*The Orphanage*) (Bayona 2007). Features in the Gothic mode from the *cine con niño* to the *nuevo cine con niño* construct a child protagonist whose sensitivity and marginality allows him or her to empathise with the suffering of other innocents and choose to serve as their advocate. These others may be spirits, ghosts, living dead, or civil dead who have been persecuted with impunity. The Gothic child protagonists engage with the disenfranchised through prosopopeia, which is 'a form of projection; a form of ventriloquism in which the living speak for or through the dead, just as the adult revisits, reshapes and retells his childhood experiences as if he were (still) a child' (Lury 2010: 111). This ventriloquial connection to the dead or otherwise maligned is the feature that most interests us in these films. Here we will explore the dialogism of films in the Gothic mode, saving their broader dialogism with regards to rites of passage for Chapter Six. Ann Davies has traced a latent Gothic mode in Spanish cinema whereby:

> apparently disparate films are in fact linked together through a Gothic sensibility that threads through them, one that explicitly or tacitly acknowledges Anglo-American concepts of Gothic landscapes and Gothic monstrosity. This then continues through into the 1980s before emerging as full-blown Gothic in the late 1990s and the early twenty-first century. In Spanish cinema before the 1990s we can detect not so

much a coherent Gothic genre, but certainly a coherent Gothic mode, ambiguously Spanish, that prefigures the 1990s and beyond. (2016: 117)

For Maria Pramaggiore, the international resonance of these films is due to the child: 'Spanish horror has succeeded as a global genre embracing Spanish cinema and Spanish language films from other national contexts partly because it uses the child to interrogate the genre's ability to represent traumatic history' (2017: 71). The child protagonists of this subgenre of the *cines con niño* repeatedly ask: '¿Es un fantasma?' ('Is he a ghost?') and '¿Qué es un fantasma?' ('What is a ghost?').[1] The Gothic children of *Marcelino pan y vino*, *El espíritu de la colmena* (*The Spirit of the Beehive*) (Erice 1973), *Urte ilunak/Los años oscuros* (*The Dark Years*) (Lazkano 1992), *Secretos del corazón* (*Secrets of the Heart*) (Armendáriz 1997), *El espinazo del diablo* (*The Devil's Backbone*) (Del Toro 2001), and *El orfanato* ascend or descend stairs or travel to the periphery of town to find answers to these questions by engaging with monsters and imaginary friends of varying stripes. Other Gothic child victims become victimisers in order to overthrow the unjust order, as in *Cría cuervos* (*Raise Ravens*) (Saura 1976).

Marcelino pan y vino (Vajda 1955)

Ladislao Vajda's National Catholic classic, *Marcelino pan y vino* (1955), is an unlikely Gothic film. Yet, Vajda's feature draws from horror film aesthetics to portray the crucifix as the boogey man in the attic. As we saw in Chapter Two, Vajda's Jewish ancestry and Hungarian origin also make him an unlikely individual to direct a National Catholic film. *Marcelino pan y vino*, based on José María Sánchez-Silva's homonymic children's book from 1952, won a Silver Bear in Berlin and Special Mention in Cannes. It takes place in a small Spanish town after the Napoleonic Wars during which the monastery was ruined. Six Franciscan friars rebuild the monastery to come across an orphaned baby, Marcelino (Pablito Calvo), left at their doorstep. Unable to find him suitable parents, the monks become the boy's foster family. The film is a hagiography in which five-year-old Marcelino engages in prosopopeia with Jesus on the cross and charitably brings the thin man with 'cara de hambre' (Marcelino is dubbed as saying: 'you look very hungry') bread and wine before Jesus grants him eternal sleep and reunion with his mother in heaven. The *Diccionario de cine español* calls *Marcelino pan y vino* an: 'irónica e irreverente incursión en el llamado Cine religioso de la época' (ironic and irreverent incursion into the so-called religious cinema of the period) (Vidal Estévez 1998: 884).

Marcelino, in fact, satisfies a number of the characteristics that Margarita Georgieva identifies in 'Gothic Child on Film':

> the death of the parents, the mystery of the child's fate, the child resisting hardships, the gravestones, spirituality, the candles, the burial ceremonies, the nightly journeys through underground passages and the final realization that comes with newly acquired knowledge, the happiness of finding love and a new family. Interestingly, the train element is present too. (2013: 168)

The mystery of his parentage is an obsession for the boy and the monks attempt to relieve his curiosity by attributing his maternal lineage to the Virgin Mary. Marcelino's curiosity is not limited to his familial origin but also to the prohibited space of the monastery's attic.

Marcelino violates the interdiction of climbing the stairs, reaching the 'desván fantasmagórico' (phantasmagoric attic) (Jolivet 2003: 137). Space in the film is organised on an axis: up to heaven, out to Marcelino's hidden treasures and the danger of a scorpion bite, and down to the town. Imanol Zumalde Arregi considers the vectors of child protagonists' movement in *Marcelino pan y vino*, *El espíritu de la colmena*, *El espinazo del diablo*, and *El laberinto del fauno* but does not interpret the religious and political meanings of vertical and horizontal axes (2013: 205). Anne-Marie Jolivet reads the spatial distribution as linked by: 'La escalera entre abajo y arriba, entre el mundo seguro de los padres y el peligroso y prohibido del desván, pasa a representar el proceso iniciático hacia el ámbito del mito y del origen' (The stairs between upstairs and downstairs, between the safe world of the priests and the dangerous and prohibited world of the attic, comes to represent a rite of initiation towards the realm of myth and origin) (2003: 137). The staircase represents a metaphorical Jacob's ladder (Prout 2005: 73; Crumbaugh 2015: 342) leading to a scary thin man, who is surrounded by spiders on cobwebs and sharp objects and from whom the monks unexpectedly try to scare Marcelino away. Marcelino reaches the top of the stairs for the first time after a scorpion bite and nightmare. In the Old Testament, Jacob has a dream about climbing stairs to heaven for God's renewed protection (Karesh and Hurvitz 2006: 244). By prefacing Marcelino's ascent with a nightmare rather than a dream, Vajda's film sets the stage for horror. Cinematography, sound, and lighting also cast the attic as a haunted space. The musical soundtrack indicates danger and Marcelino runs away when he first lays eyes on the crucifix, the effigy of Christ's lifeless body. Heavy shadows shroud the attic. From Marcelino's low-angle point-of-view, Christ's hand animates to receive the bread and wine. Since Marcelino has been a good boy, the crucifix tells him that he will grant his wish to be with his mother.

Marcelino's one-sided conversations with his imaginary friend Manuel are reminiscent of his prosopopeia with the crucifix. Marcelino meets the mother of his imaginary friend Manuel outside the monastery, but he imagines that Manuel accompanies him on his excursions to the attic. Justin Crumbaugh considers Manuel to be a 'spectral presence' that 'represents for Marcelino the childhood he would have were his parents alive. It is the spectral time of the hypothetical, of the life that never was, that never will have been' (2015: 344). He notes how Marcelino's story, for a dying girl about a child who has already died, creates an 'ominous feel' in the film (345). Marcelino is Francoist National Catholicism's Gothic child, who communicates through prosopopeia with the crucifix. Vajda's film balances precariously on a fine line between the fetishisation of sacrifice and suffering and Gothic conventions.

Fifty years later, Javier Fesser's *Camino* (2008) tells the hagiography of the ten-year-old title character who agonises from cerebral cancer and the repression of her Opus Dei mother. Fesser's moribund girl protagonist, who learns the story of Saint Bernadette, is reminiscent of Vajda's deathly ill girl character who hears the story of Marcelino. Camino fantasises with imaginary friends like the mouse from Cinderella named Marcelino, who leads her to a fantasy world, and the book character Mr Meebles, who represents an inexistent God. Both *Marcelino pan y vino* and *Camino* portray symbols of Catholicism as fearsome, but the National Catholic film affirms the existence of God while Fesser's film negates it.

El espíritu de la colmena (Erice 1973)

Like Marcelino, Víctor Erice's Ana (Ana Torrent) gravitates towards scary characters: Frankenstein's monster, the life-sized anatomy model Don José, and a fugitive from Franco's law. Ana lives with her older sister and parents in a beehive-styled house in the town of Hoyuelos on the Castilian plain in 1940, the year of the director's birth in the Basque Country and the immediate post-war. The retrospective film was released in the year of the Basque separatist group ETA assassination of Franco's successor Luis Carrero Blanco, nearing the end of Franco's dictatorship and the start of the transition to democracy (Vilarós 2005: 33). Ana's sister Isabel (Isabel Tellería) tells her that the monster who so captivated her in James Whale's *Frankenstein* (1931) lives in the abandoned building with a well on the outskirts of town and that she can even summon and visit him. The imaginative six-year-old protagonist conflates a Republican *maqui* fugitive, who takes shelter in those ruins, with the monster and befriends him before he is murdered.

Ana exhibits characteristics of the Gothic child, most prominently the mystery of her fate, her nighttime escape to visit the monster and the train element. For Ann Davies, *El espíritu de la colmena* is a Gothic film in its own right (2016: 118). Richard Curry and Antonio Lázaro-Reboll consider it a horror film (Curry 1996: 274; Lázaro-Reboll 2012: 275). E. C. Riley perceives a 'gentle haunting quality' in the Golden Seashell-winning film (1984: 491). Isabel is also a Gothic child who almost strangles a black cat, paints her lips red with blood, leaps over fire, and stages the horror scene of her death (for which she lays herself out like a supine crucifix) just to scare her younger sister. Ana and Isabel play on the train tracks and the fugitive arrives to town by jumping from a locomotive. The train is:

> an eerie combination of technology, mystery and horror. It is a cozy yet dangerous carrier and is the material representation of the child's liminality. The child is a soul in transition. This train that the child inevitably boards springs from the much older idea of the gothic quest on which the child embarks to recover memories of the past. (Georgieva 2013: 168)

Ana, like the unnamed fugitive, is a soul in transition. She moves freely from home to school to the ruins to the train tracks.

During one of Ana's nocturnal excursions, she leaves the bedroom she shares with her sister to walk out into the dark and contemplates the stone stairs upwards and the moon. A beautiful transition links the Gothic child and the train tracks. Ana's face in upwards gaze to the moon dissolves to the train tracks from the perspective of the arriving train and the sounds of the whistle and locomotion. The fugitive leaps from the train. Editing suggests that Ana has telepathically summoned him. This man is in trouble and we have little information to determine why, just his wardrobe and the politics of 1940. He appears to be dressed in a ragged Republican soldier uniform. He may be a *maqui*, or dissident who continued the armed fight against Franco into the 1950s (Curry 1996: 272). Critics have also noted the coincidence of personifications across the *maqui*, the monster, Ana's beekeeper father Fernando (Fernando Fernán Gómez), Ana, and the train (Stone 2002: 90). The symbolism of characters is polysemic and their interpretations are thus multiple. *El espíritu de la colmena* is, after all, an oppositional film released two years before Franco's death.

According to Ana's imagination, the monster and the *maqui* inhabit the same, marginal ruins. Both characters are outcasts and targets. James Whale's monster, for accidentally drowning a young playmate, and the fugitive, for resisting Franco's dictatorship, are persecuted and banished by their respective societies. The peripheral location of their abode signifies their marginality. Frankenstein's monster is a composite of cadavers while, I argue, the *maqui* is a civil dead, following Giorgio Agamben's biopolitics. Both are bare life; they have been stripped of their right to life and any other rights of protection they may have had. Agamben illuminates the connection between those banished with the dead: '"To ban" someone is to say that anyone may harm him" [Cavalca, *II banda*, p. 42]) or was even considered to be already dead (*exbannitus ad mortem de sua civitate debet haberi pro mortuo*, "Whoever is banned from his city on pain of death must be considered as dead" [ibid., p. 50])' (1998: 63). I deploy Agamben here in relation to the disenfranchisement of the *maqui* rather than with regards to historical memory, a compelling interpretation advanced by Jo Labanyi. She writes that what makes the disappeared of dictatorship:

> 'refugees from history' (one thinks of the refugee in *El espíritu de la colmena*, who leaps from a train, a classic image of history as progress) the 'living dead' is in fact that they are denied memory . . . It is crucial that the refugee in *El espíritu de la colmena* has no articulated or articulatable past. (Labanyi 1998: 8)

Spatial distribution of *El espíritu de la colmena*, as it was in *Marcelino pan y vino*, is again key for my reading.

While Hoyuelos and all of Spain are under Franco's regime in 1940, we can make further distinction between the beehive home and the ruins. For Fernando Savater: 'Quien se sale realmente de la colmena se convierte en monstruo, en espíritu, y no puede esperar piedad ni reconocimiento de parte de las abejas' (Whomever truly leaves the beehive becomes a monster, a spirit, and he cannot expect pity or recognition on the part of the bees) (1976: 18). Those who leave the beehive become monsters and spirits or, in Agamben's terms, bare life. The monster is simply a dissident: 'El monstruo no es más que la monstruosidad del Orden que le segrega, pero debe ser presentado por éste como el infractor de la ley, y su exilio vergonzoso como merecido castigo' (The monster is none other than the monstrosity of the Order that segregates him, but must be presented by this entity as an infractor of the law, and his embarrassing exile is his just punishment) (10). The beehive is a mechanism of control by patriarchal authority, whether it is Fernando's or Franco's. Savater's reading most closely approximates a biopolitical interpretation when he discusses expulsion from the beehive in relation to death:

> Todas la medidas, todos los controles de la colmena son perfectamente necesarios; tienen la irremediable presencia de la muerte, y 'muerte' es el nombre de todo lo exterior a la colmena: muerte por hambre, por miseria, por desorden, por improductividad, por revolución (o por contrarrevolución), muerte por caos. (1976: 24)

[All the measures, all the controls of the beehive are perfectly necessary; they have
an irredeemable presence of death, and 'death' is the name for everything beyond
the beehive: death by starvation, by poverty, by disorder, by non-productivity, by
revolution (or counter-revolution), death by chaos.]

In effect, civil death is the condition of the inhabitants of the ruins.

As a Gothic child, Ana identifies with these misfits and seeks them
out. Her ability and desire to communicate with the civil dead amounts
to prosopopeia with them. Like Marcelino, Ana feeds her criminalised
friend (Maqua Lara 1998: 539; Stone 2002: 92). Ana steps into the *maqui*'s
footprint as if preparing to follow in his rebellious footsteps. She does in
fact rebel. Ana runs away from her father and the beehive at night to find
the spirit. Similarly, the reflection of her face in the stream dissolves into
the monster's countenance. The monster and the *maqui* are Ana's true
family. In fact, the resemblance of her dark eyes and hair to that of the
fugitive are also suggestive of the kinship of these Gothic characters.

Cría cuervos (Saura 1976)

Ana Torrent again plays the lead in Carlos Saura's (1932–) contemporary
Gothic family romance, *Cría cuervos*, three years later. The protagonist's
name, also the actress's, is another indication of continuity from Erice's to
Saura's film, which won the Grand Jury prize in Cannes. She is a Gothic
child whose contact with the dead and death is primarily twofold: she
has flashbacks to her quality time with her deceased mother and fashions
herself an assassin able to kill authority figures like her father and aunt
with 'poisonous' baking soda or euthanise her weary grandmother. By
contrast to other Gothic children discussed thus far, seven-year-old Ana
is a victim turned victimiser (Georgieva 2013: 170) similar to the killer
children of *¿Quién puede matar a un niño?* (Narciso Ibáñez Serrador 1976),
of the same vintage. Saura's title refers to the Spanish proverb: 'cría
cuervos y te sacarán los ojos' (raise ravens and they will pluck out your
eyes). These 'children of Franco', as Marsha Kinder observes, are directors whose child protagonists retaliate against their makers:

They were led to see themselves as emotionally and politically stunted children who
were no longer young; who, because of the imposed role as 'silent witness' to a tragic
war that had divided country, family and self, had never been innocent, and who,
because of the oppressive domination of the previous generation, were obsessed with
the past and might never be ready to take responsibility for changing the future.
(Kinder 1983: 58)

Many scholars have noted the timeliness of Ana's 'killing' of her military patriarch, who betrayed and mistreated Ana's adored mother, in 1976 and Franco's natural death in 1975. Ana longs for her mother like Marcelino does his. She safeguards her treasured weapon below ground beside an empty pool. The fact that the pool is empty even in the summertime indicates a generalised void (of affection) in Ana's home life. Ana descends the staircase of her stately home for her father's 'murder' and wake. But Ana's experience with death is not limited to her mother's and father's deaths but also includes the passing of her hamster Roni (whose burial ceremony she officiates), her game of hide-and-seek with her older and younger sisters with the victory cry, '¡tienes que morir!' ('You have to die now!'), and her imagined leap from a rooftop.

While Ana Torrent plays the protagonist as a child in 1975–6, Geraldine Chaplin plays Ana twenty years later and young Ana's mother. She, like her director (Stone 2002: 102), reflects on the misery of childhood during the dictatorship:

> No entiendo que las personas dicen que la infancia es la época más feliz de su vida. En todo caso para mí no lo fue. Por eso no creí en el paraíso infantil. Ni en la inocencia, ni en la bondad de los niños. Yo recuerdo mi infancia como un período largo, interminable, triste, donde el miedo lo llenaba todo. Miedo a lo desconocido. Hay cosas que no puedo olvidar. Parece mentira que hay recuerdos que tengan tanta tanta fuerza. (Gavilán Sánchez 2002: 65)

> ['I can't understand how some people say that childhood is the happiest time of one's life. It certainly wasn't for me and that maybe is why I don't believe either in a child-like paradise or in the innocence of children. I remember my childhood as a long, interminable and sad time, filled with fear. A fear of the unknown. There are things I cannot forget. It seems unbelieveable how memories can be so . . . so strong.']

Geraldine Chaplin plays doppelgangers (Brasó 2003: 48), related to the theme of repetition and imitation that carries throughout *Cría cuervos*; Ana incarnates her scorned mother in role play with her sisters and their maid comments on how much Ana resembles her mother. Saura links imitation, the power to kill, and self-realisation:

> I don't know how we can feel proud of the fact that children imitate us; in this respect, they are merely perpetuating our errors. I think children would have to kill the adults in order to be able to be themselves. (Brasó 2003: 43)

Ana can only gain freedom (and power) by eliminating repressive authority figures.

In biopolitical terms, Ana would overthrow the sovereign, s/he who has the right over life and death (Agamben 1998: 55), in order to become sovereign herself. In fact, Agamben notes that this quality of the sovereign, which Foucault highlights in his definition (1976: 119), first described the power of the *pater* over his children. Ana's primary target is her father. Saura explains:

> Ana, the child, is not so much preoccupied with the theme of death as she is imbued with the feeling of having the power to kill, the power to make anyone she pleases disappear, and also the power to bring them back. (Brasó 2003: 44)

She indeed has the imaginative power to bring back her mother, although even then Amelia (Geraldine Chaplin) returns with a ghostly countenance. In flashbacks, Ana's insomnia is rewarded by one-on-one time with her mother, who often waits late into the night for her philandering husband to come home.

There is a phantasmal quality to Chaplin's appearances. Saura's Ana also believes that she is able to summon her mother, much like Erice's Ana, by closing her eyes. Her mother then appears pacing by the door frame of the girl's bedroom. Ghostliness turns horrific when Amelia agonises, screeching and bleeding in pained foetal position and morbidly pale, on her deathbed. With a blank look in her eyes, she tells Ana: 'Todo es mentira. No hay nada. No hay nada. Me han engañado. No quiero morir. Tengo miedo. No quiero morir. No quiero morir. Me duele.' ('It's all a lie. Nothing exists. Nothing exists. They've cheated me. I'm afraid. I don't want to die. I don't want to die. It hurts.') There is no comfort for Ana either, who mourns the death of her mother throughout the film. Ana's prosopopeia involves her ability to communicate, even if only in memories, with her deceased mother and attempt to hold the parties guilty for her mother's misery accountable.

Urte ilunak (Lazkano 1992)

Arantxa Lazkano's 1992 film, *Urte ilunak* (*Los años oscuros*), offers more nuance in the depiction of the two Spains by revealing how its child protagonist is caught between Basque and Francoist nationalism. This unique vision, recognised with a Goya nomination for best new director, can be attributed to the one-time director's (Zarautz 1949–) experience as educator and psychologist (Amatria 1992: 38). Eight-year-old Itziar (Eider Amibilia) is the youngest of three daughters whose mother is expecting a baby boy. Her father is involved in the Basque resistance to Franco's regime that requires his frequent absences and trips to France. The film contrasts and associates most of the indoor spaces with control (the school and the home) and the outdoor spaces with freedom (nature). Itziar plays by the sea, in the forest, and in the countryside. The film's action occurs during three years (1952, 1958, and 1965) and Itziar's schooling takes place during the Francoist period of National Catholicism (1953–9). In 1958, the greater part of the film, Itziar attends Catholic school where she makes friends with a new girl from Badajoz. For Itziar's health, however, she must leave the humid Basque air and study in a boarding school in France until 1965. The retrospection of the film circumvents the celebrations of Spanish nationalism in 1992, the quincentennial of Columbus's first voyage to the Americas, with a critical gaze towards Basque nationalism, similar to the better-known film of the same year, Julio Medem's *Vacas* (*Cows*).

Itziar is a Gothic child who lives, as the title indicates, in darkness. She is the target of bullying by her siblings, parents, teacher, and classmates. According to the director, there was a gender difference in the sexual and linguistic education of boys and girls in the Basque Country and repression was more severe for girls:

> Existe una cierta diferencia porque los niños de esa época no tuvieron tanta represión a nivel escolar. En este sentido, las monjas marcaron mucho más una represión de tipo sociológico que los curas o los frailes. A los niños, por ejemplo, se les enseñaban las cosas en euskera y no se dieron cuenta de ese morbo que poseía la monja con todo lo que tuviera relación con el idioma. De hecho, en esa época, los niños hablaban más entre ellos en euskera, era la lengua que habitualmente utilizaban. En cambio, las niñas tendían más hacia el castellano porque estaban más reprimidas (Mayora 1992: 6)

> [There exists a certain difference because children at that time did not experience the same repression at school. In this sense, the nuns were much more sociologically repressive than the priests or monks. Boys, for example, were taught in Basque and they had no knowledge of the obsession that the nun has with regards to language. In fact, at that time, boys spoke more in Basque to each other, it was the language that they used. By contrast, girls spoke more Castilian because they were more repressed.]

Itziar is punished at school for speaking Euskera and castigated at home for speaking Spanish. She is also the Gothic child who resists hardships and fantasises with the illusory hope of belonging to a loving family. Even play with friends engages with a macabre spirituality, including a séance-like game of awaking the dead and becoming blood sisters with the newcomer to school, Sofía (Andrea Toledo). Like Erice's Ana, Itziar feels most herself on the outskirts of town, underneath the canopy of a tree and stars rather than ruins. Like Marcelino and Saura's Ana, Itziar safeguards her treasures in this space.

Dialogism with *Marcelino pan y vino* is most notable in *Los años oscuros* because Itziar in fact goes to the movies to see Vajda's film. Itziar's childhood approximates emotional orphanhood more so than Marcelino's. There is an utter lack of affection that Itziar receives from her parents and other adults (from shopkeeper to teacher) around her by contrast to Marcelino's six adoring adoptive fathers. It is no surprise, then, that the sequence we watch Itziar viewing is where Marcelino meets Manuel's mother. She too wonders what it would be like to have a loving mother. Isolina Ballesteros interprets the intertext as one that: 'provee el consuelo para la protagonista, de padre frecuentemente ausente y siempre severo, y legítima desde el sistema la función patriarcal de la Iglesia en la educación infantil' (consoles the protagonist, whose father is frequently absent and always severe, and legitimises from within the patriarchal function of the Church in childhood education) (1996: 237). María Pilar Rodríguez elaborates on additional points of contact between the two protagonists:

> Marcelino e Iziar presentan comportamientos similares, ya que ambos inventan un amigo imaginario y se dedican a esconder objetos secretos. Frente a la conexión de *Marcelino, pan y vino* con el nacionalismo español que buscaba probar la superioridad moral del catolicismo y del sufrimiento frente al sadismo de la invasión extranjera (idea desarrollada por Kinder 241), la película de Lazcano elige privilegiar el motivo de las ausencias afectivas de los niños que les impulsan a inventar amigos imaginarios, y alude a la necesidad de crear su propio espacio vital a través de la creación del secreto y de la huida. (2002: 48)

> [Marcelino and Iziar behave similarly, since both invent an imaginary friend and dedicate their time to hiding secret objects. With respect to the connection between *Marcelino, pan y vino* and Spanish nationalism that aimed to prove the moral superiority of Catholicism and suffering from a sadistic foreign invasion (an idea developed by Kinder 241), Lazcano's film chooses to privilege the motive for the affective absences for the children that causes them to invite imaginary friends, and alludes to the necessity to create one's own space through the creation of secret and flight.]

The Church in *Urte ilunak* does not appear in loving incarnation; Itziar's teacher is a strict nun and the town's priest advises Itziar's mother to subject her to a number of sacrifices.

A series of sequences link *Marcelino* to Gothic elements in *Urte ilunak*. After viewing *Marcelino*, Itziar leaves the theater and calls out for Manuel. Surprisingly, an older gentleman answers her in song. The older man is not named Manuel but rather Cosme (Joxé Lizaso) and Itziar will soon attend his wake. Itziar and friends play a game on the staircase of pretending to awaken a dead man. The children are in a place of limbo, neither at the top of the stairs nor the bottom, from where they imagine they can contact the dead. In typical Gothic form, one child uses a scary voice to say 'estoy subiendo las escaleras' (I'm walking up the stairs) and suddenly the children hear footsteps. Stairs in Lazkano's film do not lead to heaven, as they do in *Marcelino*. Shortly thereafter, Itziar pays her respects to Cosme, peering into his casket, and returns his wallet to him eternally. Cinematography here, a low angle of Itziar from the casket, recalls Ana's behaviour at her father's wake in *Cría cuervos*, although Itziar walks up to Cosme's body of her own volition.

Itziar prefers the shadows and the countryside to the oppressive climate of her home and school. Escapades to these locales allow her some room to breathe and resist panoptic nationalist structures. Although she longed for a loving family, Itziar is exiled to boarding school in France and returns years later. She is courted by a young man whose Basque nationalism is too much like her father's. He tells her that he remembers her as a child: 'llena de secretos' (full of secrets). Family secrets lie at the heart of the next Basque film I will discuss.

Secretos del corazón (Armendáriz 1997)

Montxo Armendáriz's (1949–) Oscar-nominated and Goya-winning film from 1997 explores Javi's (Andoni Erburu) discovery of the origin of life and his true origins. The eight-year-old learns that the man he calls uncle is actually his father while his supposed father killed himself years before the action of the film. *Secretos del corazón*, set in Pamplona and a Basque town in the 1960s, pairs sexual awakening, to a greater extent, to political awakening, to a lesser extent; Javi conflates moans of ghosts to those of adults' sexual encounters. He and his older brother Juan (Álvaro Nagore) live with their aunts while attending Catholic school in Pamplona. *Secretos del corazón* dialogues with *Marcelino pan y vino* and *El espíritu de la colmena*, although its depiction of the Gothic child is closer to that of *Marcelino* with, like the *nuevo cine con niño Urte ilunak*, a critical portrayal of the Church. Javi embodies the Gothic child's characteristics in the death of his parent; spirituality and candles; the funeral of his friend's mother; his descent to the cobwebbed cellar to retrieve wine; the alarming sounds of a train; and the final realisation that comes with newly acquired knowledge of a present, loving father. Of most importance to my reading of Javi as Gothic child are the boy's exploration of his father's room and descent to the scary cellar. Prosopopeia for Javi is that that he imagines with the ghost of his supposed father.

Secretos del corazón inverts Jacob's ladder from *Marcelino pan y vino*. According to the Old Testament, a crisis in the father–son relationship incites Jacob's dream of stairs to heaven (Karesh and Hurvitz 2006: 244). Stairs are the conduit for Javi's relationship with both his fathers: upwards to his deceased 'father's' room and downwards to the barn-cellar he shares with his 'uncle'. His true parental reunion is achieved downstairs, towards or under the earth and in earthly exploits. The intertext of Marcelino during Javi's excursions to the cellar is unmistakable (Wright 2013: 111). A conversation regarding fear prefaces Javi's descent and Marcelino's ascent. The Father Superior (Rafael Rivelles) tells Fray Papilla (Juan Calvo) that it is wrong to scare Marcelino. Javi's mother consoles him atop the cellar's stairs that the secret of the brave is that: 'nunca dicen que tienen miedo' ('They never say that they are afraid'). Both boys observe a spider on its web (Figures 5.1 and 5.2). Javi retrieves wine from the cellar to bring to his father at the kitchen table while Marcelino retrieves bread and wine from Fray Papilla's kitchen to bring to his Holy father. Javi's mother tells him that it is important for him to overcome his anxiety by disregarding and silencing his fears. Javi's coming-of-age is signalled by transgressions: crossing the river, entering forbidden or scary spaces, revealing secrets, and lying to figures of religious and other authority.

Javi climbs the stairs to investigate his supposed father's room. Like

Figure 5.1 Marcelino (Pablito Calvo) explores the attic in *Marcelino pan y vino*.

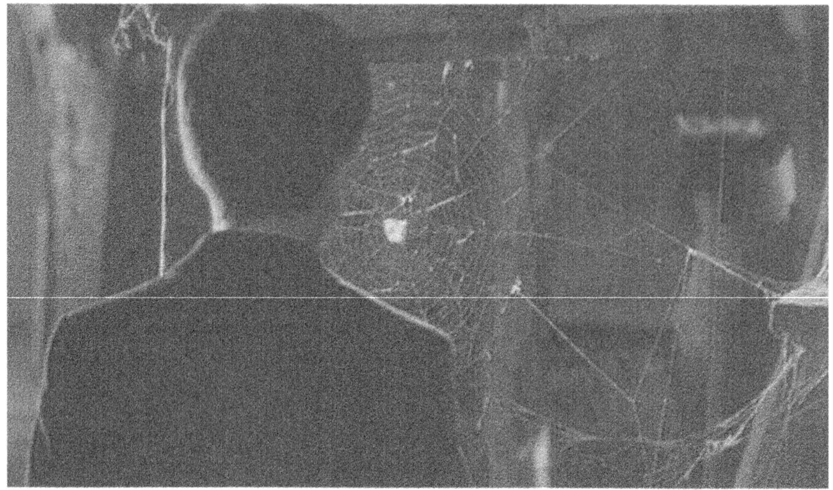

Figure 5.2 Javi (Andoni Erburu) explores the basement in *Secretos del corazón*.

Erice's Isabel, Javi's older brother fabricates a scary story in answer to his younger brother's questions. Juan tells Javi that their father died in that room and that is why it holds his secrets. A handheld camera from Javi's point-of-view approaches the door with trepidation. It is a teaser that his mother interrupts with her reiterated prohibition: 'no me gusta que entréis en esa habitación' ('I don't like you going into that room'). Javi returns to the forbidden room and camerawork over his shoulder shows how the boy takes in the shadowy space. This time, the strident sound of a noise maker that Juan wields interrupts and startles Javi's solitary exploration. Juan indicates where their father died. Like Erice's Ana, who steps into the civil dead man's footprint, Javi connects with his deceased 'father' by sitting in the armchair in which he died. According to Juan: 'Los muertos gritaban para liberarse de sus secretos. Por eso se oyen las voces' ('The dead were shouting to be free of their secrets. You heard the voices'). Javi works up the courage to listen to the voices of the dead and investigate their truth. *Secretos del corazón* sets up Javi's prosopopeia but dismantles it as he discovers that these voices are not the sounds of tormented souls but rather of love making.

The other haunted space, according to Juan, is the mansion of their Tía María's (Charo López) lover Ricardo (Chete Lera). However, this time, Javi reveals the secret of María's affair with Ricardo to Juan. This man is the monster's equivalent in *Secretos del corazón*, likened to the blow-up Michelin Man his reflection replaces in a store window while Javi strolls with María. The image recalls the transition from Ana to

Frankenstein's monster in *El espíritu de la colmena*. Javi's approach to the mansion, beyond its spider web-designed metal gate, prioritises sound over sight since Javi is unable to get a clear view of its interior. The camera shows a close-up on Javi's friend Carlos's (Íñigo Garcés) ear as he confuses the sounds of the house with hauntings. Again, a jarring noise, that of a train barrelling by, alarms the boys and interrupts their snooping. The Gothic train indicates, as Georgieva notes, mystery, horror, and a desire to uncover past secrets (2013: 168). Javi reveals the 'secrets of the heart' here as well, when he spies on María and Ricardo and discovers a heart in an ornament at the front door. The 'monster' Ricardo is no one to fear. Those tagged as monstrous (the *maqui* or Ricardo) simply do not comply with the moral standards of Francoism. Ricardo's monstrosity stems from his extramarital affair with María.

Javi's prosopopeia reveals the secrets of the past and present, although the film demonstrates ambivalence regarding righting past wrongs.[2] His approach to his 'father's' armchair allows him to expose an infidelity and his investigation at the 'uninhabited house' permits the revelation of another. These transgressions are accepted and not judged by the film, although the union of their expectant mother to their 'uncle' is sanctified by the Church in the end. Perhaps by accepting the actions of his mother and 'uncle', Javi does not fall prey to the same repressive thinking of his Tía Rosa (Vicky Peña), the Francoist moral arbiter of the family. I would argue that Javi does not ultimately follow his mother's advice to keep quiet about his fears and discoveries. In fact, his coming-of-age largely rests on his disobedience to authority figures and overcoming his fears. Javi lies to the priest director of his Salesian school play (Armendáriz also attended a Salesian school in Pamplona (Gómez 1998: 83)) in order to make possible Juan's return from expulsion to reclaim his starring role. Rob Stone contrasts *Secretos* to other films of the *cines con niño* on this subject: 'Javi's eventual crossing of the river, his triumphant breaking of the cobweb, are signs that his new generation would beat its irrational fears and soon substitute a progressive, liberal Spain for the terror of an annihilation that never happened' (2002: 103). Overcoming the fear of ghosts is central to our next film for discussion, *El espinazo del diablo*.

El espinazo del diablo (Del Toro 2001)

Mexican director Guillermo del Toro's (1964–) *El espinazo del diablo* follows Gothic convention more closely (his 2001 film is not simply in the 'Gothic mode') but embraces the marginalised. Ann Davies's assessment of the Gothic mode in Spanish cinema would consider this film as 'full-blown Gothic'. Ghosts in Del Toro exist but they do not exist to hurt the living. Twelve-year-old Carlos (Fernando Tielve) engages in prosopopeia during the Spanish Civil War with his Castilian plain orphanage's ghost Santi (Junio Valverde) in order to help Santi enact justice for his murder by Jacinto (Eduardo Noriega).[3] For Xavier Aldana Reyes:

> In their exploration of violence within the context of the Spanish Civil War, *The Devil's Backbone* and *Pan's Labyrinth* also recast the Gothic from a very fresh national angle that resonates with the Francoist cinema of metaphoric resistance (*Spirit of the Beehive*, *Raise Ravens*) and social and political concerns of a country immersed in a momentous process of historical recuperation. (2017: 220)

Guillermo del Toro (Mexico 1964–), who was mentored and befriended by Spanish Republican exiles and their children in Mexico, co-wrote the screenplay with Spanish screenwriters Antonio Trashorras and David Muñoz. Cartoonist Carlos Giménez's series *Paracuellos*, set at and inspired by the Francoist Auxilio Social orphanages in which he grew up, informs Carlos's orphanage (Lázaro-Reboll 2007: 41).[4] However, it is important to note that Santa Lucía is an institution run by Republicans and for the children of Republicans. As the director Carmen (Marisa Paredes) puts it, they are: 'rojos cuidando hijos de rojos' ('Reds looking after Reds' children'). The spectator of this Goya-nominated film in fact witnesses an institution in transition from the support of the Republican colonies to the abuse of the Auxilio Social.

Carlos (and Santi) is a parentless Gothic child who resists the hardships of orphanhood and a new hostile environment and who makes nightly journeys to the murky underground pool (*fosa*) to retrieve water and investigate Santi's disappearance. The voice-over narration of Dr Casares' (Federico Luppi) ghost begins and ends the film in circular fashion, asking: '¿Qué es un fantasma?' ('What is a ghost?'). Carlos's exploration of this research question propels the film. Ghostly characters are not limited to Santi and Dr Casares. Carmen, after all, suggests that Republicans like herself and Dr Casares towards the end of the Civil War are all living dead: 'a veces pienso que los fantasmas somos nosotros' ('Sometimes I think that we are the ghosts'). She also makes an ironic reference to phantom limb pain when she laments the weight of her amputated leg, whose prosthetic is loaded with the orphanage's gold for their getaway. David Archibald argues that all the characters are ghosts because *El espinazo del diablo* is set in the past (2012: 139). María Gil Poisa also observes that Jacinto's blurry photograph likens him to a ghost (2016: 133). Carlos, however, most closely associates with Santi, whose bed he takes, and Dr Casares, whom Carmen notes is similar to Carlos, in his quest for justice. Miriam Haddu considers how *El espinazo del diablo* engages with the Gothic tradition but also re-works it with the mundane since Santi first appears to Carlos in broad daylight (2014: 150–1). I will focus on Carlos's prosopopeial communication with the ghost Santi and how *El espinazo el diablo* highlights and exhibits the fullest expression of the Gothic mode begun in *Marcelino pan y vino*.

El espinazo del diablo is another *nuevo cine con niño* film, like *Secretos del corazón* and *Cría cuervos*, that reorients the Gothic child's explorations as a descent rather than an ascent. Carlos retrieves water while Marcelino and Javi serve wine and Erice's Ana offers honey and an apple. Saura's Ana recovers her 'poison' from beside the empty pool in her backyard while Carlos investigates another kind of pool. Del Toro's film is more akin to *Cría cuervos* (and Pedro Almodóvar's *La mala educación*) in its retribution towards repressive, even abusive authority figures. His revision of *Marcelino*'s Gothic mode is apparent in the boys' irreverent remarks on the orphanage's crucifix and in the amplification of the Gothic convention. The Republican orphanage undergoes cosmetic changes as the Nationalists, in 1938, near their victory. Since, as Carmen laments, 'la España nueva es católica y apostólica' ('new Spain is Catholic and apostolic'), administrators and orphans recover Catholic symbols from the attic. As a punishment for leaving their room the night before, the guilty parties must enact their own stations of the cross, that is, carry the crucifix out of storage. One boy cracks with a common blasphemy: 'para estar muerto, pesa la hostia' ('for a dead guy he sure weighs a lot!'). Del Toro's boys do not worship and serve the crucifix like Marcelino does. In fact, they symbolically bring the crucifix down from the attic to earth.

Carlos's deferential and charitable relationship is not with the crucifix but rather with Santi. In lieu of *Marcelino*'s Manuel and crucifix, Santi is Carlos's 'invisible' friend. Like Erice's Ana, Carlos befriends the monster. Santi almost seems afraid of Carlos at first. Carlos brings him the offering of Jacinto rather than food. Carlos hears, as Javi imagines in *Secretos*, the voice of the deceased Santi ('muchos vais a morir' ('Many of you will die')) and, like the blood sisters of *Urte ilunak*, reaches out and touches Santi's blood. As a Gothic child, Carlos chooses to listen to Santi (and the dormant bomb in the orphanage's patio) rather than fear him. He travels to the underground pit to learn what Santi wants, saying: 'quiero hablar contigo' ('I want to talk to you') and 'dime qué quieres . . . ya entiendo, voy a ayudarte' ('tell me, what do you want? . . . I understand. I'm going to help you'). Santi asks Carlos to bring him Jacinto in order to avenge his wrongful death. Carlos acts as a proxy for Santi, doing his bidding. Santi thus ventriloquises Carlos in order to enact justice at Santa Lucía.

El orfanato (Bayona 2007)

El orfanato, a horror film produced by Del Toro and set at an orphanage in the early 2000s, continues the use of the Gothic convention for the investigation of injustice inflicted upon the weakest. In Juan Antonio Bayona's (1975–) 2007 film, for which he won best new director, the protagonist is thirty-seven-year old Laura (Belén Rueda) who takes over an orphanage in Northern Spain (from where she had been adopted thirty years earlier in 1975) with her husband and seven-year-old HIV-positive adopted son Simón (Roger Príncep). His condition is a secret kept under lock and key like those that Javi is determined to discover in Armendáriz's film. It is Laura's intent to run the orphanage as a home for disabled children, but Simón disappears on the day of the open house, changing her life forever. Maligned children are central to the story even though they are not the main characters. Interestingly, however, Laura impersonates her childhood self, reminiscent in this way of José Luis López Vázquez's character in *La prima Angélica* (Carlos Saura 1974), in order to find her son who has gone missing. In her prosopopeia, Laura channels her younger self in order to communicate with the ghosts who have taken Simón captive. These are Simón's imaginary (or not) playmates, echoing Marcelino's unseen friend Manuel. Mother and son play the role of Gothic children in *El orfanato*.

The Gothic children – Laura, her peers, and Simón – of *El orfanato*, like *El espinazo del diablo*, are orphans. These children epitomise the vulnerability and injustice of the Gothic child victim turned unintentional victimiser. At the orphanage, reminiscent of the abusive Auxilio Social, the root of present-day haunting is the accidental death of the ironically named caregiver Bengina's (Montserrat Carulla) 'deformed' (*malformación*) son Tomás (Óscar Casas) by the other children just after Laura's adoption decades earlier. Unwed Benigna treated her son like a monster who had to be kept hidden and hooded in a downstairs basement. Simón is able to communicate with his mother's peers, whom presumably Benigna had poisoned for their role in Tomás's death. Laura horrifically finds the remains of the other six children in the oven of the orphanage. They are, Simón explains, children like himself that 'no pueden crecer' ('can't (grow up)'). The *Peter Pan* intertext within the horror film suggests that these children will not grow up because they die prematurely.[5] It is a Gothic twist on *Peter Pan*. Similarly, the medium, who investigates the paranormal activity at large and is played by none other than Geraldine Chaplin, tells Laura that people 'próximas a la muerte' ('who are close to death') are those who can perceive the ghosts. *El orfanato*, like *Cría cuervos*, draws on the phantasmal characteristics of the actress.[6]

In true Gothic child form, Simón befriends the ghosts and monsters. Yet, the legacy of these murders haunts Laura. She is, returning to the second part of Karen Lury's description of prosopopeia, the adult who revisits childhood experiences as if she were still a child (2010: 111). Laura learns that she must play the ghost children's treasure hunt game, even dressing in her (now inexplicably adult-sized) orphan's uniform, in order to find Simón.[7] Laura summons the ghosts with a game of hide–and–seek ('un, dos, tres, toca la pared' ('one, two, three, knock on the wall')) like the one she played as a child. It recalls the morbid version of hide–and–seek ('You have to die now!') that Ana plays with her sisters in *Cría cuervos*. Laura suspects that they have hidden Simón, her treasure, to lure her into their hunt. *El orfanato*'s Gothic children comply with the common characteristics noted by Georgieva: they do not have parents, their fate is mysterious, they resist hardship (of orphanhood), and they travel at night through underground passages (Laura finds Simón's cadaver in Tomás's basement). Ultimately, all the Gothic children reunite as a family after Laura poisons herself, now able to care for them forever. Disadvantage, deformation, disability, and illness characterise *El orfanato*'s children.

As is the case in Guillermo del Toro's *El laberinto del fauno* (2006) and Alejandro Amenábar's *The Others* (2001) there is a shuffling of and between the earthly and otherworldly planes. Protagonists do not achieve justice in the real world but rather in the otherworld; Ofelia (Ivana Baquero) gains access to her underground kingdom through martyrdom. Marcelino, of course, achieves his goal through death as well. In *The Others*, spectators learn that the protagonists are ghosts who fear the living rather than the other way around. Ann Davies notes the reversal of predator and prey in Bayona's and Amenábar's films, since Laura discovers that she accidentally locked Simón in the basement: 'the mother is confined to the house and grounds, exploring the rooms until she comes to realize that the explanation for events lies with her own murderous self' (2011: 91). Like the Gothic child protagonists of the *nuevo cine con niño*, HIV-positive Simón earns eternal life through his descent into the basement. Happy endings are not possible for most Gothic heroes and heroines in the here and now.

Conclusions: Spirits, Stairs, Ruins, Imaginary Friends and Prosopopeia of the Civil Dead

Gothic children of the *nuevo cine con niño* descend from their homes to unearth and uncover the traces of the *cine con niño*, the afterlife, and the previous lives of their peers and families. Their films discover anti-Francoist pasts with a Republican moral compass, gazing downwards and retrospectively rather than upwards as the Francoist saying, 'del Imperio hacia Dios' (from the Empire to God), would have it. The narrative adventures of children in the Gothic mode indeed resonate in subsequent productions in the form of phantom texts; Juan Antonio Bayona shares the 'moviescape of [his] childhood' in *El orfanato* (Delgado 2008: 45). This greater dialogism, one that also takes place at the macro-level of genre, is the focus of Chapter Six.

Notes

1. Translations to English are mine except those provided by the English subtitles of films, which I indicate with quotation marks around the text inside the brackets. I used the English dubbing of *Marcelino* distributed by VCI Entertainment. I provide the English translation for *Urte ilunak*.

2. *Volver*'s (Almodóvar 2004) denouement is remarkably similar. Raimunda's mother (Carmen Maura) is not actually a ghost, but rather someone who has come out of hiding to ask for forgiveness for her (negligent) role in a sexual transgression (her husband's incestuous rape of their daughter). Both are stories of redemption linked to sexual taboos and childhood trauma.

3. Santi is short for Santiago and may refer to the figure of St James moor-slayer (Santiago Matamoros). Former intern Jacinto may not be an invader, as the Moors were perceived in the Iberian Peninsula's middle ages, but he is an unwelcome presence and Santi(ago) charges himself with Jacinto's death. He takes part in the 'reconquista' of the Santa Lucía orphanage from Nationalist figures. Curiously, as the directors of the institution note, the Second Republic was secular; a reversal of the ideological and religious battle takes place during the film. Santi would thus reconquer the orphanage for the secular Republic rather than from the 'infidels'. From the Nationalist perspective, the 'infidels' were the 'reds'. Javier Domínguez García summarizes the resignifications of St James in the twenty-first century, noting: 'Western propaganda portraying the *Reconquest* of Spain as a crusade to expel the Muslims from territories rightfully belonging to Christians has been long mythologized in Spanish historiography as part of the origins of the nation' (2009: 77; emphasis in the original). *El espinazo del diablo* appropriates Catholic iconography for its Republican cause.

4. One survivor of the Auxilio Social offers testimony to a case of manslaughter that is strikingly similar to Santi's death in *El espinazo del diablo*: 'Un día que fui a los aseos oí que estaban regañando a Alfredito, un niño con el que me entendía muy bien, todo él delicado y poquita cosa. Se había hecho pis encima y una señorita le pegó un fuerte bofetón, con tan mala suerte que el niño tocó con la cabeza en la pared y quedó tendido en el suelo sin reaccionar, como un muñeco al que se le han acabado las pilas. Se lo llevaron a la enfermería, pero al día siguiente vimos cómo la furgoneta del colegio, una DKV, se llevaba a

Alfredito todo envuelto en una sábana. Nunca más lo volvimos a ver. A esa edad la muerte no existe, no crees que nadie pueda morir, pero ahora estoy convencida de que aquel niño murió' (One day I went to the bathroom and I heard that they were scolding Alfredito, a boy with whom I got along really well. He was very small and delicate. He had peed his pants and one of the staff slapped him really hard and with such bad luck that the boy hit his head on the wall and fell to the ground without a reaction, like a doll whose batteries had run out. They took him to the infirmary, but the next day we saw the school's van, a DKV, Alfredito was taken away wrapped in a sheet. We never saw him again. At that age death doesn't exist, you can't believe that anyone could die, but I am now convinced that that boy died that day) (Armengou and Belis 2016: 190). Refer to Chapter One for more on the Auxilio Social.

5. By contrast, Ana María Matute's *Primera memoria* (1959) uses the intertext of J. M. Barrie's *Peter Pan* as a means to explore the loss of childhood innocence of her pubescent protagonist Matia simultaneous to the Republic's loss in the Spanish Civil War.

6. María Delgado notes the cinematic resonances in the casting of Chaplin and the child protagonist (2008: 45). In similar Spanish film history fashion, *No-do* (Elio Quiroga 2009) casts Ana Torrent as a new mother suffering post-partum depression and the torment of ghosts in her house. These are the fictional ghosts of innocents sacrificed by the Catholic Church and accidentally uncovered in a Francoist No-do newsreel.

7. *El orfanato*'s protagonist may be inspired by Laura of *The Horrors of Oakendale Abbey* (1797), whose séjour at an abbey taps into her childhood traumas (Georgieva 2013: 171).

CHAPTER SIX

Dialogism and Ritual Function
of the *nuevo cine con niño*:
El espíritu de la colmena, *Secretos del corazón* and *El laberinto del fauno*

Introduction

The *nuevo cine con niño* often exhibits the ritual function of genre cinema. In Chapter Five, I examined the dialogism of the Gothic child across these films. I will examine broader kinship of the three films, specifically with regard to their imaginative child protagonists. In the current chapter, I analyse dialogism and the ritual function in a selection of three intricately linked films: *El espíritu de la colmena* (*The Spirit of the Beehive*) (Erice 1973) from the early transition to democracy, *Secretos del corazón* (*Secrets of the Heart*) (Armendáriz 1997) released during José María Aznar's conservative administration (1996–2004), and *El laberinto del fauno* (*Pan's Labyrinth*) (Del Toro 2006) corresponding to José Luis Zapatero's socialist government (2004–11). I am able to reveal the *nuevo cine con niño* as a genre-in-the-making with the imaginative alternatives to Francoism and its *cine con niño* that their respective historical contexts allow. These films fuse the ritual function of genre and the child's rite of passage, resting on the protagonist's liminality and ability to envision new possibilities. In historian Edward Muir's summary of the rites of passage in early modern Europe, he reviews three rites that remain relevant for our twentieth and twenty-first century child protagonists: (1) the preliminary rite of separation; (2) the liminary rite of transition that 'temporarily suspend[s] the subject betwixt and between his or her old and new state, providing an experience of the sacred or a utopian vision of an alternative social world'; and (3) the postliminary rite of aggregation or incorporation 'which bring the person into the embrace of the new community' (2005: 21). In the *nuevo cine con niño*, child protagonists embark upon rites of passage that do not simply convey them towards a generalised, biologically mature adulthood but rather into a certain political community of adults. Numerous *nuevo cine con niño* films, like *Secretos del corazón* (Armendáriz 1997), *La lengua de las mariposas* (Cuerda 1999), and *El viaje de Carol* (Uribe 2002), express the liminality, *limen* meaning threshold, of their child protagonists through the visual motif of crossing rivers and bridges to reach a new adult world. This is the community of Republicans, Francoist dissidents, or other outcasts of the dictatorship in the *nuevo cine con niño*'s political coming-of-age narratives.

Reaching the Threshold: *El espíritu de la colmena* (Erice 1973)

Ana (Ana Torrent) is the original inquisitive, observant, imaginative, sensitive, and rebellious *nuevo cine con niño* child. The six-year-old looks for meaning in and release from 1940s Castille, her sister, the cinema, and finally her imagination. Director Víctor Erice (1940–) best explains the climate that conditioned his childhood and, in turn, envelopes Ana's:

> Los años cuarenta del siglo pasado. Un escenario de ricos y pobres en el cual los niños tuvimos que aprender a sobrevivir. Sobrevivir significaba, entre otras cosas, tratar de arreglarse solo. En mi caso, fue el cine el que vino en mi ayuda: sencillamente, me adoptó. Me permitió sacar partido a todo sin exigirme nada a cambio. Más aún: me ayudó a esquivar a una sociedad regida por vencedores. A sobrellevar primero, y combatir después, sus grotescos valores. No me ofreció otro modelo de sociedad, sino algo mucho más valioso: el mundo, el mundo entero . . . (Erice 2004: n.p.)

> [The 1940s. A scene of rich and poor in which us children had to learn how to survive. Surviving meant, among other things, trying to figure things out on your own. In my case, it was the cinema that came to my aid: it simply adopted me. It permitted me to take advantage of everything without requesting anything in return. What's more: it helped me evade a society dominated by defeators. To live with it first and then to fight its grotesque values. Cinema did not offer me another model of society, but rather something much more valuable: the world, the whole world . . .][1]

Cinema became a sort of foster parent for future filmmaker Víctor Erice, whose first feature-length film tells a similar story. At the beginning of *El espíritu de la colmena*, Ana, her sister Isabel (Isabel Tellería), and the townspeople of Hoyuelos attend the screening of James Whale's *Frankenstein* (1931) in the Town Hall. Ana is captivated and curious as to why the monster kills his young playmate María (Marilyn Harris) and why the townspeople kill the monster. Isabel tells her naïve younger sister:

> No lo matan . . . Y a la niña tampoco . . . Porque en el cine todo es mentira. Es un truco. Además yo le he visto a él vivo . . . En un sitio que yo sé cerca del pueblo. La gente no le puede ver. Sólo sale por la noche . . . es un espíritu. . . . Los espíritus no tienen cuerpo. Por eso no les pueden matar

> ['They didn't kill him, and he didn't kill the girl . . . Everything in the movies is fake. It's all a trick. Besides, I've seen him alive . . . In a place I know near the village.

> People can't see him. He only comes out at night . . . No, he's a spirit . . . Yes, but
> spirits don't have bodies. That's why you can't kill them']

From that moment on, Ana seeks out the monster and confuses him with a resistance fighter that she finds hiding in the fabled monster's lair. I will examine how Ana's investigations are preliminary, arriving at the liminary in the final sequence. Spain also finds itself on the cusp of the preliminary and liminary in the year of the film's release. Scholars date 1973, two years before Franco's death, as the beginning of the transition to democracy (Vilarós 2005: 33). In this year, Franco's successor Luis Carrero Blanco is assassinated by the Basque separatist group ETA. Thus, Spain is in the process of separation from Francoism and in transition towards another political model. Ana's search for an alternative to the oppressive silence and internal exile of the immediate post-war enacts the ritual function of the *nuevo cine con niño*.

Ana seeks out foster parents in the form of the monster and the *maqui*. In accordance with the preliminary rite of separation, Ana sneaks off from her beehive-styled home to the monster's ruins in the rural outskirts of town with her sister during the day and then without her sister during the night. The presence of water where Ana communes with the spirit lends the film to a ritual reading suggesting that the ruins' well and the water beside which Ana finally meets the monster form part of a baptismal rite. Her spiritual godparents are the monster and the *maqui*. However, the *maqui* may not only be Ana's spiritual father. The girl's deep brunette hair and dark brown eyes, in a family of blondes and strawberry blondes, rather resembles the resistance fighter's complexion. Scholars debate whether there is a biological relationship between Ana and the fugitive (Labanyi 1998: 12; Curry 1996: 272). He may be the addressee of her mother's letters and her mother's former lover. While the *maqui* is killed, the monster is a spirit that can never die.

El espíritu de la colmena also tells the story of Ana's rite of initiation, one that is for Fernando Savater an initiation into the spirit. For Edward C. Riley and Javier Marzal Felici, Ana plays 'juegos de iniciación' (games of initiation) with Isabel (Riley 1984: 492; Marzal Felici 2006: 43–4). The more formal language of ritual permeates Savater's reading of the film; Ana undertakes a 'peregrinación' (pilgrimage) to the spirit's 'templo' (temple) (Savater 1976: 17). For Savater, Ana's movements are liminary: 'Allí celebra Ana sus primeras ceremonias de recogimiento, sus liminares rituales de silencio, sus invocaciones junto a ese pozo cuya chimenea une dos mundos' (That is where Ana celebrates her first ceremonies of retreat, her liminary rituals of silence, her invocations beside that well whose chimney unites two worlds) (ibid.). Muir's categorisation of rites of passage is more precise, however. What Muir calls the 'special state' occurs for Ana during the time she passes at the ruins and, most significantly, when she meets the monster. Muir explains:

> In most cases, the transitional or the liminal phase creates a special state, a moment when there is a 'pivoting of the sacred,' whereby the participant, ceremoniously and often physically separated from others, sees the rest of society from the outside, as if society itself were sacred and thus prohibited. In the transitional phase the individual crosses a threshold into another level of existence, a sacred or inverted world or sometimes a world of pure feeling. (Muir 2005: 22)

The pivoting of the sacred is achieved in *El espíritu de la colmena* in the shot-reverse shot between the monster and small Ana at night and outside of town. The camera's gaze 'pivots' from Ana's point of view, which predominates in the film, to the monster's. Both outsiders are then framed in a two-shot. Internal framing provided by tree trunks on either side, as if delineating the parameters of a projection screen, suggest that we are now watching Ana with Frankenstein in Whale's film. As the monster inclines towards Ana, the film suggests a postliminary embrace that would welcome Ana into the community of outcasts. However, the closing of Ana's eyes, the sequence is most likely a dream after all, truncates the literal and metaphorical embrace with a hard cut.

In 1973, Ana reaches the threshold of another world. Muir, by way of Arnold van Gennep, highlights the staging of such a transition: 'Van Gennep emphasized the significance of an actual physical transition to a rite of passage, the literal crossing over a threshold, accomplished in many rites by walking through a doorway. The passage is not just symbolic but a physical movement from one place to another, often from a profane to a sacred space' (2005: 22). This is indeed the case for Ana as she concludes *El espíritu de la colmena*. Ana is backlit by the moon as she stands at an open window looking out and hears her sister's instructions on how to summon the spirit (Figure 6.1). Ana orients herself towards the fantasy world, which she prefers to Franco's Spain, but does not pass through this threshold. An alternative is within reach and our on-screen child protagonist approaches it but is not shown achieving it. Erice's 'elliptical' film (Smith 1999; Curry 1996; Riley 1984), still subject to Francoist censorship laws, simply suggests the existence of another world in 1973.

More is imaginable three years later, judging from Ana Torrent's role in *Cría cuervos* (Carlos Saura 1976). Besides the casting of its child protagonist, other resonances (like mother–daughter hair-combing scenes in which characters gaze into the camera-mirror) render homage to Erice's

Figure 6.1 Ana (Ana Torrent) reaches the threshold in *El espíritu de la colmena*.

classic and re-utilises Ana Torrent as the symbol of Spain's transition to democracy. In Saura's film, released one year after Franco's death, seven-year-old Ana acts on the homicidal belief that she is able to kill with baking soda. Most importantly, Ana administers the 'poison' to her father, a soldier in Franco's military who mistreated her late mother for years. The child protagonist of the transition to democracy, advanced three years since *El espíritu de la colmena*, imagines that she kills the dictatorial father. The ritual function of *Cría cuervos* still operates within its protagonist's imagination.

Through the Threshold and Back Again: *Secretos del corazón* (Armendáriz 1997)

The spectator of *Cría cuervos* views seven-year-old Ana's daily life and gains access to her mature evaluation of her childhood as an adult. Adult Ana's (Geraldine Chaplin) memories from a future 1995–6 anticipate the memory boom of the 1990s. Montxo Armendáriz's film from 1997 takes part in this boom with its retrospection on the childhoods of Javi (Andoni Erburu) and Juan (Álvaro Nagore) in 1960s Basque Country. The memory boom of the 1990s arose in opposition to a cultural moment, that of the celebrations of the quincentennial of Columbus's first voyage to America and the Barcelona Summer Olympics, more interested in celebrating and capitalising on the historical legacy of a modernising nation rather than taking stock of the injustices of the thirty-six-year dictatorship of the same century. The *nuevo cine con niño* child Javi, curious and ultimately rebellious, investigates his family's past during the regime. His family demonstrates the division of the two Spains: his paternal grandfather is a defeated Republican and his maternal aunt adheres to the morality of Francoism. Javi discovers what may have also been one of Ana's family secrets in *El espíritu de la colmena*, that his father is another man (his 'uncle'). Armendáriz's reinterpretation of *El espíritu de la colmena* is indisputable (Pereira Zazo 2002: 234; Wright 2013: 107).[2] In my analysis of *Secretos del corazón*, I will explore how Armendáriz transforms the phantom intertexts of *El espíritu de la colmena* for 1960 and 1997 Spain. I argue that Javi's investigations require him to defiantly cross the threshold, but his findings are much more mundane and much less utopian or transformative.

Javi and Juan are the new Ana and Isabel, but fantastic answers to the younger sibling's inquisitions are denied in *Secretos del corazón*. Armendáriz's feature, produced by Imanol Uribe's Aiete Films, presents Catholic ritual as superstition to dismiss and Javi's coming-of-age rests in part on his willingness to defy religious authorities. The bedroom that each pair of siblings shares (like in *La lengua de las mariposas* (Cuerda 1999)) facilitates their pillow talk and is adorned with painting of a guardian angel and her charge. Spirits for Ana are ghosts for Javi: the ghost of his deceased 'father' and the phantasmal inhabitants of the supposedly haunted house. Juan plays scary tricks on Javi that make him imagine tortured souls in their father's room in the town and in the haunted house in Pamplona. Javi passes through the threshold of his 'father's' room and peers through the window to the 'haunted' house to see his Tía María (Charo López) making love with the would-be monster Ricardo (Chete Lera). The *Garbancito* school play recalls the villagers' hunt of Frankenstein's monster from Whale's and Erice's films.

The more significant liminal space for our discussion is the stone pathway that crosses the river. The film is circular in the sense that it opens with Javi's final obstacle to overcome: his fear of crossing the river. He is too afraid to cross the stone bridge after his brother in the daytime at the beginning of the film. The bridge has an important narrative function within the geography of Pamplona, where the boys live with their Aunts Rosa (Vicky Peña) and María while their Salesian school is in session. María is finally fed up with Rosa's moralistic harping on her personal life and storms out of their apartment to meet up with her married lover Ricardo at night. Javi runs after her, afraid that she has left for good, to the same liminal bridge. Javi's love for and identification with Tía María

Figure 6.2 The postliminary embrace of Javi (Andoni Erburu) and Tía María (Charo López) in *Secretos del corazón*.

encourage him to overcome his fear. He is now able to cross the bridge even at night. A high- and low-angle shot-reverse shot from the river with the sound of rushing water dramatises Javi's hesitation. When he reaches María, he receives from her the postliminary embrace. But, this threshold is two-way since María says that she will return, and we see Javi crossing again to go home to Tía Rosa, who is a much less sympathetic character than María (Figure 6.2). He, too, is now a part of the community of non-conformists to Francoism. Javi further proves his new affiliation by lying to the priest director of the school play so that his brother Juan can regain his starring role in the performance.

While there is an anti-Franco political undertone to Javi's rite of passage, it is much more mundane than Ana's initiation into fantasy. *Secretos del corazón* offers earthly answers to more spiritual questions and life goes on. To a certain extent, I agree with Rob Stone that: 'the child protagonist is relieved of his function as catalyst for the development of a political analogy and becomes instead an observer, a listener with his own problems to concern him' (2002: 103). In fact, I argue that Javi is relieved to a certain extent, but not entirely, from his role in political allegory. Javi's rite of passage holds the crux of the film's political message of liberation, set in a decade in which Spain began to open ever so slightly. *Secretos del corazón* leans towards Republican Spain but its cast of characters straddles both outlooks; just as María lives and loves out of wedlock, Javi's parents (mother and 'uncle') marry in the church since they are expecting a child.

For Sarah Wright, *Secretos del corazón* espouses a message of historical reconciliation (2013: 112). Yet, the film's ambiguity allows for another interpretation as well. We are told that María will live with Ricardo and no longer with Rosa. She may return only to visit, or she may fall back into her old pattern. The sisters will likely forgive each other but María may never live under Rosa's house rules again. Armendáriz's film engages in the ritual function of the *nuevo cine con niño* by proposing the alternative of Tía María's non-conformism and Javi's pursuit of this way of life. *Secretos del corazón* is a film of the memory boom that precedes, by a decade, the 2007 Law of Historical Memory and that is still careful, like the law, not to alienate either of the two Spains.

Crossing the Threshold Forever:
El laberinto del fauno (Del Toro 2006)

Mexican director Guillermo del Toro's Spanish films – *El espinazo del diablo* (2001) and *El laberinto del fauno* (2006) – engage with Spanish film history and intensify the latent Gothic and fantastic elements, respectively, from their precursors. In Chapter Five, I argue that *El espinazo del diablo* reincarnates the mode of Gothic child protagonist from *Marcelino pan y vino* (Vajda 1955) for its fullest expression in a horror film. Currently, I focus on how *El laberinto del fauno* draws on the imaginative child from *El espíritu de la colmena* to take fantasy, and therefore also the ritual function of the *nuevo cine con niño*, further. Ana's fantasy arises from *Frankenstein* and twelve-year-old Ofelia's (Ivana Baquero) emerges from the pages of fairy tales and children's literature. I will focus on *El laberinto del fauno*'s phantom intertexts from Erice's film, although it is important to note that Del Toro's Oscar-winning feature exhibits rich dialogism with centuries of folk tales.[3] Ana simply imagines, and the spectator must as well since her visions are not visualised, the world of Frankenstein's monster. By contrast, spectators follow Ofelia as she crosses the threshold into the fantastic worlds of the labyrinth and underground kingdom.

Both films, set in 1940 and 1944, begin as if fairy tales (with versions of 'Érase una vez', or Once upon a time), follow their girl protagonist's engagement with fantasy and *maqui*(s) that the father figure often hinders, have a patriarch associated with a pocket watch, and conclude with the heroine's life in fantasy. When, in a sort of cinematic game of Russian dolls, Ofelia places the eye stone into the sculpture at the entrance of the labyrinth, *El laberinto del fauno* cites Ana's gift of sight to the life-sized anatomy classroom model Don José in *El espíritu de la colmena* (Smith 2007: 5) and the importance of the child protagonist's point of view.

Ofelia's replacement of one eye is not only a wink to Erice's film, it also speaks fundamentally to *El laberinto del fauno*'s own situation within Spanish film history.

As a *nuevo cine con niño* film, *El laberinto del fauno*, more so than *El espíritu de la colmena*, depicts the two Spains and amplifies their polarisation. The Republicans are noble, good guys and the Fascists are the worst of villains. Ofelia arrives to her stepfather Capitán Vidal's (Sergi López) headquarters with her mother and fairy tales in hand. Fairies help Ofelia find the entrance to the labyrinth and Ofelia will complete tasks assigned by the Faun in order to reclaim her throne as Princess Moana of the underground kingdom. Meanwhile, on the ground, Vidal fights to suppress the resistance of the *maquis* who take refuge in the forest. Her pregnant mother will die in childbirth and Ofelia will be alone with her baby brother and associate more closely with Mercedes and the other *maquis*. Vidal shoots and kills his stepdaughter, but Ofelia lives on in her fantastic kingdom. Pre-pubescent Ofelia is a liminal child who first extricates herself from the mill headquarters (preliminary), crosses over into the labyrinth for trials (liminary), and finally lives eternally among a new collective (postliminary). Marcelino's saintly death in Vajda's National Catholic film echoes in Ofelia's martyrdom for the Republic, having made offerings to the Faun rather than the crucifix, in *El laberinto del fauno*. This victory for the Republic (in which the resistance fighters then kill Vidal and appropriate his son) participates fully in the ritual function as a more utopian and a historically inaccurate outcome to the fight against Fascism, which is also defeated by children in *El espinazo del diablo*.

I argue that *El laberinto del fauno* forms part of the *nuevo cine con niño*, given its characteristics, dialogism, and ritual function. Guillermo del Toro, in fact, cites *El espíritu de la colmena*, foundational of the *nuevo cine con niño*, during a conversation regarding his 2006 feature as one of his 'favorite horror films'.[4] The two films also share the admiration of James Whale's picture since, as in *Frankenstein*, Del Toro sets his film at a mill. Tanya Jones attributes *El laberinto del fauno* to 'two genre pools' – fantasy and horror – and recognises a 'theme of childhood' and message of 'imagination' (2010: 21, 27, 35). Guillermo del Toro insists on the generic heterogeneity of his Spanish-language films:

> I don't mind anyone remaking any of my Hollywood efforts, because they are comfortably sat within one genre or another. For me, 'Cronos' is and it isn't a vampire movie; 'Devil's Backbone' is and it isn't a ghost story; and 'Pan's Labyrinth' is and it isn't a fantasy film. I don't want them to be homogenised into a genre. (Jenkins 2006: n.p.)

However, I find that *Espinazo* and *Laberinto* fall squarely in the, admittedly heterogeneous, *nuevo cine con niño* genre. The child protagonists are the key.

Critics have noted the echoes of Ana Torrent in Ofelia (Diestro-Dópido 2013: 15), have listed *El laberinto del fauno* among recent child-starred Spanish films (71), and enumerated a number of commonalities between the films (Lie 2009; Miles 2011; Gavela Ramos 2011; Vargas 2014: 191). Yet, Robert J. Miles contrasts the films and finds fault with *El laberinto del fauno*'s glossy visualisation of Ofelia's fantasies when compared to *El espíritu de la colmena*:

> In the visibly stitched-togetherness, the reflexivity, and not just clever intertextuality, of Frankenstein's monster, *The Spirit of the Beehive* still generates an awareness of the fundamental potential likeness of our damaged selves to the threat, the enemy, our Others. By contrast, *Pan's Labyrinth* is a mesmerizing open wound into history. It is timely, expertly executed, but, paradoxically – and despite its global exposure – like the name of the monster the film so conspicuously vilifies, perhaps more easily forgotten. (Miles 2011: 203)

This is the same complaint that Óscar Pereira Zazo lodges against *Secretos del corazón*'s dialogism with Erice's film:

> A pesar de que los detalles que *Secretos* toma prestados de la película de Erice, el espíritu de ambas películas no es el mismo. He aquí una de las causas: el punto de vista de la protagonista se construye en *El espíritu* mediante la negación del focalizador; o matizándolo más, mediante la superación dialéctica del tipo de mirada que caracteriza a la cámar. (Pereira Zazo 2002: 234)

> [Despite the fact that *Secretos* borrows details from Erice's film, the spirit of both films is not the same. Here is one of the reasons: the perspective of the protagonist is constructed in *El espíritu* by virtue of the negation of the focaliser; or nuancing it more, through the dialectic overcoming of the kind of gaze that characterises the camera.]

For Miles and Pereira Zazo, subsequent films do not leave enough to the spectator's imagination.

I contend that Ofelia post-liminarily continues, crossing the threshold forever, Ana's preliminary footsteps. Where, in 1973, Ana just reaches the window, Ofelia, in 2006, passes through like a latter-day Alice in Wonderland. Ofelia, the eldest of the three protagonists I discuss in this chapter, is liminal in a number of ways. She is on the cusp of puberty and thus betwixt and between childhood and womanhood. The bleeding pages of the magical *Libro de la encrucijadas*, in fact, hint at the onset of menses (Lindsay 2012: 15). But, she proves not to be, as her mother chides with regards to Ofelia's fairy tales: 'mayor para llenar[se] la cabeza con tantas zarandejas' ('you're a bit old to be filling your head with such nonsense'). It is important to consider the woman she chooses to become, more closely following Mercedes's than her mother's model. Ofelia undertakes the preliminary rite of separation by leaving the walls of the mill and exploring the labyrinth. In doing so, Ofelia also makes a political orientation against traditional, domestic womanhood and for resistance to Fascism, as the forest is the home to both the labyrinth and the *maquis*. As Ofelia enters the labyrinth, she gains access to the 'utopian vision of an alternative social world' (Muir 2005: 21) of the underground kingdom where: 'no existe ni la mentira ni el dolor' ('there are no lies or pain'). Her death marks another part of the transitional phase (54). Finally, when she is reincarnated as Princess Moana, Ofelia is reunited with her family, much like Marcelino. Ofelia's political rite-of-passage asks her to associate with 'los del bosque', her spiritual godparents, and her Republican family. These are the communities that embrace her (and her baby brother). Like Ana, Ofelia chooses an alternative family and her affiliation with this family is symbolically tied to opposition to the dictatorship. Fantasy is a mode of resistance for Ana and Ofelia, who is able in 2006 to realise Ana's initial explorations.

El laberinto del fauno was released at the height of the historical memory debates, whose resulting law was passed the following year in 2007. Stephanie R. Golob calls the Law of Historical Memory 'innovative but incomplete' since it 'shies away from determining criminal responsibility of perpetrators of past human rights violations protected by the transitional amnesty' (2008: 136–7). Its 'innovations' declare Franco's military courts 'illegitimate' and allow for reshaping the confines of public sphere to address such past injustices in the future (137). Erice's and Del Toro's films take part in memory; according to Yvonne Gavela Ramos they: 'mediatizan el recordar colectivo de la posguerra española' (mediate the collective remembering of the Spanish post-war) (2011: 184). Princess Moana had, in fact, fallen victim to oblivion upon reaching the surface: 'borró de su memoria cualquier indicio de su pasado. La princesa olvidó quién era, de dónde venía' ('erased her memory. She forgot who she was and where she came from'). *El laberinto del fauno* argues that Ofelia must undergo a series of trials in order to recuperate her memory as Princess Moana. All of this, according to the film, is only possible in the fantasy world. Del Toro's film engages in the ritual function by visualising an alternative to Vidal's and Franco's Spain. Ofelia's fantastic victory is aspirational for Spain's politics of memory. Del Toro's film participates in what Golob calls 'transitional justice culture' (2008: 128). Golob assesses the years of 2006–8: 'Clearly influenced by ideas and beliefs central to transitional justice culture, the goal of advocates for post-transitional justice politics in Spain remains the inclusion of "the other Spain" in the ongoing (and admittedly contested) construction of a national grand narrative. Democracy is not just about rights; it is also about *belonging* to, and in, a self-governing community' (135; emphasis in the original). Del Toro's *nuevo cine con niño* film privileges the 'other Spain' and its community, although they may still be 'underground'.

Conclusions: The Dialogism and Ritual Function of the *nuevo cine con niño*

Nuevo cine con niño films visualise the past of Republican Spain and offer alternatives to Francoist Spain. *El espíritu de la colmena*, *Secretos del corazón*, and *El laberinto del fauno* dialogue among themselves and, beyond themselves, with transitional justice culture at three distinct moments during the early Transition and memory boom. The visions of these child protagonists fuse their power of fantasy with the 'imaginative solutions' of the *nuevo cine con niño*'s ritual function. Their rites of passage reveal the complexity of transitional justice. Where Ana is only able to reach the threshold, Ofelia charges through never to return, thirty-three years later. *El laberinto del fauno* and *Secretos del corazón* push the envelope further. Ofelia's and Javi's triumphs are tempered, however. Javi successfully crosses through the door to his 'father's' room and the river's bridge. But his role model Tía María is an ambiguous one. She may return to the fold (Javi's Catholic school play is indeed pastoral) or she may be irremediably taken by the 'wolf'. Yet, Javi's deception of the priest director at the end of the film suggests that he, too, from the perspective of Francoism, becomes a wayward sheep. Ofelia follows in the footsteps of her Republican role model Mercedes but her happy ending is only possible in the fantasy world.

Notes

1. All translations in Chapter Six are mine except those provided in the English subtitles for the films, which I denote with quotation marks around the text inside the brackets.
2. See Chapter Five for a discussion of the phantom intertexts in *Secretos del corazón* of *Marcelino pan y vino*.
3. See Jones (2010), Diestro-Dópido (2013), and Deveny (2014), for instance. For a discussion of the complex relationship among myth, ritual, and the folk tale, see Goody (2010).

4. Gavin Smith interviewed Guillermo del Toro for *Pan's Labyrinth* at the New York Film Festival's Directors Dialogues on 14 October 2006. The podcast was released to iTunes in four instalments, and this reference corresponds to part II, on 6 December 2006. I downloaded it on 30 November 2007.

Queering Post-war Childhood in
Urte ilunak and *Pa negre*[1]

Introduction: Beyond the Two Spains

In Chapter Seven, we investigate films that challenge the binary of the two Spains, two *cines con niño*, and genre films. The concept of the two Spains is centralist and elides the country's complex history with plurinationalism. The Second Republic (1932–9) approved the autonomous status of Catalonia in 1932 and the Basque Country in 1935, which were annulled with Franco's victory in the Spanish Civil War and then re-established by the constitution of 1978 (Pereira-Muro 2003: 236, 244, 247). In Fernando León Solís's overview of the binary, he considers the conflict between the two Spains and the country's historic nationalities:

> The strength of the ideological divisions is epitomized by the Manichean and almost mythological struggle between 'The Two Spains' (*Las dos Españas*) – the conservative and the liberal. Two groups that fight 'for the appropriation of the identity of the nation' (Morón Arroyo, 1996: 180), and whose strong opposition has been pointed out (rather simplistically, one might say) as the reason for the breakout of the Spanish Civil War (1936–1939). This divide has haunted Spanish society for so long and with such intensity that bringing it to an end was one of the greatest aims of the 1978 Constitution of the new democracy after the death of Franco. (León Solís 2003: 1–2)

Over the course of *The Two* cines, we have followed how the conflict over appropriation of the child and nation has played out in the narrative of Spain's child-starred cinemas. The majority of these productions, however, collectively contribute to the cultural marginalisation of the periphery of Spain, its languages, its cultures, and its historic nationalities through exclusion. Agustí Villaronga's *Pa negre* (*Black Bread*) (2010) and Arantxa Lazkano's *Urte ilunak* (*The Dark Years*) (1992) respond to portrayals of the two Spains by problematising and deconstructing the binary through heteroglossia, dialogism, and hybridity.

I will argue that Mallorcan director Agustí Villaronga's *Pa negre* (2010) shares commonalities with earlier features – *El espíritu de la colmena* (Víctor Erice 1973), *Cría cuervos* (Carlos Saura 1976), *Urte ilunak* (Arantxa Lazkano 1993), *Secretos del corazón* (Montxo Armendáriz 1997) and *La mala educación* (Pedro Almodóvar 2004) – but is unique in the *nuevo cine con niño* for its queering of childhood. The figure of the queer child, and particularly that of the ghostly gay child per Kathryn Bond Stockton's concept, is key to understanding the difference of *Pa negre*, the first Catalan-language feature to win a Best Film Goya. This chapter explores how the feature's queering of the main character relates to a wider spectrum of difference during Franco's dictatorship and how its queer approach also distinguishes the feature from its *nuevo cine con niño* peers. Much like *Pa negre*, Arantxa Lazkano's *Urte ilunak* problematises the binary of the two Spains in her regional film in Basque but also offers an alternative to the *nuevo cine con niño bildungsfilm*.

Alterity is a unifying theme in Villaronga's film and Emili Teixidor's works – his novels *Pa negre*, first published in 2003, and *Retrat d'un assassí d'ocells*, from 1988, and stories from *Sic transit Gloria Swanson*, first published in 1975 – on which the feature is based. Teixidor (1933–2012), whose childhood in Osona (Catalonia) inspired his literary works, is twenty years Villaronga's senior (Anonymous 2012: n.p.). The director adapted the work of Teixidor during a period in which the Partido Socialista Obrero Español (PSOE), led by former President José Luis Rodríguez Zapatero (2004–11), elaborated: 'a whole progressive politics of civic engagement and indeed the very principle of the social inclusion of *difference*' (Graham 2012: 135; italics in the original). Notably, Zapatero's administration extended the right of marriage to include same-sex couples in 2005. While Teixidor's novel makes evident the heteroglossia of Andreu's communities, exploring the boy's attention to the uses of language that surround him and the inclusions and exclusions they indicate, Villaronga's adaptation highlights the related theme of difference in Teixidor's *Pa negre* and *Retrat d'un assassí d'ocells* and renders its exploration of insiders, outsiders, and abjection through character development and the visual composition of its mise en scène.

In *Pa negre*, the ten-year-old protagonist gains awareness of his own sexual difference alongside the taboo sexual and political dealings of a hate crime – the castrating and killing of a gay man – in which his father and fellow townspeople in rural Catalonia participated. During the early post-war years of hunger, social vengeance, black market, and black bread, Andreu (Francesc Colomer) also discovers the complexity of his parents' lives, past and present. In their own ways, they sacrifice themselves and others for their son's future. His father Farriol (Roger Casamajor) colludes with the Francoist Manubens family for the attack on Pitorliua (Joan Carles Suau) and is executed for killing another man and his son. His mother Florència (Nora Navas) engages in taxing work at a textile factory and begs for the mercy of the Manubens, her family's rich and powerful overseers. To ensure Andreu's promising future, they encourage their son to accept the offer of adoption – with all of its political, sexual, linguistic, and socio-economic repercussions – by the childless Manubens at the end of the film. By joining this family, Andreu disavows his homosexual, Republican, Catalan, and working-class difference.

Agustí Villaronga's Difference

Agustí Villaronga is a self-identifying 'oddity' (*bicho raro*) (Carrón and Seoane 2011).[2] Born in 1953 in Palma de Mallorca, Villaronga had a happy, solitary, and reserved childhood by contrast to that of his and Teixidor's young protagonists (Pedraza 2007: 9). Villaronga moved to Barcelona in the 1970s, a noted time and place of gay activism in the country, to study art history and to work in the theatre and cinema (9–10). With *Pa negre*, the director adds to his filmography of difference and 'strange cinema' (*cine raro*) (13) apparent in his earlier films such as *Tras el cristal* (*In a Glass Cage*) (1986), *El niño de la luna* (*Moon Child*) (1989), and *El mar* (*The Sea*) (2000), an adaptation of Blai Bonet's 1958 novel by the same title. Eccentric and killer children, homoeroticism, and illness link Villaronga's earlier features to *Pa negre* and set the Mallorcan director's works apart from the more common sentimental and nostalgic portrayals of childhood.

El mar in particular emanates from a similar climate and narrative world to *Pa negre*. The feature, set in Mallorca, begins during the Civil War with the revenge killing of a young peer, whose father executed another child's father. The action of *El mar* resumes ten years later to explore the long-term psychological and emotional effects of the murder on the young people, two of whom become a self-immolating gay man and a seductive sociopath and meet again in their early twenties as tuberculosis patients at a sanatorium. Similar to *Pa negre*, *El mar* depicts child characters that problematise the trope of the innocent child, illness (tuberculosis) that pathologises same-sex desire in Franco's Spain, and a more neutral view of the Spanish Civil War that is similarly critical of Nationalists and Republicans.

In this section, I will outline difference with regards to *Pa negre*'s cinematic context and the criticism of his work and my difference vis-à-vis the scholarship on *Pa negre*. Studies of the Mallorcan director's portfolio prior to *Pa negre* have been limited, have noted his eccentricity, and have compared Villaronga's cinema to that of foreign filmmakers or set his films apart and studied them in isolation. The most extensive study on Villaronga's work, by Pilar Pedraza from 2007, compares the child protagonists of the Mallorcan filmmaker to those of the Italian Neorealist director Roberto Rossellini, for example, and shares a number of insights that also come to bear on *Pa negre* from 2010. Most notably, Pedraza affirms that 'Los niños de Villaronga son cómplices o testigos ciegos del mal' (Villaronga's children are accomplices or blind witnesses to evil) (2007: 22). Andreu's role indeed transforms from witness to accomplice in *Pa negre*.

The growing scholarship on *Pa negre* discusses historical memory and coming-of-age with a focus on commonalities. Thomas Deveny discusses *Pa negre* as a *bildungsfilm* and contextualises Villaronga's feature within the debates of historical memory and child-starred films since the 1970s: 'El hecho de tener cuatro décadas de *bildungsfilms* relacionados con la Guerra civil española manifiesta la importancia del género y de la memoria histórica de este conflicto y la posguerra' (The fact that there are four decades of *bildungsfilms* related to the Spanish Civil War indicates the importance of the genre and historical memory of the conflict and the post-war) (2012: 397). For Samuel Amago, viewer identification with Andreu through the child protagonist's point of view is related to Villaronga's concern for 'recovering in some way the historical memory of a Catalan experience of the postwar' (2013: 100). Sarah Wright similarly approaches *Pa negre* from a framework of historical memory to explore the cinematic child in Alison Landsberg's terms of prosthetic memory. Wright contextualises the recent child-starred films within the memory boom: 'Recent years have witnessed an increase in Spanish films featuring child protagonists which focus on memory, a response doubtless, to the "memory boom" in Spain (Delgado, 2008)' (2013: 93). I have argued that the *nuevo cine con niño* responds to the *cine con niño*, by virtue of intertext and other similarities, and dialogues with the cinematic productions' immediate context of historical memory but also challenges it, extending beyond it. I will explore how *Pa negre*, in particular, defies the common narratives of historical memory *bildungsfilms* and the *nuevo cine con niño*.

Other scholars note Villaronga's rejection of political Manichaeism, prevalent in both *cines con niño*, but not his problematisation of childhood innocence. Dean Allbritton's insight on pathology, death, and the traumatised child in Villaronga's distinctly pessimistic film stands out for its unique focus (2014). Part of the greater trend, Nekane E. Zubiaur departs from the premise of childhood innocence to examine Andreu's coming-of-age with lessons in being and seeming as a perversion: 'Andreu aprende enseguida que ser y parecer no son la misma cosa' (Andreu learns quickly that being and seeming are not the same thing) (2013: 72). Nekane E. Zubiaur (2013: 19) and Samuel Amago (2013: 110) affirm that *Pa negre* distinguishes its portrayal of the war and post-war by rejecting the more common Manichean representations. Indeed, *Pa negre*'s resolution and even-handed demonisation of Francoists and Republicans deviates from the most common conclusions of the *nuevo cine con niño*. Guillermo del Toro's *El laberinto del fauno* (2006), for instance, represents this trend in its celebration of the historically inaccurate triumph of the morally righteous *maquis* over the villainous Fascist Captain and their appropriation of his son.

Chapter Seven is primarily concerned with *Pa negre*'s narrative departures from the *nuevo cine con niño*, in other words *Pa negre*'s difference and Andreu's sexual difference. As is most common in the *bildungsfilms* of the *nuevo cine con niño* (for example, *Secretos del corazón*, *La lengua de las mariposas* (José Luis Cuerda 1999) and *El viaje de Carol* (Imanol Uribe 2002)) that we explore in further detail in Chapter Eight, the child protagonist becomes aware of adult behaviours (both sexual and political) and begins to participate in them by experiencing first (heterosexual) love and aligning him or herself with the Republican cause. The claim of the innocent, and particularly the sexually innocent child, does not ultimately prove valid for Andreu and his peers in *Pa negre*. The protagonist discovers his own homosexual stirrings only to deny them and join the political right.

Andreu performs sexual orientation: 'seeming' heterosexual but 'being' homosexual. Comparing denouements of what I call the *nuevo cine con niño*, Sarah Wright argues: 'Andreu has made a choice to join the Manubens and we have no hint that this is a mere performance hiding an alternative way of thinking (as in *La lengua de las mariposas*)' (2013: 126). While I agree that Francesc Colomer's acting does not suggest that the protagonist will sabotage the regime from within, I find that the character's obligatory performance of heterosexual orientation serves to mask his sexual difference. My contention is that the protagonist is indeed hiding an alternative way of feeling. Andreu's homosexuality is of paramount importance both to the climate of repression and disenfranchisement in the film and to understanding *Pa negre*'s queering of the retrospective *bildungsfilm*.

Before outlining the ghostly gay child and referencing textual and intertextual allusions to abjection and monstrous childhood, I would like to consider two queer-minded films in the *nuevo cine con niño*: Lazkano's *Urte ilunak* (1993) and Almodóvar's *La mala educación* (2004). Despite the appearance of gay child characters in Almodóvar's feature, *Pa negre*'s portrayal of childhood during the dictatorship is less similar to *La mala educación* than it is to *Urte ilunak*. *La mala educación*, as discussed in Chapter Two, takes for granted the Catholic schoolboy's homosexuality in 1964, which the film communicates through the character's voice-over narration and same-sex mutual masturbation scene. As opposed to *La mala educación*, Andreu exercises his agency in the negation of his homosexuality. *Pa negre*, quite to the contrary of Almodóvar's feature, subtly reveals the protagonist's sexual orientation through association, namely his affiliation with the queer characters of Marcel Saurí, nicknamed Pitorliua, and the unnamed young consumptive patient.

Heteroglossia and *Urte ilunak*'s Queer Child

Villaronga's treatment of Andreu in rural Catalonia has a certain affinity with Lazkano's approach to Itziar (Eider Amibilia) in the small Basque town of Zumaia. With the example of the Basque-language coming-of-age film, *Urte ilunak*, queer also translates to that that is non-normative in terms of Spanish centralist identity and language. *Urte ilunak* is Lazkano's (1949–), who has worked as a psychologist and educator (Amatria 1992: 38), first and only film. Itziar is strange, always out-of-place, and estranged from her family and often from her local community. Therefore, it is fitting that *Pa negre* and *Urte ilunak*, depicting marginalised regions and languages from the periphery of Spain and Franco's dictatorship, recognise their difference and scepticism towards nationalism's master narratives. In fact, Ricardo Llamas and Francisco Javier Vidarte attribute the origin in Catalonia and the Basque Country of the first gay rights movements in the 1970s to a regional awareness of the imposition of a certain identity, whether cultural or sexual (Fouz-Hernández 2004: 63). These films from Catalonia and the Basque Country coincide in their scepticism towards political and linguistic Manichaeism and in their preference for open, natural spaces.

The protagonist of Lazkano's feature, set in the years 1952, 1958, and 1965, is queer in a more general sense than the child protagonist of *La mala educación* since her difference relates to marginalisation in her Basque nationalist family and in the greater family of Franco's Spain. She is at odds with both populations since language is a subject for scolding at home, for not speaking Basque, and at her Catholic school, for not speaking Spanish. Villaronga's film, whose characters speak Catalan freely outside the classroom, implicitly contrasts the language of instructors and civil guards with the greater film as the only Spanish-language interventions in the feature. *Pa negre* naturalises Catalan dialogue as *La mala educación* similarly naturalises child homosexuality.

Urte ilunak dramatises the clashing of ideologies and explores the disciplinary spaces of the school and the home to show that Itziar and her new classmate, like the marginalised characters of *Pa negre*, enjoy greater freedom outdoors. Receiving reprimands rather than affection from her parents, Itziar identifies with the title character's search for a loving mother in *Marcelino pan y vino*, a classic of Spanish cinema and representative of National Catholic ideology that we discussed in Chapter Five, and befriends another misfit, the newcomer from Badajoz. Lazkano's film corroborates the sickly young heroine's outsider standing and incompatibility with her immediate environment when her parents send her away to a boarding school, reportedly for its healthier climate, in an ellipsis between 1958 and 1965. While *Urte ilunak* focuses on language and nationalism, sexual rather than linguistic repression is of greater import to *Pa negre*, although Itziar's curiosity about her body is punished upon her mother's counsel with a priest.

Itziar is doubly ostracised, and finally symbolically exiled for schooling, on account of languages and nationalisms. She is the internal outsider who sympathises with the 'foreigner' from Badajoz. *Urte ilunak* portrays the inclusions and, more often, the exclusions of heteroglossic linguistic communities and Itziar's carnivalesque resistance primarily through silence. Itziar's ostracism begins as a toddler in her home; the camera adopts her low-level gaze from the hallway as her sisters and cousin taunt her in Basque from inside a room. In the next sequence, Itziar's nun schoolteacher singles her and classmate Miren (Amalia Basurto) out as Basque speakers. The classmate seated next to Itziar further identifies, enquiring in Spanish, her as persona non-grata since her father sided with the Republic during the war, with both girls self-consciously appearing from a worm's eye view from inside their desks. When Miren and Itziar play with their girl dolls at Itziar's home in Spanish, Itziar's father demands they speak in Basque, to which she questions 'Zergatik?' (Why?), even though (as Itxiar overhears) behind closed doors he and his wife converse in Spanish. Itziar's parents treat her with suspicion, and violently – slamming her hands in a drawer – punish her.

Itziar resists the two nationalisms through inclusion, questioning, and silence. At school, she befriends another subject of difference, her new classmate from Badajoz Sofía (Andrea Toledo). They are both misunderstood by their peers. Sofía is taken by her new classmates for Korean. Teenaged Itziar explains to a suitor: 'No estoy triste. Soy así' (I do not feel sad. This is how I am).[3] As children, Itziar shares her favourite place, beneath a tree reminiscent of the Basque Guernica symbol (Martí-Olivella 1997: 230; Davies 2009: 366), with Sofía and even invites her into a sanguine sisterhood. Itziar fashions her own inclusive community. In this sense, my reading of this communal act as one that transcends the politics of authorities and peers coincides with Ann Davies's, where the: 'symbolism of the tree can be quite coercive: the bonding of the girls under the tree may equally be a challenge to Basque nationalism' (2009: 366). When Itziar asks her father why she must speak Basque, she exercises her carnivalesque resistance to his demands on her expression and for her obedience. However, as Christina A. Buckley notes, she also resists through silence: 'the silences in *Los años oscuros*, both Itziar's and the film's, represent presence in agency: Itziar is steeped in the continual process of achieving her identity through silent discourse' (1998: 140). At times, her resistance takes the form of back talk, and, at others, it amounts to disobeying orders to speak.

Itziar's path to coming-of-age consists of her negotiation of these clashing ideologies. *Urte ilunak*'s denouement represents a queering of the post-war *bildungsfilm* and rejection of the ritual genre function of unity. The *nuevo cine con niño*'s common coming-of-age narratives, as we will explore further in Chapter Eight, depict the child protagonist's destination in his or her rites of passage as a bifurcating road leading to one political community of adults or another. Itziar, upon return from boarding school, chooses a third way, opting neither for her father's and suitor's Basque nationalism nor her school's and mother's Spanish nationalism. Itziar's solitary surrender below her favourite tree represents neither nationalism. It is the spatial equivalent to Itziar's resistant silence. The ending's ambiguity – whether Itziar rejects Basque nationalism but accepts Basque symbols, takes her life below the tree with her father's razor blade, or commits a form of social suicide (Martí-Olivella 1997: 230-1; Martín 2005: 107; Davies 2009: 368) – richly muddles the Manichean nature of nationalist narratives. *Pa negre* presents another outcome by inverting expectations in its carnivalesque resistance to the two *cines*; its protagonist chooses the path less travelled in the *nuevo cine con niño*.

Ghostly Gay Childhood in *Pa negre*

Each adjective in Kathryn Bond Stockton's compound noun – the ghostly gay child – provides interlocking lines of enquiry in my discussion of Villaronga's film. For Stockton, all children are queer, but the gay child is particularly elucidating of childhood: 'even though the troubles of this specific child seem to be unique. This strange child particularly leads us to perceive ghosts and the darkening of children' (2009: 2). Stockton's understanding challenges the construct of the innocent child and is apt for Villaronga's problematisation of this child.

Departing from the ghostly gay child, I will expand upon Stockton's adjective 'ghostly' to explore abjection and monstrosity in *Pa negre*, although I will also touch upon semantically related concepts of phantom texts and homo-spectrality. 'Ghostly,' within the scholarship on contemporary Spain, is a term that first requires disambiguation. Jo Labanyi's work on hauntology illuminates an important line of enquiry that contrasts with my study on sexual difference in *Pa negre*:

> The trope of haunting, which elides direct representation of the past in favor of the representation of its aftereffects, stresses the legacy of the past to the present: a legacy which – as in most ghost stories – is one of injustice requiring reparation. (Labanyi 2007: 113)

The dialogism of Villaronga's feature acknowledges but deviates from the canonical representation of the wrongs of the past that Labanyi identifies.

These ghost children are found elsewhere in *El espinazo del diablo*'s Santi (Junio Valverde in Guillermo del Toro's 2001 feature) and the playmates of *El orfanato*'s (2007) Simón (Roger Príncep in Juan Antonio Bayona's 2007 film). *Pa negre*'s closest approximation to *El espinazo del diablo* is in the invocation of young Culet's (Miquel Borràs) dying word, 'Pitorliua', to Andreu in the fourth minute of the film, relating and implicating Andreu's father in the deaths of Culet, Culet's father Dionís (Andrés Herrera), and Pitorliua. Culet piques Andreu's curiosity here as Santi does Carlos's (Fernando Tielve) in *El espinazo del diablo*.

My argument is concerned with a certain kind of ghostliness rather than ghosts. Homo-spectrality, by virtue of Pitorliua's appearances, and phantom intertexts in *Pa negre* reveal Villaronga's ironic distance from the more typical hauntological narratives. Pitorliua does not return from the grave, as does Santi, to demand justice for his wrongful death. Rather, allusions to Pitorliua's story hint at Andreu's sexual stirrings and warn the boy to escape a similar fate. While Andreu shares Carlos's investigative and empathetic impulses, his aim is not related to liberating Pitorliua. In similar fashion, although Andreu uncovers the truth about his father like Javi (Andoni Erburu) from *Pa negre*'s phantom intertext *Secretos del corazón*, I suggest that *Pa negre*'s conclusion is not concerned with Andreu's exposure of secrets and half-truths but rather with the boy's hiding of his own secrets and truths. *Pa negre*'s difference exposes the vast heteronormativity of the *nuevo cine con niño*.

Under the category of gay, I will examine difference such as the queer, non-heteronormative, non-compliant with reproductive futurity and otherwise non-normative, including the sexual and disabled child, the infirm, and the abject. Stockton's conception allows for such expansions:

> The ghostly gay child, as a matter of fact, makes *gay* far more liquid and labile than it has seemed in recent years, when queer theory has been rightfully critiquing it. Odd as it may seem, gay in this context, the context of the child, is the new queer – a term that touts its problems and shares them with anyone. (Stockton 2009: 4; emphasis in the original)

However, Stockton's theorisation of the protogay child does not take into account the self-aware closeted queer child that Andreu chooses to become.

In *Pa negre*, the tragic fate of Pitorliua serves as a cautionary tale for Andreu that inhibits his future retroaction as a gay child. Lee Edelman's concept of reproductive futurity and Judith Halberstam's theorisation of reproductive temporality come to bear on the Francoist context in which Andreu chooses to closet himself by joining a family adherent to the regime. Andreu complies with reproductive futurism, which preserves 'the absolute privilege of heteronormativity by rendering unthinkable, by casting outside the political domain, the possibility of a queer resistance to this organizing principle of communal relations' (Edelman 2004: 2), and makes impossible his backwards birth as a gay child, in Stockton's terminology, upon his agreement to adoption by the Manubens.

The homophobic record of the Manubens family exhibits what Halberstam calls the 'middle-class logic of reproductive temporality' (2005: 4). The power-wielding family brutally ended the relationship between Pitorliua and Mrs Manubens's (Mercè Arànega) brother by ordering the attack on Pitorliua and marrying off the brother and exiling him to France with his new wife. Mrs Manubens, after her brother dies, asks Dionís Seguí (Andrés Herrera) to destroy the marriage papers so that she may inherit her brother's fortune. When Dionís attempts to blackmail Mrs Manubens with the documents, Mrs Manubens orders Farriol to kill Dionís. She first attempts to ensure reproductive futurity through her brother's marriage, which produces no heirs. Mrs Manubens then denies her sister-in-law's right to inherit. Farriol's execution for Dionís Seguí's murder is the condition for Andreu's adoption, whereby the Manubens family at last secures a descendant.

There is no doubt that Franco's Spain upheld reproductive futurism and temporality. Francoism's temporality, contrary to queer time, is that of inheritance as:

> generational time within which values, wealth, goods, and morals are passed through family ties from one generation to the next. It also connects the family to the histori-

cal past of the nation, and glances ahead to connect the family to the future of both familial and national stability. (Halberstam 2005: 5)

The ideology of Francoism, informed by Doctor Antonio Vallejo Nágera's promotion of racial purity and eugenics (1938), violently enforced heter-onormativity and reproductive futurity for the sake of the regime's own continuity.

As Andreu forges his identity in this *bildungsfilm* set during the post-war, negation and exclusion play a central role and manifest themselves in the visual composition of *Pa negre*. Spanish queer theorist David Córdoba García notes that identity is forged on such a basis: 'El proceso de la negación es, pues, doble: de un lado, la exclusión de un afuera, de un(os) otro(s) frente a los que toda identidad se constituye; y de otro, la represión de las huellas de esa operación de exclusión' (The process of negation is, thus, double: on the one hand, the exclusion from the outside, of some other(s) versus those constituted by an entire identity, and on the other hand, the repression of the traces of this exclusionary process) (2005: 60). Representatives of Franco's Spain violently marginalised Republicans and homosexuals, both of whom hygienic thinkers of the regime like Vallejo Nágera considered infectious. Andreu, the ghostly gay child, compre-hends the life-or-death impossibility of his sexuality under conditions in which Francoist authorities and family members imposed borders marking inside/outside divisions.

Nevertheless, many borders are crossed, including heterosexual/homosexual, child/adult, ill/well, and Republican/Nationalist, and engender abjection in *Pa negre*'s investigation of binary thinking. Pitorliua represents a border-crosser as the homo-spectre that haunts Andreu's ghostly gay childhood and breaches the sexual border of hetero-normativ-ity. Julia Kristeva reminds us: 'It is thus not lack of cleanliness or health that causes abjection but what disturbs identity, system, order. What does not respect borders, positions, rules. The in-between, the ambiguous, the composite' (1982: 4). Pitorliua gives phantasmal shape to Andreu's queer childhood, representing the 'telling kind of ghostliness [that] hung about [the gay child's] growth' (Stockton 2009: 6). Andreu's one-handed cousin Núria (Marina Comas) suggests his likeness to Pitorliua when she initially appreciates and articulates that Andreu is 'different'. After Andreu rebuffs her sexual advances, she hatefully hisses a specific slur in his ear: 'Pitorliua.' Núria indicates thereby that Andreu is not attracted to her on account of his homosexuality.

Pa negre explores abjection through the imagery of birds, angels, homo-sexuals, and pubescent children. Pitorliua's nickname and appearance indicate his abjection; his name refers to a bird indigenous to the region (Deveny 2012: 405) that, according to the film's characters, is part-person and part-bird. Similarly, his angel carnival costume indicates a certain fluidity since Andreu's father explains that birds are 'Como los ángeles, que no tienen fronteras' ('Like angels, they have no borders'). The gay character of Pitorliua and the bird motifs, which originate in *Retrat d'un assassí d'ocells*, reinforce the suggestion of Andreu's sexual difference in Villaronga's fusion of Teixidor's *Pa negre* and *Retrat*. Andreu struggles with his orientation, lashing out against his father's hypocrisy and against his own same-sex desire when he attacks the birds that his father raises in the attic.

The Monstrosity of Núria, Aunt Enriqueta and Andreu

Monstrosity is an expression of exclusion, difference, and pubescence in *Pa negre*. It is also one of the subjects that *Pa negre* shares with its phantom literary and cinematic intertexts *Primera memoria* (Matute 2011), *The Odyssey*, *Cría cuervos* (Carlos Saura 1976), and *El espíritu de la colmena* (Víctor Erice 1973). The pubescent child is perhaps the ideal figure with which to explore the abjection of monstrosity. The young person undergoing bodily transformation – neither child nor adult – incarnates the liminality characteristic of abjection and hybridity. The monstrosity of the protagonist is the most explicit in the novel and film. Yet, sympathetic secondary characters, such as Núria and Aunt Enriqueta (Marina Gatella), display complementary marginality. These female characters illustrate that sexual difference and monstrosity, in Elaine Scarry's terms, do not exclusively relate to homosexuality in Franco's Spain, but also to extramarital sexuality and to disability.

Núria incarnates Elaine Scarry's conception of difference in terms of additions and subtractions and of underexposure and overexposure (1999: 288). Over-exposure is evident in Núria's topless sunbathing from her balcony and in her sexual relationship with the schoolteacher, both of which mark her difference from her peers and from the concept of the sexually innocent child. Most visibly apparent, however, is her anatomical subtraction. Núria, based on Roger in *Retrat d'un assassí d'ocells*, lost a hand from a grenade during the Civil War. For this reason, Núria is able to appreciate Andreu's otherness and to understand the meaning of Pitorliua's deductive castration in which the townspeople punish Marcel's body for its difference and subtract him socially through castration and murder.

While Pitorliua represents Andreu's dismal future, Aunt Enriqueta exercises a similar function for Núria's characterisation. To this effect, one of the town's children, Roviretas (Andrea Caro), comments that Núria will grow up to be like her aunt. Andreu's cousin Quirze (Jordi Pla) suggests the same of Andreu and Pitorliua. Núria and Enriqueta are similar in their non-conformist sexual practices. Enriqueta's sexual and political transgression consists of her extramarital intimate relationship with a Civil Guard. She further defies the expectations of reproductive futurism held by her family (and greater Francoist society) for her gender by working in a textile factory and refusing to marry a wealthy townsman in order to relieve her peasant kin's strained economics. She is an outsider like the monster she embodies during the grandmother's bedtime storytelling to Núria, Andreu, and Quirze.

Among the cast of characters, Andreu's monstrosity is most explicit. The protagonist of Teixidor's novel culminates in his adoption of his new monstrous identity. His language in the final lines of the novel indicates a transition, a border-crossing, and repeatedly declares that he is becoming a monster. The boy owns his abjection:

[C]omprendí, fascinado por mi propia transformación, con una mezcla de vanidad y de miedo, que empezaba a convertirme en un monstruo. En el monstruo que habían planificado que fuera. En un monstruo capaz de reunir en un solo cuerpo, en una sola vida, dos naturalezas distintas, dos experiencias contrarias. Un monstruo que yo mismo no sabía que me habitara. Un monstruo. (Teixidor 2011: 430)

[I understood, fascinated by my own transformation, with a mixture of vanity and fear, that I had begun to become a monster. The kind of monster that they had wanted me to be. The kind of monster capable of uniting in one body, in one life, two different natures, two contradictory experiences. The kind of monster that I did not even know could inhabit me. A monster.]

Andreu recognises that external pressures conflict with his nature and produce in him an abjection, an unnatural and thus monstrous being. His corruption amounts to a deformation in accordance with the self-sacrificing wishes of his parents and self-serving hopes of the childless Manubens family. Furthermore, in the duality of Andreu's hybridity he internalises the conflict and embodies the binary in an uneasy union. Andreu expresses the asynchronous self-relation, out-of-sync internally in order to comply with external expectations, characteristic of Stockton's queer child:

The protogay child has only appeared through an act of retrospection and after a death. For this queer child, whatever its conscious grasp of itself, has not been able to present itself according to the category 'gay' or 'homosexual' – categories culturally deemed too adult, since they are sexual, though we do presume every child to be straight. The effect for the child who already feels queer (different, odd, out-of-sync, and attracted to same-sex peers) is an asynchronous self-relation. (Stockton 2009: 6)

Yet, in a reversal of the protogay child's manifestation after a death, Andreu's ghostly gay childhood appears briefly only to be immediately interred for his closeting and entry in Franco's Spain. The film evidences the protagonist's ghostly gay childhood through haunting and morbid visuals: the camera blurs his school photo, which Núria subsequently buries. The gay child's effigy, rather than that of Stockton's presumed heterosexual child, is laid to rest.

Andreu's monstrosity recalls the symbolism of the pubescent girl protagonist of *generación de los niños de la guerra* writer Ana María Matute's *Primera memoria*. Matute's 1959 Premio Nadal-winning novel explores the conflict among child protagonists in Mallorca and in parallel to the Civil War (in fact, the onset of Matia's puberty coincides with the Republic's loss in the war) and is reminiscent of the climate of cruelty and violence in Villaronga's *El mar*. Matute's protagonist worries: '¿Qué clase de monstruo [soy] que ya no tengo mi niñez y no soy, de ninguna manera, una mujer?' (What kind of monster am I, no longer a child nor a woman?) (Matute 2011: 128). Matia, who would be another of Stockton's queer children, feels that maturation is a betrayal of her childhood self and her playthings. Andreu also experiences this abjection, but his monstrosity relates to a betrayal of his family and of his queer sexuality.

Villaronga's film concludes its exposition of difference and monstrosity, similarly alluding to corruption, with reference to another literary character, *The Odyssey*'s Polyphemus. The one-eyed giant is a monster of over-exposure and subtraction. The boy's teacher at his new Catholic school provides a reading in the film of the monoculous character's significance: 'representa lo monstruoso' ('represents what is monstrous') because 'su naturaleza humana se había corrompido hasta convertirlo en un ser de naturaleza diferente a la que antes tenía y llevaba escondida' ('its human nature was corrupted until becoming a being of a nature different from the one it had or that was hidden within'). The voice-over of this lesson is accompanied with a zoom-in to a medium close-up of the boy in order to identify his monstrosity. Andrés, no longer a Catalonian peasant even by name but rather christened as a member of the ruling and Spanish-speaking class, chooses to eradicate his queer nature yet remains an outsider. The teacher's words, original to the film, express the child protagonist's self-realisation of his own monstrous hybridity and border crossing found at the end of Teixidor's novel.

Sexual and Political Difference as Abjection and Contagion: The Cases of Pitorliua, Andreu and the Consumptive Patient

The mise en scène's establishment of space is essential to the film's exposure of exclusionary practices, the regulation of the body, and the interdiction of abjection and contagion. *Pa negre* displays Michel Foucault's theorisations of biopower and Doctor Vallejo Nágera's exemplification of them in Franco's Spain on the subject of hygiene, medicine, and power. During Francoism, regulation related to gender and sexuality. Accordingly, Gema Pérez-Sánchez observes: 'The oppositional pairs male/female, heterosexual/homosexual must remain well-defined and carefully contained for fascism to successfully carry out its ideological apparatus' (2007: 11). Andreu inhabits the border between the two Spains. The permeation of barriers in the film risks contagion, either of the tuberculosis that afflicts a population convalescing at the town's monastery or of Republican politics. *Pa negre* stages the conceptual and physical borders delineating identities and spaces in its mise en scène.

The institutional spaces of the church and the school (or the Catholic school as in *Urte ilunak* and the end of *Pa negre*) play a significant role in marking the borders of identity and regulating bodily comportment. The film's interiors at educational and religious institutions strictly correspond with the ideology of Francoism that Vallejo Nágera advanced. By contrast, the forest, on the outside, is a space of greater freedom, as is the case in *Urte ilunak*, and sexual permissiveness where unmarried Aunt Enriqueta rendezvouses with her Civil Guard lover and Núria and her teacher have sexual relations. It is also there that Andreu first spies a new friend, whom he will discover suffers from tuberculosis and is quarantined at the monastery to die, bathing nude and flapping his imaginary angel's wings.

School lessons, which discuss politics in terms of illness, establish borders and prescribe appropriate behaviour. Andreu's first teacher in the small town's school, a drunk engaged in a sexual relationship with underaged Núria, dictates in the film that it is necessary to: 'alejarse de los vencidos como se aleja uno de la peste' ('You must avoid the defeated like you would the plague'). The instructor's dictation likens Republicanism to the plague and is laden with the rhetoric of Franco's regime like that published in 1938 by Vallejo Nágera. The doctor warns against the dangers of contagion, linking tuberculosis to sexuality:

> Postulado importante de la Higiene racial es la creación y mantenimiento de un medio ambiente social favorable a la expansión biopsíquica de la Raza. La atmósfera

infectada de bacilos tuberculosos constituye un medio ambiente favorable a la tuber-
culinación de las personas que viven en él. Un medio ambiente paganizado, sensual,
muelle, materializado contribuirá necesariamente, a la degradación del individuo y,
consecutivamente, a la degeneración de la Raza. (1938: 3)

[An important hypothesis of racial hygiene is the creation and maintenance of a
social environment that is favourable to the biopsychic expansion of the Race. The
atmosphere with tuberculate bacteria constitutes a contagious environment for all
the people who live in it. A pagan, sensual, hedonistic, materialised environment
will surely contribute to the degradation of the individual and, consequently, to the
degeneration of the Race.]

Vallejo Nágera's theories articulate Francoist biopower and the reproductive futurity of the regime. Medicine and hygiene intersect in Vallejo
Nágera's Spain as 'political intervention-technique[s] with specific power
effects' that address sexuality as the source of disease, degeneracy and 'the
precise point where the disciplinary and the regulatory, the body and the
population, are articulated' (Foucault 2003: 252). The doctor's pseudo-
medical conjectures are presumably the basis of the boy protagonist's
future education in medicine, made possible by his adoption.

Pa negre's characters subscribe to Vallejo Nágera's and Susan Sontag's
eroticised understanding of tuberculosis, an illness that they attribute to
the adolescent patient's sexuality. Consumption is symbolically a disease
of passion and excess (Sontag 1978: 20–2). Sontag's study of the metaphor
of tuberculosis provides further explanation for the imagery of angels in
the film. Pitorliua, good and angelic, and Andreu's infirm friend manifest
qualities associated with the metaphor of tuberculosis that:

described the death of someone (like a child) thought to be too 'good' to be sexual:
the assertion of an angelic psychology. It was also a way of describing sexual feelings
– while lifting the responsibility for libertinism, which is blamed on a state of
objective, physiological decadence or deliquescence. It was both a way of describing
sensuality and promoting the claims of passion and a way of describing repression
and advertising the claims of sublimation. (Sontag 1978: 25–6)

The photo of Pitorliua dressed as an angel for Carnival combines the
clichés of illness, same-sex desire, and the child that the consumptive
patient, Pitorliua, and Andreu incarnate. On-screen, the boy's mother
cherishes this picture, remembering her friend as: 'La persona más buena
que he conocido. ¡Y alegre! Nos queríamos como hermanos pero era muy
. . . muy delicado. No estaba hecho para este pueblo y le hicieron la vida
imposible' ('Marcel was the nicest person I ever [met] and cheerful! We
loved each other like brother and sister, but he was too delicate. He wasn't
cut out for this and they made his life hell'). With platitudes evoking the

angelic psychology noted in Sontag's scholarship, Florència suggests that Pitorliua was a target of homophobia. His photo is entombed and hidden away similar to Andreu's school picture.

By contrast to Florència's euphemisms, Quirze employs derogatory and inflammatory language to describe homosexuals in the community. Quirze conflates same-sex desire and illness, giving Pitorliua as an example, when he tells Andreu that patients at the monastery are ill due to their sexual orientation and excessive masturbation. In the film, Quirze expounds with diction referring to sexual relations ('to be rotten' (*estar podrido*) (Teixidor 2011: 395)) that homosexuals are:

> Podridos, como las peras o las manzanas. Y por fuera parecen que están bien pero por dentro están llenas de mierda . . . El vicio se les ha pegado. Parecen angelitos pero cuando es de noche saltan como demonios de una cama a otra.

> [Rotting, like apples or pears, that look good outside but are full of shit inside . . . They're infected by vice. They look like angels, but I bet they go bed hopping at night.]

Quirze's words regarding the undisciplined sexual body echo Vallejo Nágera's hygienist rhetoric and epitomise Foucault's thesis. Medicine, according to Foucault, attends to so-called undisciplined and irregular sexuality and degeneracy: 'At the level of the body, of the undisciplined body that is immediately sanctioned by all the diseases that the sexual debauchee brings down upon himself' (2003: 252). While illness punishes the adolescent's homosexual body, the townspeople discipline Pitorliua's same-sex desiring body. Andreu's subconscious, influenced by his cousin's words, makes a connection between the patient and Pitorliua on the basis of their sexual orientation when it recreates the assault scene with a point-of-view shot that substitutes the consumptive adolescent for Pitorliua.

The inside/outside dyad manifest in Quirze's words is also apparent in the Catalan publication and language track of the film and in the visual composition of Andreu's first conversation with the tubercular convalescent (Figure 7.1). From the inside of the religious structure, Andreu meets the patient who is on the outside when one of his aunts brings him on her errand to the monastery. Andreu shows his curiosity and sympathy for the infirm young man from within a space of strict control and clear mandates regarding sexuality. His friend, who appears only in exteriors, is depicted with the greater freedom that natural spaces afford him. The boy's identification with the patient motivates him to risk contagion by literally and metaphorically embracing him on the outside before crossing over to the metaphorical inside, the space populated by

Figure 7.1 Andreu (Francesc Colomer) conversing with his consumptive friend from within the monastery in *Pa negre*.

the Manubens family and other members of the ruling class in Franco's power structure.

The novel, like the film, intimates Andreu's sexual difference through association with the tubercular adolescent. The main character discovers that he is more attracted to the consumptive patient than the girl with whom he has sexual relations:

En cambio [de la Lloramicos] la extraña fascinación del muchacho tísico – o lo que fuera – bajo el olmo, la delicadeza de sus movimientos, la armonía de sus rasgos, el misterio de todo lo que ocultaba bajo la sábana, que no hubiera tenido que representar ningún misterio para mí, y aun así la elegancia distante y algo desdeñosa con que trataba a los demás enfermos y el punto de rechazo que me parecía detectar del grupo hacia él . . ., todos los detalles que podía observar, se me quedaban grabados en el cerebro como impresiones más fuertes y de algún modo más importantes para mí que la aventura con la Lloramicos. (Teixidor 2011: 201)

[By contrast [to Lloramicos], the strange fascination with the consumptive boy – or whatever he was – below the elm tree, the delicacy of his movements, the harmony of his features, the mystery of all that was hidden under the sheet, that should not have been a mystery for me, and yet the still distant and somewhat disdainful elegance with which he treated the other sick people and the rejection that I seemed to detect from the group towards him . . ., all the details that I could observe, became etched in my brain like stronger and somehow more important impressions for me than my adventure with Lloramicos.]

The linking of illness and 'o lo que fuera' is significant in the protagonist's words that similarly confuse tuberculosis and same-sex desire. Andreu notes the distancing of the other convalescents from the adolescent, suggesting that the teenager's unnamed difference is his sexual otherness. The novel's protagonist begins to understand that he is love sick, recognising: 'La locura de amor, como la locura del juego, debía de ser una infección, una enfermedad como la tuberculosis, que secaba los pulmones a unos y en cambio dejaba respirar tranquilos y sosegados a otros, un misterio' (The madness of love, like a gambling obsession, had to be an infection, an illness like tuberculosis, that dried up the lungs of some and left others breathing easily, was a mystery) (Teixidor 2011: 400). Andreu is 'afflicted' with same-sex love, likened to tuberculosis, for the elegant, delicate, and disdainful adolescent.

The earlier sequence marking inside/outside divisions at the monastery prefigures Andrés's break with his mother from within his new Catholic school. At his new school, Andrés, no longer Andreu, proves insensitive to his mother's backbreaking work and arduous journey. The novel's protagonist explains his distaste for his mother's sycophancy and prefigures his choice to distinguish himself from her: 'el mejor modo de sobrevivir era guardar las convicciones propias e incluso toda la dignidad personal y arrodillarse de buen grado a lamer las botas de los amos' (the best survival strategy was to keep one's convictions to oneself, forgo personal dignity and lick the masters' boots on one's knees) (Teixidor 2011: 134). He also observes her suffering from love and vows not to make the same mistake: 'Aprendí una lección para huir de cualquier compromiso sentimental' (I learned a lesson to flee from any kind of sentimental commitment) (136). Villaronga's Andrés makes good on these promises when he rebuffs his mother and the former life that she represents, only able to afford rationed black bread, upon her visit at his school. Doors and windows form barriers between the two and intensify the boy's closeting. Such enclosures, reminiscent of Andreu's visit with his mother to Farriol in jail before his father's execution, suggest that the boy has chosen his own sort of prison. The cool palette and tight framing on Andrés's blurred close-up in Figure 7.2 contrast the more open framing (even considering the barred windows in the closed monastic space) with warm colours in the setting of Figure 7.1. To further underscore Andrés's enclosure and desire to obliterate his past, the boy fogs up the window through which he glimpses his mother hunched over and hobbling out of the school. Andrés literally compounds the division by making opaque the barrier between his new self and his old life. He internalises his abjection and reinforces the border so as to render it impermeable henceforth. His path defies the expectations repeatedly confirmed in other *nuevo cine con niño* films.

Figure 7.2 Andrés (Francesc Colomer) fogs up the window between himself and his
mother, upon her exit from his new school in *Pa negre*.

Phantom Intertexts

Pa negre's phantoms, besides Pitorliua's homo-spectrality, are primarily
those of film history rather than the spectres of past wrongs as is the case
in canonical hauntological cultural products that we examined in Chapter
Five. For Jacques Derrida, *Pa negre* would amount to a 'phantom-text'
wherein 'these distinctions, these quotation marks, references, or citations
[of the intertexts] become irremediably precarious; they leave only traces,
and we shall never define the trace or the phantom without, ironically or
allegorically, appealing from one to the other' (1986: 80). Given the highly
intertextual nature of *Pa negre*, a discussion of monstrosity and spectrality
in the film also requires a brief exploration of select phantom cinematic
intertexts *Cría cuervos* (Carlos Saura 1976), *El espíritu de la colmena* (Víctor
Erice 1973), and *Secretos del corazón* (Montxo Armendáriz 1997).

Pa negre's promotional material invokes *Cría cuervos* and recalls childhood monstrosity in the cinematic arts. Saura's feature in many ways
foresees the boom of the *nuevo cine con niño* since the 1990s through its
portrayal of a young girl who, in 1975, defies her repressive upbringing and twenty years later, in 1995, shares the memories of her terrible
and fearful childhood. The elliptical narration of *Pa negre* recalls that of
Cría cuervos and of contemporaneous features from late Francoism, like
Erice's *El espíritu de la colmena* and Saura's *El jardín de las delicias* (1970).
Saura's title refers to the proverb, 'cría cuervos y te sacarán los ojos' (raise
ravens and they will pluck out your eyes), and the film's young protagonist

who attempts to poison her father for his mistreatment of her mother and militaristic *machismo*. Saura's child protagonist Ana (Ana Torrent), observes, judges, and rebels against paternal authority. Marvin D'Lugo reads the family dynamic of Saura's film allegorically in terms of the death of the Francoesque father making way for the new generation eager for change (1991: 136–8). Similarly, *Pa negre* and its tagline allude to birds and indicate intergenerational conflict: the lies of adults raise little monsters ('mentiras de los adultos crían pequeños monstrous'). Remarkably for the *nuevo cine con niño*, however, Andreu's judgement rules in favour of representatives of Francoism rather than the Republic.

Pa negre's sequence of story-telling by Andreu's grandmother, which addresses the subjects of difference, ghosts, and monstrosity, is key to understanding Villaronga's queering of the historical memory *bildungsfilm*. The grandmother tells Andreu and Núria a story reminiscent of James Whale's *Frankenstein* (1931), a principal intertext in *El espíritu de la colmena*, in which villagers storm a tower to apprehend and kill a monster. The grandmother emphasises her lesson in the film with a question: '¿Sabéis por qué querían matarle?' ('So why did they want to kill him?'). Andreu answers: 'Porque era un monstruo' ('He was a monster'). She corrects: 'Porque era diferente' ('Because he was different'). Their answers are complementary because difference and monstrosity are synonymous in *Pa negre*. The story's primary audience, Andreu and Núria, are different and misunderstood like the monster. Yet, *Pa negre* and the intercalated scary story both avoid Manichaeism. Villaronga's film, unlike *El espíritu de la colmena*, exposes the repression and even culpability of the monster rather than romanticise the misfit as a symbol of resistance. Quirze in fact attributes the persecution to the fact that the monster had eaten a girl. Rather than suffer the monster's fate, Andreu succumbs to Francoist social pressure and becomes complicit to its structure of power.

Secretos del corazón represents another phantom intertext that haunts *Pa negre*'s embedded ghost story. Noises coming from the attic, where Andreu's father is in hiding from the authorities for killing Seguí and his son, interrupt the story. The grandmother explains them away by attributing them to ghosts that she claims haunt the house. Family secrets may assume ghostly forms, as they do for Armendáriz's child protagonist in *Secretos del corazón*, on account of their unspoken yet lingering effects. Javi, who confuses lovers with ghosts, discovers that his father is not who he thought he was but rather is the man he calls uncle. Andreu also learns that his father is not the uncompromising idealist he claimed to be. It is not long before Andreu discovers his father's hiding place, to which Núria, wise beyond her years, evaluates: 'Ya no hay más fantasmas, eh'

('No more ghosts, huh?'). During the first third of the film and shortly after the suspicious noises from above, Andreu uncovers the truth of his father's whereabouts. *Pa negre* and Núria diffuse the suspense and the potential impact of the explanation of the attic's mysterious noises.

Pa negre's deconstructive dialogism continues. The parodic relationship between *Pa negre* and earlier child-starred films, which Sarah Wright identifies with respect to the gaze (2013: 125), is apparent in broader terms in the scary story sequence when Aunt Enriqueta, with dish-washing gloves on the hands of her outstretched arms, mockingly embodies the stiff gait of Frankenstein's monster as the grandmother narrates. Villaronga thereby pokes fun at the hauntological storylines depicting the dictatorship. *Pa negre* is a phantom-text that dialogues with, recognising then disavowing, a number of phantom cinematic and literary intertexts. Núria's lapidary comment, 'Ya no hay más fantasmas, eh', exorcises the most common hauntological narratives, the phantom intertexts of *Pa negre*.

Conclusions

Pa negre is the exception that proves the representational rules of contemporary Spanish-language cinema's heteronormative and politically partial retrospection on childhood during Franco's dictatorship. Villaronga's film queers post-war childhood and the now canonical hauntological narratives of the *nuevo cine con niño* by virtue of a cast of marginalised characters led by a ghostly gay child and a collection of phantom intertexts. Such literary and cinematic references depicting childhood from the dictatorship allow *Pa negre* to herald its difference. The ghostly gay child protagonist likewise relates to and embodies alterity – that of homo-spectrality, monstrosity, and abjection. Andreu asserts perhaps the only agency he can wield under the repressive conditions of the post-war by purposefully rejecting sexual, political, and class marginality in favour of Francoist reproductive temporality and futurity represented in the Manubens family, his new school, and future career in medicine. In the composition of its mise en scène, Agustí Villaronga's cinematic adaptation of Emili Teixidor's written works reflects the exclusionary practices of such familial, scholastic, and medical institutions, whose entry thresholds the boy resolves to cross and whose mandates he agrees to adopt. *Pa negre*'s main character thereby charts a course from sympathetic difference to callous indifference in his transformation from Andreu to Andrés.

Andrés, however, remains the 'monstrous' embodiment of duality. The child dummy's body is the site of national and plurinational conflict, the two Spains and beyond. The Catalonian peasant boy is subsumed by

Francoist National Catholic schooling upon his limited choice. *Pa negre* reveals the *nuevo cine con niño*'s affinity with the Republic by producing a contrary ending in which its child protagonist sides with the Nationalists and self-imposes heteronormativity. The film itself, however, exposes Andrés's decision as a betrayal to his family and himself. While *Urte ilunak*, in accordance with the ritual genre function, proposes an alternative to the child protagonist's coming-of-age within either nationalism, *Pa negre* rejects the Republic, its recognition of Catalonian autonomy, and the union of the ritual function by underscoring disunion and rupture. Andrés, incarnating the conflicts of conservative, liberal, and plurinational Spain, chooses Franco's Spain, one that was purportedly, on the walls of Farriol's jail no less, 'una, grande y libre'.

Notes

1. Part of this chapter first appeared in the *Hispanic Research Journal*'s Screen Arts IV 17.1 (2016: 1–18) as 'Queering Post-war Childhood: *Pa negre* (Agustí Villaronga, Spain 2010)'.
2. All translations to English in Chapter Seven are mine except those provided in the English subtitles of *Pa negre*, which I denote with quotation marks around the text inside the brackets.
3. Translations to English of *Urte ilunak*'s Spanish subtitles are my own.

CHAPTER EIGHT

The Transatlantic Dialogism in Narrative and Aesthetics of *Bildungsfilms*: *La lengua de las mariposas*, *Machuca*, *El espíritu de la colmena*, *El premio*, *El laberinto del fauno* and *Infancia clandestina*

Introduction

In this monograph, I have thus far illuminated the rich dialogism of child-starred cinemas in Spain. The final chapter will broaden this study's geographic scope to provide an overview of the dialogism and aesthetics of *bildungsfilms* across the Atlantic in the 2000s. Latin American cinema, with films hailing from Argentina, Brazil, Cuba, Mexico, Peru, and Venezuela, has enjoyed its own bumper crop of approximately fourteen child-starred *bildungsfilms* over eleven years.[1] The *bildungsfilms*, defined as 'películas de aprendizaje o formación con protagonistas que son niños' (Deveny 2012: 397) (coming-of-age films with child protagonists), that I will examine here link sexual and political awakening at the time of military or paramilitary coups in Spain, Chile, and Argentina.[2] Compared with other subgenres of the *nuevo cine con niño* enumerated in the monograph's introduction, the *bildungsfilm* is the variant that most closely resembles the definition of cinema of 'childhood' in the *Diccionario temático del cine*:

> [C]ontrasta con retratos más realistas, imaginativos o con mayor voluntad de indagación en el estadio infantil con historias sobre la nostalgia del paraíso perdido de la infancia, los recuerdos filtrados por la memoria, experiencias sorprendentes (felices o traumáticas), procesos de aprendizaje y conocimiento del mundo, etc. Obviamente, en muchos de ellos es el punto de vista cognitivo del niño–más o menos verosímil – lo que otorga a la historia un carácter híbrido, muy capaz de combinar la tragedia con la mirada ingenua, la fabulación sobre realidades cotidianas con la distorsión de los hechos. (Sánchez Noriega 2004: 270)

> [[I]t contrasts with more realistic, imaginative or critical portrayals of the phase of childhood and stories of the nostalgia of the lost paradise of childhood, recollections filtered by memory, surprising (happy or traumatic), processes of learning and discovery of the world, etc. Obviously, in many of them it is the cognitive point of view of the child – more or less credible – that which grants the story a hybrid character, very capable of combining tragedy with the naïf gaze, story-telling of daily realities with distortion of the facts.]

The motifs of the lost paradise of childhood beside gained knowledge of the adult world pervade the *bildungsfilms* at the heart of this chapter. With attention to national acculturations, I will pair select Spanish and Latin American films to reveal common political use, motifs, and aesthetics of cinematic childhood across national cinemas.

Scholarship on contemporary Latin American cinema falls on both sides of the genre studies divide. These features correspond to Stephen M. Hart's nation-image in contemporary Latin American cinema: 'The emergence of the protagonist-as-nation genre . . . it was that the 35mm paradigm of the 1970s to 1990s tipped Latin American films into a tried and tested genre of the "national drama"' (2015: 65). By contrast, Carolina Rocha and Georgia Seminet resist defining child-starred films in generic terms: 'they represent a hybrid of existing genres and share particular, identifiable features; however, they do not constitute any single cinematic genre' (2012: 15). By contrast, *The Two* cines has followed Altman's insistence on genre as process and not as an immutable category with fixed definition and borders: 'Genres are not just *post facto* categories, then but part of the constant category-splitting/category-creating dialectic that constitutes the history of types and terminology' (Altman 1999: 65; italics in the original). Therefore, my genre study shares more commonality with the observations of Stephen M. Hart, Jay Beck, and Vicente Rodríguez Ortega; the latter two: 'provide a thorough investigation of contemporary Spanish cinema within a transnational framework by positing cinematic genres as the meeting spaces between a variety of diverse forces that necessarily operate within but also across territorial spaces' (Beck and Rodríguez Ortega 2008: 1). I set out to show how national cinemas drink from the font of international genre cinema, specifically the *bildungsfilm* in this chapter, to paradoxically address national specificities. Thereby, the binary at the heart of genre cinema readily transforms from the two Spains to the two Chiles and even two Argentinas.

In the first part of the current chapter, I analyse the narrative and aesthetic similarities of an enriching if unlikely friendship and its devastating betrayal at the time of Generals Francisco Franco's 1936 and Augusto Pinochet's 1973 coups, respectively, in *La lengua de las mariposas* (*Butterfly*) (José Luis Cuerda 1999 Spain) and *Machuca* (Andrés Wood 2004 Chile).[3] I will argue that national division and duality appear as organising concepts in the two Spains of *La lengua de las mariposas* and the two Chiles of *Machuca*. The focus on schooling in both films highlights the first noun of the compound noun, *bildungs-film*, meaning education. In the second part of this chapter, I compare two pairs of features that display two main aesthetic trends in the representation of childhood and resistance under military dictatorship: the arthouse, naturalist aesthetics of biopolitical childhood in *El espíritu de la colmena* and *El premio* (*The Prize*) (Paula Markovitch 2011 Mexico-Argentina) versus the fantastic, expressionist aesthetics of the paramilitarised child in *El laberinto del fauno* (*Pan's Labyrinth*) (Guillermo del Toro 2006 Mexico-Spain) and *Infancia clandestina* (*Clandestine Childhood*) (Benjamín Ávila 2011 Argentina). I will contend that each aesthetic mobilises the child protagonist in the cultural memory wars. My theoretical framework in this chapter continues to be informed by Bakhtin's dialogism and Altman's dualism (1999: 24), considering how states, now plural, and genre interact across the Atlantic.

Two Spains, Two Chiles

With forty years between the Nationalist and military junta coups and five years between these filmic representations, *La lengua de las mariposas* and *Machuca* exhibit striking similarities regarding cinematic responses to their respective national conflicts. *La lengua de las mariposas* belongs to the robust *nuevo cine con niño* genre and to a longer tradition of child-starred filmmaking in Spain, where film censorship ended in 1977. *Machuca*, released two years following the abolition of censorship (Sorensen 2009: 79), is rather unique within Chilean filmmaking, which does not abound in child protagonists but rather in exceptional documentary filmmaking.[4] Two Chilean films of note with child protagonists are *Largo viaje* (Patricio Kaulen 1967) and *Gringuito* (Sergio M. Castilla 1998). *Machuca*'s and *Lengua*'s trajectories are not only cinematic, however, since both are literary adaptations. *Lengua* won the Goya for Best Adapted Screenplay while *Machuca* won awards for Best Film, Director, Actor (Ariel Mateluna), Actress (Manuela Martelli), and Cinematographer in festivals around the world and was nominated for a Best Spanish Language Foreign Film Goya.[5] Nevertheless, *Machuca* is less unique and a better indication of genre convention when examined within the wider tradition of *bildungsfilms* in Spanish. Spain and Chile nationalise the *bildungsfilm* by appropriately contextualising the binary involved in the conflict.

Comparisons in this chapter fall under the umbrella of transatlantic studies, which have examined, for better or for worse, Spain's transition to democracy as a model for Latin American countries who descended into military dictatorship in the 1970s as Spain was emerging from its own. The most renowned link between Spain and Chile within the context of human rights abuses under dictatorship is of course Spanish former judge Baltasar Garzón's warrant for Pinochet's arrest in 1998, while the former head of state was in London, for the human rights violations of Spanish nationals under his seventeen-year regime. Pinochet led a United States-backed coup on 11 September 1973 that deposed the Americas' first democratically elected Socialist President, Salvador Allende. Pinochet imprisoned, tortured, and disappeared more than 3,000 dissidents (Skidmore et al. 2014: 289). While Spain's transition to democracy has long been considered exemplary, Chile's 1988 referendum, which voted Pinochet out of the presidency, and subsequent efforts to adjudicate human rights abusers, primarily in Argentina, could have been instructive for Spain. Luis Martín-Cabrera observes the impunity of transatlantic dictatorships:

> [O]ne of the functions of the dictatorship on both sides of the Atlantic was to suspend the previous legal apparatus in order to implement a radical redefinition of sovereignty. The aim of such a redefinition was to increase the biopolitical powers of the state in order to authorize the extinction of lives without punishment. (Martín-Cabrera 2011: 86)

Indeed, Franco's regime concluded due only to his death and Garzón's attempts forty years later to investigate the crimes of Francoism led to his disbarment in 2012.[6] Although Pinochet had been removed from the highest office, he was still awarded the position of 'senator for life'. Following Garzón's warrant, Pinochet was allowed to return to Chile and placed under house arrest until his death in 2006. Garzón's work encouraged the initiation of transitional justice within Chile and faced paralysing opposition in Spain.

We return now to the concept of the two Spains, which I first presented in the introduction of this book, and take into consideration its comparison with the theory of the 'two demons' in Latin American dictatorships. Spanish poet Antonio Machado (1875–1939) addresses the two Spains in *Campos de Castilla* (1910). The polarisation of the nation grew in the nineteenth century and came to a head with the Spanish Civil War from 1936 to 1939 (Pereira-Muro 2003: 179). Machado's understanding of his culture is illuminating and particularly insightful for a discussion of *La lengua de las mariposas* given his biographical similarities with the character Don Gregorio (Fernando Fernán Gómez) and the poetic intertexts in Cuerda's film and Rivas's story. In both LIII of *Proverbios y cantares* (Machado 1998: 158) and 'Recuerdo infantil' (1903) of *Soledades* (Machado 1983: 18–19), childhood is juxtaposed with two Spains or other suggestions of national fratricide. LIII warns that one of the two Spains, the dying or the yawning nation, would freeze the heart of a younger Spain that wants to live (Machado 1998: 158; Machado 1982: 145).[7] The conflict begins at birth, according to Machado, and continues, at the least, into early schooling. 'Recuerdo infantil' depicts a tedious math lesson accompanied by the monotonous sound of rain and the teacher's voice and by the decoration of biblical Cain's murder of his brother Abel (Machado 1977: 21). Childhood figured in Machado's poetry, including one of his final verses (Gibson 2006: 628–9). The two Spains, portrayed as brothers in a fight to the death, prefigure the onset of the Spanish Civil War at the end of the *La lengua de las mariposas*. Most films of the *nuevo cine con niño*, as I noted in the book's introduction, reify the two Spains despite historical realities that are more than two dimensional.

Cuerda's feature focuses on the eight- or nine-year-old Moncho (Manuel Lozano), his family, and his friendship with teacher Don Gregorio, who is reminiscent of Antonio Machado and other instructors of the Second Republic (1931–9), in the months leading to the onset of the Civil War. Don Gregorio's quotation of Machado's Soneto V 'Huye del triste amor' (Gibson 2006: 376) likens grief for his twenty-two-year-old wife to the death of Leonor, Machado's wife, at the age of eighteen. The educational thought that most heavily influenced the schools of the Restoration and Second Republic was Krausism, a philosophy founded by the German thinker Karl Christian Friedrich Krause (1781–1832). Spanish jurist Julián Sanz del Río championed Krause's ideas in speeches from 1857 to 1859 (Puelles Benítez 1986: 283) and Krausism informed the Instituto Libre de Enseñanza (ILE), which Francisco Giner de los Ríos founded. *La lengua de las mariposas* is an excellent example of the ILE's commitment to secular education and the 'active or intuitive' methodology of putting the student in contact with nature through field trips and science lessons. According to education scholar Manuel de Puelles Benítez, the ILE adapted to the student:

> [F]rente al intento de la escuela nueva de crear un mundo al niño, la Institución respetaba su propio mundo tratando de ponerlo en relación con el de la sociedad en que el niño nace y donde ha de forjarse su personalidad. (Puelles Benítez 1986: 289–90)

> [[F]aced with the new school's attempt to create a world for the child, the Institution respected the child's world by trying to relate the child to the world into which he was born and in which he will form his personality.]

Antonio Machado was not only a product of the Institución and an educator (in Soria and Segovia, Castilla and Baeza, Andalusia) but also becomes an icon of the Institución in *Lengua* and the inspiration for Don Gregorio's character.

Moncho is an asthmatic boy whose condition has delayed his incorporation into public schooling before the action of the film. Raised in a loving family, Moncho's socialisation into 1936 Galicia, the region of Franco's birth, takes place before the spectator's eyes. Moncho's mother presents him on the first day of school to Don Gregorio: 'es como un gorrión y esta es la primera vez que sale del nido' ('he's a sparrow out of the nest for the first time'). His parents represent the two Spains: his mother Rosa (Uxía Blanco) is a church-goer while his father Ramón (Gonzalo Uriarte) is an atheist affiliated with the Republic. Ramón, a tailor, recognises teachers as 'las luces de la República' ('They're the light of the Republic') and gifts Don Gregorio the suit that the persecuted teacher will ultimately wear as he is carted off at the end of the film for presumed execution. Moncho's relationship and bedtime conversations with his older brother Andrés (Alexis de los Santos) are reminiscent, but more encouraging, of sibling pairs from *El espíritu de la colmena* and *Secretos del corazón*. The figures surrounding Moncho foster his growth. Moncho learns that there is nothing to fear in Republican schooling because the teachers do not use corporal punishment (like his father's) but rather allow their pupils to explore nature. Moncho learns lessons in human nature through the natural sciences.

Birds, bees, butterflies and bridges feature prominently as coming-of-age motifs of transition and growth in the Spanish films discussed here and in Chapter Six: *El espíritu de la colmena* (Víctor Erice 1973 Spain), *Secretos del corazón* (Montxo Armendáriz 1997 Spain), and *El viaje de Carol* (Imanol Uribe 2002 Spain). In Cuerda's film, Don Gregorio's first lesson on butterfly tongues facilitates the pupils' contact with nature and teaches about butterflies and pollination. In class, Don Gregorio explains human nature via the natural sciences: birds, bees, and butterfly tongues. For instance, Moncho learns about a bird, the *tilonorrinco*, that gives its mate an orchid. Avian nicknames associate Moncho to birds: 'gorrión' and 'pardal.' As Moncho comes of age, his interests shift from the animal to human world. On an outing with Don Gregorio during which Moncho uses his teacher's gift of the butterfly net, the sounds of girls bathing in the river draw his attention away from butterflies to the birds and the bees. As he approaches Aurora (Lara López), Don Gregorio encourages Moncho to bestow a flower upon his first love by reminding him of the *tilonorrinco*'s romantic behaviour. At the time of the coup, when Don Gregorio is captured, Moncho's new vocabulary ('tilonorrinco', 'espiritrompa') acquires ambiguous new meanings.

Before engaging in the comparison of the two Spains and two Chiles, I would like to give further background on the 'two demons' theory and

Machuca. The two demons, a conception that Carlos Demasi has traced within Uruguayan dictatorship and transitional justice, illuminates points of contact and of divergence in the interpretation of national conflicts across the Atlantic. The theory describes the 'quiebre de las instituciones' (breakdown of institutions) (Demasi and Marchesi 2004: 67) at the time of Uruguay's 1973 coup but it is a concept that appeared post-facto as a means, Demasi argues, to justify the coup as inevitable (67–70). Highly sceptical of the interpretation, Demasi notes that it emerged in tandem with amnesty politics and exculpated the military and civil society alike (70–1). The editors of *Dictatorships in the Hispanic World: Transatlantic and Transnational Perspectives* compare Chile to Uruguay, observing: 'Although Chile has been more successful than their neighbouring country Uruguay in the confrontation of a harrowing political past, the post-dictatorial era witnessed an overall climate of social amnesia' (Swier and Riordan-Goncalves 2013: 7). Differing from the two demons, the two Spains is not a post-facto (post-war), reconciliatory concept and is, I suggest, a better descriptor of alternating discourse in Spanish politics that shuffles the responsibility from one band to the other.[8] Put in another way, historian Julián Casanova argues that contemporary Spain now needs to move beyond testimonials and memory narratives to educate its citizenry of the history of the war, categorically stating: 'Without the military uprising of July 1936, there would not have been a civil war in Spain' (2016: 217). Thus, other demons (Cainite brothers) plague Manuel Gutiérrez Aragón's *Demonios en el jardín* (1982 Spain) from Chapter One. But, in accordance with Demasi's reading of Uruguayan politics, the two demons are to blame for the downfall of childhood paradise in *Paisito*'s (Ana Díez 2008) Montevideo (Hogan 2012). In this sense, what I am calling the two Chiles has more in common with Spanish cultural politics than Latin American.

The social experiment defeated in *Machuca*, like *Lengua*, also celebrates the value of education and particularly its potential for social justice. Instead of the Spanish Instituto Libre de Enseñanza, *Machuca*'s spectator witnesses the Escuela Nacional Unificada (ENU) that makes possible the interactions and subsequent friendship of eleven-year-old children representing the two Chiles: middle-class and fair-skinned Gonzalo Infante (Matías Quer) and lower-class and darker-skinned Pedro Machuca (Ariel Mateluna). Father McEnroe (Ernesto Malbran) of St. Patrick's School, based on filmmaker Andrés Wood's (1965-) school director Father Gerardo Whelan at St. George's School (Sorensen 2009: 90), teaches lessons in mutual respect and community that echo Allende's democratisation policies and were inspired by Marxist thought (Núñez Prieto 2003: 16, 41,

99). The ENU's aims were to: achieve equality in education, encourage childhood development, regularise the education system, and tie it to the social, cultural, and economic development of the country, decentralise school administration, guarantee the best working conditions for educators, and promote the democratic participation of all the educators and community in the transformation of the education system (Núñez Prieto 2003: 16–17). Pedro Machuca was inspired by Carlos Fariña, perhaps the youngest dissident (at thirteen years old) whose remains from 1973 were found thirty years later in the La Pincoya neighbourhood of Santiago with twelve bullet wounds.[9]

As another political *bildungsfilm*, the boys' social awakening, learning about class struggle in 1973 Chile, takes place alongside their sexual awakening, both early adolescents being infatuated with Pedro's neighbour Silvana (Manuela Martelli). The boys' friendship is, similar to *Lengua*'s storyline, truncated at the time of Pinochet's coup. The military takes control of St Patrick's, ousting Father McEnroe, and raids Machuca's village. Concerned about his friend's absence from school, Gonzalo goes to Pedro's shantytown where he witnesses the harassment and execution of its inhabitants and even the murders of Silvana and her father. In betrayal of the friendship between the boys, Gonzalo utilises the markers of his privilege, his physical appearance and wardrobe, to allow him to escape the scene relatively unscathed while Pedro is not to be seen again, erased like the roadside graffiti that bears witness to the civil unrest.

Despite their narratives' points of contact, a comparison of *La lengua de las mariposas* and *Machuca* is uncommon. Each film is typically discussed within its respective country's politics of memory and with attention to narrative rather than form. One exception notes the destruction of the educational sphere and importance of each film for Spanish and Chilean historical memory. The authors argue:

> Este despertar para o passado que os filmes mobilizam num momento de reestruturação da memória e da identidade social destes países é de extrema relevância para a reflexão e para a reescrita de uma história até então adormecida nas mentes traumatizadas das sociedades em questão. É como o reescrever no simbólico muro mostrado em *Machuca*. (Braggio et al. 2014: 200)

> [This awakening to the past that the films mobilise in a moment of restructuring of memory or social identity of these countries is of extreme relevance to the reflection and rewriting of a history thus far dormant in the traumatised minds in question. It is like the rewriting on the symbolic wall in *Machuca*.]

Braggio, Fiuza, and Magalhães Debiazi refer to the aforementioned roadside graffiti that, over the course of the film, reads: 'No a la guerra civil' ('No Civil War'), 'guerra civil' ('Civil War'), and is finally blank. They argue that both features fill in this blank in the traumatic national histories of coup and dictatorship. Ho-Joon Yim paradoxically compares *La lengua de las mariposas* and *Machuca* to argue *Machuca*'s uniqueness within Chilean film and its role in educating the national public (2017: 212). Similarly, Kristin Sorensen contends that *Machuca*: 'works through posttraumatic Chilean memories that have been sanitized by other forms of media in a manner that is deeply affective yet also inclusive of a diverse and divergent audience' (2009: 83). Moisés Park focuses on the child protagonists of this history from below: '*Machuca* es una representación de la historia por parte de los derrotados, que–como se explicará–no son meramente los pobres, los militantes, la izquierda o los allendistas, sino los niños' (*Machuca* is a representation of the history told by the defeated, that – as will be explained – are not only the poor, the militants, the left or Allende supporters, but rather the children) (2014: 117). Translated from the Chilean into the Spanish context, from 'derrotados' to 'vencidos', *La lengua de las mariposas*, like other *nuevo cine con niño* films, focalises through the perspective of history's defeated. As scholarship and Sorensen's overview of reception indicate, *Machuca* allows for debate of issues central to historical memory.

Despite the film's success in the box office and at festivals, there are differences of opinion with regards to *Machuca*'s politics of representation. Reception of the film has been overwhelmingly positive, noting that the feature serves to educate Chileans today about the coup, but some rightly note that United States involvement in the coup is overlooked (Martín-Cabrera and Voionmaa 2007: 69; Sorensen 2009: 93–101). For others, the use of child protagonists infantilises and simplifies the complex history. Tzvi Tal critiques this use in *Machuca*, which 'politiza la memoria e infantiliza la historia' (politicises memory and infantilises history) (2005: 137). Rita De Grandis, in an interpretative inversion, finds: 'The child's perspective renders that traumatic past simpler and more palatable for transnational and national audiences, contributing to the official discourses that stigmatize and occlude this past so as to foster democratic cohesion' (2011: 236). As I have demonstrated in this book, child protagonists more often (re)politicise rather than depoliticise national conflicts through sentimental portrayals that disarm spectators' critical apparati. In fact, as I will note with *Infancia clandestina* (and *Viva Cuba*), the press of such films often insists that they are apolitical.

La lengua de las mariposas utilises animal imagery to symbolise national division while *Machuca* expresses class division through fruit analogies. Moncho is a sparrow who is introduced not only to the 'espiritrompa' and 'tilonorrinco' of the birds and the bees but also to the law of nature between the wolf and the lamb. Don Gregorio's retirement speech to students and parents, the film's thesis sequence, makes reference to this truth and to his condition as lamb while reaction shots identify the two Spains of the Galician town. Don Gregorio's musings on freedom annoy the town's priest and Guardia Civil officer and offend the town cacique Don Avelino (Jesús Castejón) and his school-aged son, both of whom storm out of the classroom. Don Gregorio is certain, after all, that 'el lobo nunca dormirá en la misma cama con el cordero' ('the wolf will never lie down with the lamb'). The parable of the wolf and lamb is also told through the story of the Chinese girl ('la niña china'), which precedes Don Gregorio's conclusion speech, from Rivas's 'Un saxo en la niebla', in which a Chinese girl is adopted as a wife and loses her voice when she escapes and is attacked by wolves. She is, nevertheless, married to a wolf. The marriage of the sheepish Chinese girl to her wolfish husband exemplifies the mismatched couple that school teacher Don Gregorio fancifully wills never come to pass in Spain. The earlier carnivalesque inversions of the Second Republic, the film's characters are even shown celebrating Carnival, return to the status quo with the Nationalist coup and victory. The division between Republicans and Nationalists is latent in the film (Yim 2017: 205). Boal's (Roberto Vidal Bolaño) marriage to 'Nena' (Milagros Jiménez, named 'Carolina' in Rivas) is reminiscent of livestock ownership and colonialism.

Boal appears and acts like a wolf. The short story includes more of the husband's physical and verbal violence towards the girl than the film. Boal threatens her: 'Te abro la crisma, *Carolina*!' ('I'll box your ears, *Caroline*! You know I will!') (Rivas 2000: 44; Rivas 2006: 34; emphasis in the original original). Rivas describes Boal's hairy fist as 'una enorme maza peluda' ('an enormous, hairy hammer swinging through the air') (2000: 44; 2006: 34). Boal devours his food like a wolf: 'masticó de forma voraz' ('he chewed voraciously') (Rivas 2000: 49; Rivas 2006: 41). He manhandles his wife to unbutton her blouse and show Andrés and Moncho the scars on her back from the wolf bites. The narrator fears for Carolina in Boal's hands: 'Temí que se quebrase como un ala de ave en las manos de un carnicero' ('I was afraid she would snap like a bird's wing in a butcher's grasp') (Rivas 2000: 50; Rivas 2006: 41). Boal guards his wife, who is dressed in a 'woolen shawl' ('chal de lana') 'como un inquieto pastor de Ganado' ('like a shepherd anxious about his flock') (Rivas 2000: 53; Rivas 2006: 45). Finally, as the narrator (Andrés in the film) imagines fleeing with the girl, he visualises the brute on his knees howling with the wool shawl in his paws: 'Boal aullaba en la noche, cuando la niebla se despejaba, de rodil-las en el campo de la feria y con el chal de lana entre las pezuñas' ('Boal howled in the night, as the mist cleared, on his knees in the fairground, holding the woolen shawl in his paws') (Rivas 2000: 53; Rivas 2006: 46). Rivas most clearly describes Boal as a wolf in this final sentence. This pair indicates the world that Don Gregorio has known is, in 1936, about to be turned upside down.

La lengua de las mariposas tells the history of the coup as a tale of two Spains with visual language in addition to the dialogue, narrative, and characterisation that we have just examined. The opening intertitles of Cuerda's film also prefigure the split between two opposing forces, since they tell that the Spanish people were 'caught in the middle'. Cuerda stages the competition for Moncho's education between religious and secular representatives in a sequence outside school. Moncho represents the Spanish people caught between his secular teacher (on the left both physically and ideologically) and the priest (on the right). The priest com-plains that Moncho was slated for *monaguillo* (altar boy) before he started attending Don Gregorio's class. Don Gregorio and the priest compete for influence over Moncho in Latin. The priest first tests Moncho's retention of ecclesiastical responses in Latin. In doing so, he acts as an appropria-tive ventriloquist that treats Moncho as a dummy for the performance of church ceremony, a practice suggested earlier in *Tómbola* (1962). Moncho, on the eve of the Civil War, has forgotten the response requesting peace: 'dona nobis pacem'. The priest, like Moncho's mother who calls him a sparrow, describes Moncho's experiences: 'las aves saltan del calor de los nidos' ('birds leave the warmth of their nests'). Birds, and other air-borne creatures, symbolise freedom for Moncho and Don Gregorio, who invites the children to 'volar' ('fly free') following his speech. Don Gregorio responds (also in Latin) that freedom only makes men stronger: 'la liber-tad estimula el espíritu de los hombres fuertes' ('freedom stimulates the spirits of strong men'). The priest's authority does not allow, as does Don Gregorio's approach, for liberty. Don Gregorio, in fact, does not elicit any rote-memory replies from his students but rather engages them in active learning. Their discussion illustrates tenets of the ILE: 'la necesidad de la neutralidad religiosa, que no supone escepticismo o indiferencia, sino estímulo del sentimiento religioso, abierto a los grandes problemas de la humanidad' (the necessity of religious neutrality, which does not presume scepticism nor indifference, but rather stimulation of religious sentiment, open to the great dilemmas of humanity) (Puelles Benítez 1986: 289). In another sequence, Moncho asks his new spiritual leader Don Gregorio, who has replaced the priest, about life after death. Don Gregorio cautiously asks what his parents have told him; Moncho's mother believes in heaven and his father cynically jokes that the rich will bring their lawyers to Judgement Day. Don Gregorio confides that he does not believe in the afterlife and believes that people may choose to make the here and now Hell. Moncho's teacher does not impose his opinion on his student.[10]

In *Machuca's* thesis sequence, another school assembly scene, Gonzalo's mother María Luisa (Aline Küppenheim) articulates her perplexity at the school's philosophy of mixing the social classes: 'pears and apples'. The social composition of a private school in Santiago de Chile in 1973 and a public school in small town Galicia in 1936 are indeed different but it is precisely greater diversity in the Chilean classroom to which privileged parents object. The only racial diversity found in *Lengua* takes the form of the Chinese girl, who is silenced and enslaved to her husband rather than educated.[11] Following the Eucharist, Father McEnroe addresses the growing unrest at the school, which mirrors conditions beyond the school's gate. The debate that unfolds about social justice, integration, and paternalism supports and questions, by opposing camps, Allende's social policies. María Luisa challenges St Patrick's and the *Unidad Popular's* policies and in fact marches with the Patria y Libertad party: '¿Cuál es la idea de mezclar las peras con las manzanas? Porque yo quisiera saber por qué se empeñan tanto . . . No digo que seamos mejores ni peores pero, pucha, que somos distintos' ('what's the whole idea of mixing pears and apples? I'd like to know why it is you try so hard . . . I'm not saying that we're better or worse, just different'). Her analogy points to skin colour and difference. Machuca's mother Juana (Tamara Acosta), seated with the other disadvantaged newcomers to the community in the back of the church, defends her convictions on the basis of her life experience:

Yo me vine así a Santiago a los quince porque no quería que mis hijos fueran los culpables de todo siempre. Pero parece que aquí en la ciudad es igual. Los culpables siempre somos los mismos. Así es como tiene que ser. Y a ustedes nadie los va a culpar por seguir con la misma historia. Yo me pregunto no más, ¿cuándo se van a hacer las cosas de otra manera? ¿Cuándo se van a atrever a hacer algo distinto?

['I came here to Santiago when I was fifteen because I didn't want my children to be blamed for everything. But I can see things here are the same. Everything is always our fault. That's just how it is. No one will blame you for not changing. Sometimes I ask myself, when will things change? When will we dare to do things differently?']

Juana, as McEnroe instructed her son, must speak up in order to be heard. Her humble home is decorated with posters depicting Allende's initiatives as she supports his efforts to change the status quo. For *Machuca*, María Luisa, Juana, and their sons represent the two Chiles divided into pears and apples. Juana's viewpoint is privileged in the film named after her fictional son; however, the dualism of the fruit analogy is mirrored in the co-protagonists Gonzalo and Pedro. Park recognises and refutes *Machuca*'s polarity:

> La dicotomía pobre-allendista y rico-pinochetista no se refleja con claridad en la ya película; esta ilusión de que Chile estaba dividido en dos y que las clases sociales determinaban la posición ideológica se niega en el filme. De hecho, Wood enfatiza las contradicciones y la paradoja que niega la bipolaridad en Chile.' (Park 2014: 132)

> [The dichotomy poor-Allende supporter and rich-Pinochet supporter is not clearly reflected in the film; this illusion that Chile was divided in two and that social class determined ideology is negated in the film. In fact, Wood emphasises the contradictions and paradox that negates bipolarity in Chile.]

While assembly seating reveals some blending of the two Chiles, Machuca's community is still seated at the back and the film itself is divided between Gonzalo's and Machuca's worlds.

Each film's climax takes place at the moment of betrayal. The beautiful friendships formed between Moncho and Don Gregorio, Gonzalo and Machuca are conquered by self-preservation and fear. Moncho's mother (in the film, father in Rivas) encourages her husband and sons to cast aspersions at Don Gregorio in order to publicly affiliate themselves with the new order. Reaction shots reveal self-contentment on the faces of Nationalist characters and anguish on the faces of Republican characters. Moncho shouts 'ateo', 'rojo', and finally the ambiguous 'tilonorrinco' and 'espiritrompa' as he follows the other boys running after the truck with the prisoners and throwing rocks. His new vocabulary may be directed in anger at Don Gregorio or in anger at his abandonment. Moncho's run transforms into slow motion and then freeze frame and then black and white. His forward movement, his growth through education over the course of the film, arrives at a sudden halt. His development is truncated as the coup occurs and the film arrives at its conclusion.

Cinematography also heightens the climax scene in *Machuca*. Following the military takeover of St Patrick's, Gonzalo goes to Machuca's community to check on him. Colour is dampened in the image of the lethal military raid on Machuca's neighbourhood. Victims are yanked out into the open for execution. Shot-reverse shot editing reveals the reaction shots of both Machuca and Gonzalo (Figure 8.1). The terrifying and violent chaos is shot mostly from Gonzalo's point-of-view with an unsteady hand-held camera. In *Machuca*, we witness with Gonzalo and Pedro the killing of Silvana and her father. A soldier, who blocks Gonzalo's escape, prompts

Figure 8.1 Gonzalo (Matías Quer) witnesses vivid violence in muted colour in *Machuca*.

Gonzalo's betrayal in appeal to his appearance of privilege. Gonzalo's flight occurs in an emotionally charged slow motion, like Moncho's final minutes; however, the friendship and lives of some of these friends ends here in *Machuca* but the feature does not. Wood's film continues in order to show Gonzalo's new normal under Pinochet. His parents have split, and he now lives with his sister, his mother, and her older lover in a mansion, ostensibly having benefited from Pinochet's rise to power. Ho-Joon Yim sees *La lengua de las mariposas* as offering a more nostalgic, mythic representation of the days leading to the national conflict and *Machuca* as more of a historic microcosm of the precipitating events (2017: 201). This scholar explains the differences, considering that the creators of *Machuca* felt a greater responsibility to educate their audience:

> Las políticas diferentes de ambas películas hacia el pasado traumático, en cierto grado, provienen de la tendencia o situación del cine nacional. *Machuca*, siendo una de las pocas obras chilenas que abordan el pasado, no podía ignorar la responsabilidad de reflejar la verdad histórica, mientras que *La lengua* se sitúa en la tendencia prevaleciente del cine español contemporáneo. (Yim 2017: 212)

> [Differing politics in the two films with regards to the traumatic past, to a certain degree, come from the tendency or situation of national cinema. *Machuca*, one of the few Chilean works to deal with the past, could not ignore its responsibility to reflect historic truth, while *La lengua* is situated within a prevailing tendency of contemporary Spanish cinema.]

I insist on narratives as mediations of history; why not tell *Machuca* in Chilean cinema's more prevalent documentary form? I suspect that the creators of both *La lengua de las mariposas* and *Machuca*, in varying degrees, wish to educate a younger audience and emotionally engage an older one with memories of their youths and visions of the future for their children.

The two Spains and two Chiles, in my view, do not serve to justify their respective coups, as Demasi argues of the two demons theory, but rather to recognise suffering during the violent repression of military dictatorship by showcasing its most vulnerable citizens. If indeed Gonzalo does not have any other choice than to extricate himself from the danger of an 'insurmountable' coup (Tal 2005: 148), Moncho does what he is told. Cuerda directed Manuel Lozano in the final scene to attack Don Gregorio on the orders of his character's mother, who intended to shield Moncho's Republican father.[12] Instead of exculpating both Spains and Chiles, these films utilise their child protagonists to move and educate their spectators with regard to their respective social projects quashed by military coups. *La lengua de las mariposas* and *Machuca* explore politicised coming-of-age where the child protagonist, Moncho or Gonzalo, is obligated to affiliate with one of the two Spains or Chiles. This affiliation of both characters with the triumphant right represents the defeat of their growth and squandered potential, a negation of who they could have become in more inclusive societies. Becoming is central to *bildungsfilms* and, in the next set, child protagonists undertake a different trajectory, becoming dissidents and militants in varying degrees.

Transatlantic Aesthetics of *Bildungsfilms*: *El espíritu de la colmena* (Erice 1973), *El premio* (Markovitch 2011), *El laberinto del fauno* (Del Toro 2006), and *Infancia clandestina* (Ávila 2011)

Our comparative perspective progresses chronologically from coups in Spain and Chile to the years following military takeover in Spain and Argentina. *El espíritu de la colmena*, set on the arid Castilian plain in 1940, and *El laberinto del fauno*, set at the foot of a lush Spanish hillside in 1944, take place during the early post-war years in Spain, as does *Pa negre* analysed in the previous chapter. The protagonists of *El premio*, set in coastal San Clemente del Tuyú in 1977, and *Infancia clandestina*, set in Buenos Aires in 1979, are children of militants fighting the Junta regime of Argentina's Dirty War (1976–83). The Spanish films herein discussed make reference to the *maquis* resistance to Franco's dictatorship while the Argentine films refer to dissidence that includes the *montonero* paramilitary group fighting Jorge Rafael Videla's military regime. The filmmakers draw upon their childhoods during these periods: Víctor Erice (1940–) grew up in 1940s and 1950s Basque Country (Heredero 1998: 312–13); Paula Markovitch (Buenos Aires 1968–) grew up the daughter of 'semi-clandestinos' in San Clemente del Tuyú (Casas 2013); Benjamín Ávila's (Buenos Aires 1972–) *montonero* parents and younger brother were disappeared by the regime; and, with a more remote connection, Guillermo del Toro (Mexico 1964–) was mentored and befriended by Spanish Republican exiles and their children in Mexico (Anonymous 2006b: 20). Overarching themes of obedience and disobedience, celebrating the latter, are shared among the four films discussed in this section. *El espíritu*'s Ana (Ana Torrent) befriends a *maqui* and *El laberinto del fauno*'s twelve-year-old Ofelia (Ivana Baquero), I argue, becomes a fantastic version of a *maqui*.

Secundio Serrano defines *maqui* as metonymical for the Galicism for bush, hence the resistance fighters based in the bushes, and notes the pejorative evaluation, painting them as cowardly and unruly, of these fighters in the *Diccionario de la Real Academia*: 'Maquis. – Persona que, huida a los montes vive en rebeldía y oposición armada al sistema político establecido' (Maqui. – a person who, having fled to the hills lives in rebellion and armed opposition to the established political system) (2001: 1–2). Thus, the *maqui* is defined by his or her hide-out in the forest, marginality to the Francoist system, and open rebellion against it. In historian Paul Preston's more positive assessment, by contrast to the *Diccionario*'s, the *maquis* continued their valiant armed efforts against the Franco regime into the early 1950s:

> Hasta finales de la década de los cuarenta, las fuerzas armadas de Franco se vieron obligadas a emprender operaciones militares contra grupos armados que se habían implicado en un vano sino heroico intento de cambiar el resultado de la guerra. De modo esporádico, la Guerra Civil, o la violenta resistencia contra el establecimiento de un Estado franquista, continuó hasta la retirada de las últimas unidades que componían la guerrilla a principios de los cincuenta (2001: vii).

> [Until the end of the 1940s, Franco's armed forces were obligated to undertake military operations against armed groups that had tried not in vain but in a heroic attempt to change the result of the war. Sporadically, the Civil War, or the violent resistance to the Francoist State, continued until the withdrawal of the last military units that composed the guerrilla at the beginning of the 1950s.]

El laberinto del fauno's affiliations mirror Preston's; Captain Vidal (Sergi López), the villain, leads the Nationalist defence against *maquis* Mercedes (Maribel Verdú), her brother, Doctor Ferrerio (Álex Ángulo), and Ofelia in *El laberinto del fauno*.

Argentina's so-called Dirty War is the period in which 10,000 to

20,000 Argentines were disappeared by General Jorge Rafael Videla's regime, installed by virtue of coup in 1976 (Skidmore et al. 2014: 259).[13] In Ávila's film, twelve-year-old Juan (Teo Gutiérrez Moreno) and his family, like other *montoneros*, took exile in Cuba for training before returning to Argentina to continue their clandestine warfare in 1979 (Gillespie 2008: 22, 139). Rather than comparing 'sibling films' – *El premio*'s girl protagonist and *Infancia clandestina*'s boy protagonist – of the same release year and setting, I will focus on the aesthetic affinities of the motion pictures set in Argentina with those set in Spain for the purpose of showing the wider trend of mobilising child protagonists for the cause of historical memory.

Having discussed *El espíritu de la colmena* at greater length and with a focus on the biopolitics of the Gothic child in Chapter Five and fantasy in coming-of-age in Chapter Six, in the current chapter I will compare the auteur aesthetics of Erice's film in comparison to those of Cecilia's (Paula Galinelli Hertzog) biopolitical climate of clandestine childhood in *El premio*. As I discussed in Chapter Five, we can read Ana as a Gothic child whose sensitivity and curiosity encourage her sympathy with the unnamed *maqui*, a civil dead persecuted and devoid of right to life in Franco's Spain. In this chapter we will focus on the inhospitable environments of each film as indicators of their hostile political climates. The fabulations of Ana's older sister Isabel (Isabel Tellería) ignite seven-year-old Ana's imagination, which conflates the re-warmed cadaver that is Frankenstein's monster with the *maqui* in hiding in an abandoned and isolated building on the meseta. In *El premio*, seven-year-old Cecilia Edelstein and her mother have fled Buenos Aires in the winter of 1977 to the remote seaside locale of San Clemente del Tuyú in fear of their safety following the disappearance of the girl's political dissident father. While *bildungsfilm* boy protagonists learn the meaning of the verb 'chingar' (*La lengua de las mariposas* and *Secretos del corazón*) or that parental 'vacation' means 'disappearance' (*O Ano em Que Meus Pais Saíram de Férias*), Cecilia learns that 'pesimista' means that her father will likely never return and has probably been killed. *El premio* witnesses the transformation of the bright schoolgirl from bare life to biopolitical discipline through enrolment and lessons at school, where she wins a prize from the military for best patriotic essay. The film itself, produced by the director's country of residence, won numerous awards: Mexican Ariels for production, screenplay, and first work as well as awards in Armenia, Cuba, France, Germany, and Israel. I wish to explore how the naturalist aesthetics of the film communicate the bleakness of their home country through the destructive wind and sea elements that assail their dilapidated refuge. The elements of repression, more subtly portrayed in *El espíritu de la colmena* under Franco's censorship, nearly reach gale force in Markovitch's 2011 film.

Unlike Chilean film but like Spanish cinema, Argentina has a tradition of child-starred cinema. While Spain from the 1940s to the 1960s had *niños prodigio* Pablito Calvo, Joselito, and Marisol, followed by adolescent stars, Argentina had its own *pibes prodigio* of the 1940s and 1950s in the figures of Toscanito (Andrés Poggio 1934–) and Adrianita (Adriana Bianco 1941–), likewise followed by adolescent stars. Spanish and Argentine cinema also had some cross-over, evidenced in Adrianita's photographed appearance with Pablito Calvo (Anonymous 1998: n.p.) and Joselito's performance alongside adult Argentine actress Libertad Lamarque (1908–2000) in the Spanish film *Bello recuerdo* (Antonio del Amo 1961).[14] Toscanito, Adrianita, and later Polín (Diego Puente 1953–) in *Crónica de un niño solo* (Leonardo Favio 1965) portray the life of children on the street. Children as victims of appropriations begin to appear in the 1980s in representations of the Dirty War with *La historia oficial* (Luis Puenzo 1985). The significance of the child within this historical backdrop, during which approximately 500 babies were kidnapped (Haberman 2015: n.p.), continues in the posterior films I discuss in this chapter.

Aesthetic similarities between *El espíritu de la colmena* and *El premio* have not escaped the critics nor has the dialogical relationship between *El espíritu de la colmena* and Spanish cinema depicting the post-war, including *El laberinto del fauno*, as I analyse in Chapter Six. Paul Julian Smith notes: 'This premise of the child as unknowing witness to historical horror is well-known in Spanish-language cinema. Since Erice's masterful *The Spirit of the Beehive*, there have been almost forty years of films from Spain on the theme. And 2011 brought, in addition to *The Prize*, contributions to the genre from as far apart as Buenos Aires and rural Colombia' (Smith 2014: 221).[15] Although the approach to periods of political conflict through the child's gaze and coming-of-age are quite common, I contend that *El premio* distinguishes itself from other Argentine films with similar subject matter due to its stark, naturalist aesthetics. Thus, I disagree with Verónica Inés Garibotto that *El premio* corresponds to recent Argentine filmography that 'build[s] a privatized and romanticized version of recent Argentine history and [is] (thus) acclaimed worldwide' (2015: 269). *El premio* is, like *Pa negre* (Villaronga 2010 Spain), the exception that proves the rule. The naturalist aesthetics and acoustics of *El premio* neither romanticise Cecilia's clandestine childhood nor the militant's struggle but rather communicate the bare life of the child protagonist.

El espíritu de la colmena and *El premio* resemble each other in their sombre colour palette, sparse dialogue, and blustery soundtrack. I will focus my

Figure 8.2 Cecilia (Paula Galinelli Hertzog) of *El premio* stubbornly roller skates on the beach of San Clemente del Tuyú in the winter.

comparison on the ambient sound of bare life in the features. They divide their explorations of post-war and Dirty War bare life among their rebellious girl protagonists' homes, schools, and natural surroundings. While Ana's beehive-like home is expansive, if empty, and comfortable, Cecilia's seaside shack is the epitome of precariousness and her school exemplifies Dirty War indoctrination. The films are most similar in their artistry of absence and emptiness, which are beautifully expressed in the girls' solitary scenes on the meseta and beach (Figure 8.2). Ambient sound and musical soundtrack are the focus of these sequences and the means to express the vulnerability of bare life, embodied by outcasts and clandestine individuals.

Sound design in the first of the meseta sequences is comprised of the wind and wind instruments, accompanied by the cello, in the instrumental popular children's song 'Vamos a contar mentiras' (Let's tell lies). Ana and her sister stand gazing upon the well and abandoned building, Isabel's fabled homestead for Frankenstein's monster and the coming hideout for the *maqui*. Wind represents exposure, vulnerability, and danger beyond the beehive. Screenwriters Ángel Fernández Santos and Víctor Erice give the element of air the prominence of a character in the screenplay, describing the prominence of the wind in this sequence:

El sonido del viento. El viento que penetra a través del tejado desvencijado, entre las vigas, a través de los marcos de las ventanas destrozadas. Entre los escombros, una gorra, apergaminada y sucia, restos de loza . . . las huellas del paso de seres humanos. Estas imágenes de la desolación, del abandono, se diría que proporcionan a Ana un instintivo sentimiento de desamparo, de malestar. (1976: 72)

[The sound of the wind. The wind that penetrates the ramshackle roof, between the rafters, through the frames of the destroyed windows. Between the debris, a dirty parchment-like cap, shards of crockery . . . the remnants of the passage of human beings. It could be said that these images of desolation and abandonment, provide Ana with an instinctive feeling of neglect and discomfort.]

The wind invades the space of the abandoned building and reveals absence, remains, and abandonment. It intensifies the sensation of neglect in this place where a clandestine fighter finds temporary shelter. It is true for both films that 'the wind is air in its active and violent aspects' (Cirlot 2002: 373). The building and well represent spaces made dangerous by a hostile and repressive regime. As is the case with symbolism of the monster, however, air is also polysemic. At other times, within the confines of state institutions, asphyxiation is the threat. A classmate at school recites the verses of Rosalía de Castro's poem XIII from *New Leaves* (*Follas novas* 1880) that refer to the need for air to breathe (Castro 1991: 71).

Absence of air, affection, or free speech characterises Ana's surroundings. According to Erice's experience, a vacuum replaced the presence of adults in the aftermath of the Civil War:

A veces pienso que para quienes en su infancia han vivido a fondo ese vacío que, en tantos aspectos básicos, heredamos los que nacimos inmediatamente después de una guerra civil como la nuestra, los mayores eran con frecuencia eso: un vacío, una ausencia. Estaban –los que estaban–, pero no estaban. Y ¿por qué no estaban? Pues porque habían muerto, se habían marchado o bien eran unos seres ensimismados desprovistos radicalmente de sus más elementales modos de expresión. (Erice 1976: 144)

[Sometimes I think that for those of us whose childhood was lived fundamentally in that vacuum that, in so many basic ways, those of us who were born immediately after a civil war like ours inherited, the grown-ups were frequently that: an emptiness, an absence. They were there – those who were – , but they were not present. And why weren't they present? Because they had died, they had left, or they were consumed and radically devoid of ways to express themselves.]

Erice describes Ana's parents and the emptiness that the young girl aims at filling with her investigations and associations with the *maqui* and Frankenstein's monster.

Markovitch turns up the volume of the blustery soundtrack from *El espíritu de la colmena* in *El premio*. The opening sequence of *El premio* masterfully introduces the bare life of the refugee, Cecilia. We see that the stubborn and solitary girl is out of place, obstinately attempting to roller skate on a beach in the winter. The soundtrack of the discordant piano tune over ocean waves further indicates the dissonance of the image. The threatening tide ultimately sinks the wheels of her skates. Cecilia finds herself in this inhospitable environment on account of a government hostile to the politics of her parents. When the forces of the wind and ocean strike again halfway through the film, they reach and inundate Cecilia's and her mother's dilapidated shelter. The presumed politically compromising literature they had buried in the sand is dredged up by the ocean current and Cecilia's mother attempts with great determination the futile task of sweeping the water out and placing blankets under the front door as a stop-gap measure. They are exposed. Markovitch explicates her use of the weather metaphor: 'Incluso con la metáfora del agua que entra a la casa, del viento, de que todo entra, es expresar esa sensación de desamparo de que el alma no está a salvo' (Even with the metaphor of the water that enters the house, the wind, everything that enters, is to express that sensation of abandon, that not a soul is safe) (Acevedo Kanopa 2012: n.p.). As the seawater inches closer to their home, so does the military. Their house is flooded right before Sargento Estévez (Diego Alfonso) appears at Cecilia's school to announce the patriotic essay contest.

Cecilia's school is a laboratory for techniques of state coercion. As such, *El premio* portrays power, embodied by the Sargent and Cecilia's teacher, through certain camera angles and disciplinary practices. During the class visit, the teacher and Sargent stand side by side as the officer asks whether the children love their country and the instructor enthusiastically coaches them that they in fact do. The teacher instructs her students that they are soldiers and should therefore stand at attention. The discrepancy in camera angles communicates the power of the military, from a high angle, over the school children, from a low angle (Figure 8.3). This visit details the biopolitics of childhood during the Dirty War in so far as it demonstrates the utilisation of school children for the reproduction of state ideology. Michel Foucault's *Discipline and Punish* also reminds us

Figure 8.3 Sargento Estévez (Diego Alfonso) addresses the schoolchildren in *El premio*.

that school pedagogy was adapted from military discipline in the first place (1979: 159). Bribed with hot chocolate amidst the damp cold and the opportunity to win a prize, the docile and dutiful schoolchildren comply with the mechanisms and calculations of the military regime.

Cecilia, the stubborn seaside roller skater, rebels against her mother's authority but is readily coerced by school and military influence. During her integration to the new school and among new peers, Cecilia Edelstein learns new things like how to make the sign of the cross and how to love the country that killed her cousin and disappeared her father. However, in a first draft of her essay, she writes the unthinkable: an indictment of the military. In a panic, Cecilia and her mother beg the teacher during the middle of the night to allow her to re-write the essay. The submission, for which her mother suggests that she write 'Lo contrario . . . Que los militares son buenos y valientes. Cualquier bobada dices' ('The opposite . . . That the soldiers are good and brave. Any nonsense!'), wins Cecilia the prize. Her mother also becomes complicit in the biopolitics of the regime out of fear, as Eduardo Bustelo observes: 'La biopolítica consigue transformar la infancia no como responsabilidad de los adultos sino de acuerdo con la inseguridad de éstos' (Biopolitics transforms childhood not into the responsibility of adults but rather in accordance with adult insecurity) (2007: 52).

A series of painful coercions act upon Cecilia's docile body to prepare her for the prize ceremony. The student does not have formal shoes and clothes to wear for the event, so the teacher loans Cecilia her daughter's shoes, which are one size too small. We see the painful grimacing on Cecilia's face as she learns to march like a soldier in these restrictive shoes. Cecilia undergoes reform for her biopolitical rebirth. Her body, requiring correction, represents that of the dissidents. Bustelo notes: 'La biopolítica toma la vida como si la sociedad ahora tuviese un único cuerpo. Y el biopoder se expresa como un control que invade las profundidades de las conciencias de los adultos y de los cuerpos de la infancia' (Biopolitics understands life as if a society had one body. And biopower expresses itself as the control that invades the deepest consciences of adults and the bodies of children) (2007: 51). The teacher proceeds to forcefully dress Cecilia in a more formal school apron, which buttons in the back and is therefore more reminiscent of a strait jacket than her earlier uniform. Her biopolitical transformation is also gendered since her teacher wants Cecilia to look beautiful for the sargeant. Cecilia appears less and less elated by the prize as she comes to realise what her mother had been trying to teach her: that she is receiving an award from those responsible for her father's likely death. Defeatedly rather than triumphantly, Cecilia sings the words of the national anthem before the voice-over addresses her and the other children as soldiers.

The ceremony at the military headquarters is the culmination of a number of disciplinary techniques that the teacher employs over the course of the film. These include determining who aided and abetted a cheater by condemning the entire class to walk under the rain until the culprit confesses. The schoolyard, also where the military distributed the hot chocolate, is the place of reward and punishment according to the values of the military state. Cecilia's only friend, Silvia (Sharon Herrera), identifies her as the guilty party. The teacher applauds Silvia for informing on Cecilia and asks the girls to forgive each other. Enacted on a smaller scale, the surveillance of classmates that leads to punitive action and forgiveness for betrayal is indicative of the more violent repression of adult dissidents like Cecilia's father and cousin.

Infancia clandestina, like *El premio*, follows the militarisation of its child protagonist but does so with political and aesthetic differences that bring to mind *El laberinto del fauno*. *El premio* observes Cecilia's incorporation into the power of the state while *Infancia clandestina* witnesses Juan's mobilisation for resistance to the state as a soldier for Perón. Juan's trajectory is similar to Ofelia's since both young people fight their respective authoritarian regimes. Just as *El premio*, filmed in Argentina with Argentine actors by an Argentine director living and financing her film in Mexico, is difficult to categorise geographically, so is Guillermo del Toro's *El laberinto del fauno*, filmed in Spain as a Spanish-Mexican co-production with Spanish actors by a Mexican director. *El laberinto fauno* is transnational in its production and highly dialogical with *El espíritu de la colmena*, as discussed in Chapter Six, and with fairy tales and children's literature (Clark and McDonald 2010; Diestro-Dópido 2013: 15–16; Hubner 2010: 51).

Del Toro's and Ávila's films explore connections between *infancia* and infantry. However, Ávila's feature is more explicit in terms of the militarisation of its child protagonist but not as overt as in the forced inscription of child soldiers by Peru's Shining Path in *Paloma de papel* (Fabrizio Aguilar 2003) or by the Farabundo Martín National Liberation Front during the Salvadoran civil war in *Voces inocentes* (Mandoki 2004). *El laberinto del fauno*'s and *Infancia clandestina*'s militarisation of children inhabits to varying degrees the realm of the symbolic obscured by expressionistic fairy tale and comic book aesthetics. Del Toro's Ariel, Goya, Argentine academy award and Oscar-winning film is constructed according to juxtaposed binaries – one pair consisting of the house headquarters of Ofelia's stepfather Captain Vidal (Sergi López) opposed to the forest hideout of the *maquis* resistance and the other pair composed of Franco's Spain in 1944 and Princess Moana's timeless underground kingdom. These are the two Spains whose mapping in Del Toro's mise en scène and characterisation is mutually revealing with regards to Ofelia's mobilisation.

In the film, the young and avid reader of fairy tales arrives with her expectant mother to Captain Vidal's headquarters to discover that she is the long-lost Princess Moana who nevertheless needs to prove herself through a series of tests assigned in the forest's labyrinth by the wily faun. Ofelia's mother dies in childbirth and Ofelia is killed by Captain Vidal but is reborn as Princess Moana. The *maquis* triumphantly kill Vidal and appropriate his newborn son, concluding the film. Although martyrdom is Captain Vidal's military career aspiration and he is indeed killed at the conclusion of *El laberinto del fauno*, I will argue that, in this revisionist heroine's tale, the martyred soldier is Ofelia rather than Vidal.

Under the orders of the faun, Ofelia receives training in obedience and disobedience. I wish to denaturalise Ofelia's instruction in resistance in accordance with the *maquis*' Republican ideals and to reject the assumption of childhood innocence. Thus, I dispute Antonio Gómez López-Quiñones' argument: 'Ofelia functions in *Pan's Labyrinth* as an entity non-normalized (at least not completely) by institutions designed for the progressive transformation of children into citizens of a specific collective project' (2012: 51). By contrast, I suggest that Ofelia is indeed normalised into the diegetic collective project of the *maquis*, an adult political community, and the extra-diegetic agenda of Republican historical memory. Sarah Wright argues that recent child-starred films are highly invested in historical memory: 'The child is therefore symbolic not only of the loss of historical memory and its recuperation after a time-lag but also it is often a site of trauma in contemporary memory wars' (2013: 14). Ofelia, like Moncho, is one of many recent child protagonists of the *nuevo cine con niño* to be mobilised by and for the vanquished of the Spanish Civil War. The child protagonist is not only a site but also a militant in the memory wars.

El laberinto del fauno and *Infancia clandestina* are alike in their colour scheme, their protagonist's element of disguise, and their militarisation of childhood. Ávila's Argentine-Spanish-Brazilian co-production also belongs to a collective project, that of historical memory valuing resistance during the Dirty War and more specifically the participation of family members in this homage. Still, materials accompanying Film Movement's DVD of the feature propose a de-politicised reading of childhood, stating: 'This is not a political film. It is essentially a coming of age love story, set in a time that was politically significant.'[16] I beg to differ that the personal is political in Ávila's autobiographical film; the militarisation of a child politicises the young person. The director affirms that, although politicising childhood was not his film's aim, it is unavoidable: 'No quise que la película fuera ni política ni dramática, pero sabía que iba a serlo, inevitablemente' (I did not want the film to be political nor dramatic, but I knew that it inevitably would be) (Ranzani 2012: n.p.). Over the course of the Argentine Academy and Film Critics award-winning and Goya-nominated film, Juan struggles with his identification with his family's cause and his desire to lead a life of greater freedom to pursue childhood things like a class camping trip and first love. However, the deaths of his father and uncle and the disappearances of his mother and baby sister leave Juan to draw strength from his *montonero* training.

It is my contention that *El laberinto del fauno* and *Infancia clandestina* disguise political violence and the militarisation of their twelve-year-old protagonists with graphic novel-style aesthetics that may encourage de-politicised readings of childhood. Verónica Inés Garibotto is another critic sceptical of the use of the child's perspective in the *bildungsfilm*: 'The child's perspective allows for a coming-of-age narrative that – rather than bringing the political dimension of left-leaning violence to the fore – privatizes, romanticizes, and converts revolutionary violence into an individual trait' (2015: 269). Conversely, other scholars like Sarah Thomas appreciate the role that 'graphic violence' (Thomas 2015) plays in problematising memory. Geoffrey Maguire sees value in the aesthetic: 'these animated sequences highlight the medium's potential to express not the inherent gaps in the postmemorial narration of the past, but the richness and vibrancy of the child's reiteration of such intense and forma-tive memories' (2017: 153). Similar to Garibotto's scepticism towards *Infancia clandestina*, Francisco J. Sánchez argues that *El laberinto del fauno* commercialises and capitalises on Spanish history: 'by silencing the Republic, the film displaces the political context of the nation of Spain into a trans-Atlantic Spanish region in which Spanish functions as a brand of cultural goods' (2012: 142). Deborah Shaw has been of two minds regarding the fairy-tale fireworks of *El laberinto del fauno*, first arguing in her 2013 monograph that they distort history. She revised her interpreta-tion from 2013 in 'Reading *Pan's Labyrinth* in the Era of Neo-fascism' at the University of Houston on 4 April 2017, contending that fantasy ele-ments create a transcendent, anti-fascist document that transnationalises the national and transhistoricises the historical thereby offering 'hope and resistance for current and future generations' (Shaw 2013: 83).[17] Shaw would now advance that *El laberinto del fauno* has made its politics more universal rather than dismantle them. I will argue that the expression of the child's perspective through animated aesthetics obscures the political significance and use, particularly in Ofelia's case, of the child protagonists' representations.

El laberinto del fauno translates chronological precision, that of Captain Vidal's obsession with time and meticulous care for his deceased father's pocket watch, into the parlance of fairy tales in the Pale Man sequence. Michel Foucault's study of the adaptation of military discipline, in particular the utilitarian use of time, to the classroom shed light on Ofelia's schooling:

> It is this disciplinary time that was gradually imposed on pedagogical practice – specializing the time of training and detaching it from the adult time, from the time of mastery; arranging different stages, separated from one another by graded examinations; drawing up programmes, each of which must take place during a particular stage and which involves exercises of increasing difficulty; qualifying individuals according to the way in which they progress through these series. (Foucault 1979: 159)

Ofelia's timed fairy-tale trials recall the training that Foucault describes here and are a point of intersection between the girl's training in the disciplines of military obedience and *maqui* disobedience.

The mission involving Ofelia's retrieval of a dagger from the ogre's den, Ofelia's second of four interlocking tasks of increasing difficulty, is timed with an hourglass and mandated by fairy-tale instructions and interdictions. The faun and his guidebook (*libro de las encrucijadas*) direct the following:

> Con la tiza, trazaréis un contorno de una puerta en cualquier parte de vuestra habitación. Una vez abierta la puerta, iniciad el reloj de arena. Dejaos guiar por las hadas. No comáis ni bebáis nada durante vuestra estancia y aseguraos de volver antes de que caiga el último grano de arena.

> ['Use the chalk to trace a door anywhere in your room. Once the door's open, start the hourglass. Let the fairies guide you. Don't eat or drink anything during your stay, and come back before the last grain of sand falls.']

Ofelia, of course, does not follow these instructions. Her training under the faun, although presented as an apprenticeship in obedience, prepares her in the skills of disobedience that are primary for the *maquis*. The Pale Man's banquet table exposes the ugliness of Captain Vidal's dinner party, while the fairy-tale magic dresses up Ofelia's *maquis* mobilisation.

Although Manichaeism is maintained through the affiliations of *El laberinto del fauno*'s characters, Ofelia's *maqui* mobilisation undermines their opposition. For instance, the *maqui* doctor's last words categorically distinguish between the two camps: 'Obedecer, por obedecer – así sin pensarlo – sólo lo hacen gentes como usted, Capitán' ('to obey – just like that – for the sake of obeying, without questioning, that's something only people like you can do, Captain']. But, Ofelia's childhood is not unlike that celebrated by Franco's regime, whose March 1938 Boletín del Estado announced: 'Que el niño perciba que la vida es milicia, o sea, disciplina, sacrificio, lucha y austeridad' (The child should perceive life as militancy, that is, discipline, sacrifice, struggle and austerity) (Martín Gaite 1987: 21). Indeed, Ofelia/Moana makes the ultimate sacrifice of her own life for her brother's. She follows the *maquis*' play book of disobedience that wins her brother for the resistance fighters.

In *Infancia clandestina*, the boy's initiation into the *montonero* resistance is shown through his own drawings of a series of disguises worn by Cuban revolutionary Che Guevara. The ease with which Juan transforms the appearance of his illustration of Che prefigures his own docility as a child soldier for the *montoneros*. A chain of command is evident in the narration by Juan's parents Horacio (César Troncoso) and Charo (Natalia Oreiro) that explains and directs their son's 'mission'. Juan, named after former president Perón (1946–55 and 1973–4), assumes the disguise of Ernesto, named after Guevara. Juan's parents belong to the generation to which Peronism attended for its measures promoting childhood well-being and education:

> Perón significantly dedicated to youth what was his last annual address to congress, stressing that the young people of 1955 were the 'first product of the Revolution' and that they would carry the burden of perpetuating it on their shoulders. The reasoning attributed a historical responsibility to a particular age group envisioned as molded by the social well-being that Peronism had impressed upon the country. (Manzano 2014: 23)

Montoneros such as Juan's parents answered Perón's call to perpetuate the revolution.

The body of a soldier of any age is trained in instrumentality; it is a docile body. Not fully cognisant of the sacrifice and danger of the *montonero* endeavour, Juan demonstrates his docility and utility by clicking his heels and answering his remarkably carefree Coronel-uncle and joyfully shining his shoes. There is a sense that Juan is a toy soldier who at first plays at *guerrillero*, not unlike the child protagonists of *Paloma de papel* and *Voces inocentes*, before greater sacrifice is required of him. The boy's maternal grandmother Amalia (Cristina Banegas) expresses the only words óf concern questioning the normalcy of Juan's false identity and militarisation: 'You want your children to be guerrilleros?' ('¿Querés que tus hijos sean guerrilleros?'). Her enquiry makes room for a third

Figure 8.4 María (Violeta Palukas) blindfolds Juan/Ernesto (Teo Gutiérrez Moreno) for a camp game in *Infancia clandestina*.

Argentina that prefers not to engage in the conflict. Amalia's stance suggests that, if the film's action were to continue, it is unlikely that she would join the activism of the Grandmothers of the Plaza de Mayo who have clamoured for justice for their disappeared children and grandchildren.

The common political vision shared by Juan and his parents manifests in the feature's motif of eyeglasses, in turn evoking the common trope of the child's gaze in film, and impersonation that carry across Juan's role models of Che Guevara and his father Horacio. Juan/Ernesto does not share the perspective of his classmates. He and his girlfriend are at first blinded by their feelings for each other (Figure 8.4) but María's (Violeta Palukas) miming of 'lentes de gente decente' ('decent folks' eyeglasses'), a certain competing conservative and Euro-centric perspective, foreshadows their split. Juan resists what dominant ideology, indicated in lyrics of the school camp song, sees as improvements but demonstrates his docility for *montonero* instruction. In a key sequence for Juan/Ernesto's political coming-of-age, the boy's imagination refashions the campfire song in conjunction with a fantasy of his father's and his own funerals on television. Juan/Ernesto's substitution for his father indicates his acceptance of a more engaged role in the fight. While Juan/Ernesto does not wear his father's glasses, he does share Horacio's political viewpoint. Juan/Ernesto follows in his father's footsteps, unlike *Pa negre*'s protagonist who tries on his father's eyewear at the beginning of the film only to reject his father and all he represents in the end. Although Juan/Ernesto earlier plotted a getaway from the *montonero* lifestyle with his girlfriend, he progressively assumes a larger role in the *guerrilla* when he shelters his baby sister in their panic room and is captured upon his parents' disappearance. This is not to say, however, that Juan's affective experience is equal to that of his parents.

Vision and the child's point-of-view are also primary to Ávila's short film, *Veo veo* (2011), although its more mundane aesthetics recall Markovitch's film more than *Infancia clandestina*. The short film's eight-year-old protagonist Juancho (Lucas Esteban Rodríguez) relocates to a new home and school in 1977 due to his father's *montonero* ties. There is no animation in the film, also dedicated to Ávila's mother, yet Juancho like Del Toro's Ofelia and Erice's Ana makes sense of his father's two-year absence through fable. In fact, his older sister explains that their militant father, whose death Juancho like Juan/Ernesto later learns about on television, is like Robin Hood. Like Cecilia, Juancho compromises the safety of his father and his family as a result of a school assignment. The students are asked to bring in a photo of their father for the class's family tree. Juancho's father had been excised from all photos except, by accident, one remaining negative. He and his new neighbour and classmate Eva (María Agostina Gatabria), whose mother had died a while before, develop the photo with her father. In *Veo veo*, visuality regards not how the son sees, as in *Infancia clandestina*, but what he is able to see, namely the countenance of his father. It is forbidden fruit of the family tree, developed by Eva's photographer father.

Animation signals a journey into the surreal and, with this departure, Juan's subjectivity vis-à-vis the violence and loss surrounding him. The colour-coding that signifies a contrast between the real and magical worlds in *El laberinto del fauno* finds a different expression in *Infancia clandestina*. Live action pertaining to the resistance is often bathed in green lighting that recalls sequences animated in a complementary red and green colour scheme. Juan's subjectivity to a certain extent literally and figuratively colours the events of the film according to his experience of the traumatic events around him in a slow motion non-linear stream of consciousness fashion that imitates snapshots, like the family photos that Juan burns in the previous scene, or comic-strip frames. Its soundtrack recalls carousel music and the fair funhouse to which Juan/Ernesto and María temporarily escaped. The animated sequences that open and close the film depict violence, first, crossfire between the military and Juan's parents that precipitates their exile and, second, Juan's apprehension for questioning. It would be incorrect to assert that all traumatic incidents in Juan's life are depicted in animation, given that the interrogation sequence is shot in similar lighting to his imagined funeral, or that coloured lighting is absent in other moments, as during the boy's vision of his deceased uncle and observation of intergenerational arguments regarding the importance and safety of the militia.

Infancia clandestina more directly explores the militarisation of children than *El laberinto del fauno* but does not martyr its child protagonist. Both characters are orphaned, and their baby siblings are seized, but Juan's is a story of survival. He is ultimately released to his only remaining immediate family, his maternal grandmother to whom he surprisingly self-identifies as Juan rather than Ernesto. In an interview, Ávila states his response to the political climate of fear espoused on-screen by the grandmother:

> La construcción del discurso del miedo que se terminó de instalar en los '80 en la Argentina asoció a la militancia con la muerte . . . En la situación política que se está viviendo hoy, se empieza a entender que la militancia no es sinónimo de muerte sino sinónimo de cre[c]er. (Ranzani 2012: n.p.)

> [The construction of the discourse of fear that was entrenched by the 1980s in Argentina associated militancy with death . . . In today's political situation, we are beginning to understand that militancy is not a synonym for death but rather for growth.][18]

Infancia clandestina commemorates to a greater extent the lives rather than the deaths of the militants. However, the protagonist's self-identification to his grandmother as Juan rather than Ernesto suggests that the boy rather than the militant survives.

The historical contexts of each film shed light on why militancy is a synonym for death in *El laberinto del fauno* and an indication of growth in *Infancia clandestina*. These quest films set in 1944 and 1979 situate themselves within the politics, biopolitics, and political economy of memory of 2006 Spain and 2011 Argentina. Greater progress has been made in Argentina with regards to transitional justice and human rights. *Infancia clandestina* was first released in 2011 on the tails of two decades of investigations, prosecutions, and convictions of those responsible for the disappearance of dissidents and their children during the Dirty War. *El laberinto del fauno*, on the other hand, precedes Spain's Law of Historical Memory by a year but a very entrenched policy of forgetting remains. As discussed in Chapter Six, the 2007 Spanish law is limited to a more, although not entirely, symbolic recognition of the crimes committed against the Republican side of the Spanish Civil War.

These films, then, wage a battle on the symbolic plane, or a cinematic biopolitics in which child protagonists are incorporated into a political struggle on-screen rather than, in the case of Spain, or in addition to, Argentina's example, in a courtroom. After Baltasar Garzón's disbarment, Argentine judge María Servini de Cubría made efforts to investigate and then try Spanish human rights violators in Argentina (Anonymous 2014: n.p.) but the Spanish State obstructed these efforts (Ryan 2016: 6). The politicisation of child characters may be disguised by fairy tales and graphic art but these films politically deploy their child protagonists nonetheless. Like the *maquis*, who continued battling decades after the Spanish Civil War was lost, the child militant protagonists Ofelia/Moana and Juan/Ernesto are drafted, as soldiers and graphic images, to carry on the resistance and the quest for justice in the cinematic memory wars.

Conclusions: Rites of Passage and Motifs of Transatlantic Dialogism

In this chapter, I have explored the common biopolitical use and aesthetics of *bildungsfilms* across the Atlantic to illuminate the pervasive and far-reaching use of the child protagonist in the cinematic memory wars. My analysis of the two Spains and two Chiles in this genre study of the *bildungsfilm* reiterates the dualism that Rick Altman observes as central to genre cinema. It is clearly the case of Spanish-language *bildungsfilms* of national conflict that: '[c]onstantly opposing cultural values to countercultural values, genre films regularly depend on dual protagonists and *dualistic* structures (producing what I have called dual-focus texts)' (Altman 1999: 24; emphasis in the original). Child protagonists of these films must choose one of the two Spains, two Chiles, and two Argentinas: the regime or the resistance. They must mobilise and take strides for one or the other camp at great sacrifice to their well-being for a potential greater good or to its detriment. Growth and well-being are contingent upon political freedom in *La lengua de las mariposas* and *Machuca* and brought to a halting end in both features. *El espíritu de la colmena* and *El premio* reveal defeat and absence in the years of military dictatorship. *El laberinto del fauno* and *Infancia clandestina* explore rebellion in fantastic dimension to these dictatorial regimes. Tragic conclusions of the films herein discussed amount to a misalignment with the repressive regime and, as I will now explore as an extension of Chapters Six and Eight, in thwarted rites of passage.

I have noted how these coming-of-age films deal in becoming, or, articulated in the terms of Chapter Six, rites of passage. My reading of *El espíritu de la colmena* and *El laberinto del fauno* in Chapter Six focuses on fantasy, rites of passage, and the ritual function. In the current conclusion to Chapter Eight, I would like to explore briefly how deviations from rites of passages produce tragic endings in *La lengua de las mariposas*, *Machuca*, *El premio*, and *Infancia clandestina*. In review, a completed rite of passage occurs along three stages: the preliminary in which the child undergoes separation, the liminary in which the child is in between states, and the postliminary in which the child is embraced by a new community (Muir 2005: 21). Moncho separates from his family to attend school with Don Gregorio (preliminary), learns new ways of thinking thanks to Don Gregorio and the ILE that he implements in early indications of pubescence (liminary), but he separates again (in the end from the Republican community) in order to demonstrate membership among the Nationalists (postliminary). Moncho's political rites of passage deviate, and turn tragic, in the sense that the community to which he is incorporated is not Don Gregorio's. The same is true for *Machuca*: Gonzalo separates from his family through schooling and visits Machuca's neighbourhood (preliminary), Gonzalo's comings and goings to Machuca's community and pubescence indicate that he is in between two worlds (liminary), but Gonzalo extricates himself from Machuca's world to return to a somewhat changed home life (postliminary). Machuca's preliminary and liminary steps (towards Gonzalo's family) follow along the same lines until his disappearance. The tragedy resides in the deaths and disappearances and Gonzalo's abrupt deviation from his trajectory towards Machuca in accordance with St Patrick's School's teachings. The embrace of Gonzalo's mother upon his, perhaps, reluctant return indicates his incorporation into Pinochet's Chile.

El premio and *Infancia clandestina* espouse another kind of reversal in the rites of passage of their protagonists. Cecilia's separation from Buenos Aires for San Clemente del Tuyú is one of forced exile. Like Moncho, Gonzalo, Machuca, and Juan/Ernesto, Cecilia preliminarily separates from her mother for school where she learns another way (that of the military regime) of thinking. Betwixt and between (liminary) the regime and its dissent, she fights her mother in order to receive the military's prize while also engaging in prepubescent flirtation with a classmate. Her tragedy consists of receiving the prize that signifies her postliminary acceptance of and into the regime. Although Cecilia, it seems, finally changes her mind, it is too late: she receives the award, and nothing will bring back her father. Juan/Ernesto's postliminary rite of passage is somewhat more complex. First, he and his family return to Argentina from Cuba and he separates from them for school (preliminary). Unlike Cecilia, he is more aware of and at odds with the ideology of his school. Still, he finds himself betwixt and between two worlds in his pubescent infatuation with María. This represents a seduction, in the etymological sense, away from his family's political convictions. Juan/Ernesto proves his adherence to the *montonero* community during capture (postliminary). But, in his tragedy, Juan/Ernesto has no other family to return to other than his grandmother, whose politics do not align with his parents'. Like Gonzalo,

Juan/Ernesto does not reunite with the family of his choice. In accordance with the politics of the features, Moncho, Gonzalo, Machuca, Cecilia, and Juan/Ernesto end up misplaced. Their rites of passage suddenly re-orient, taking a sharp turn right particularly in the cases of Moncho and Gonzalo.

Footwear and wardrobe indicate by metonymy the chosen trajectories of the (anti-)heroes and heroines and what they become. Shoes relate to identity formation, the political path, and the rites of passage that child protagonists travel in each film. I would like to conclude my reflection on the transatlantic *bildungsfilms* with a final examination of these motifs in the characterisation of child protagonists. Ana does not follow in her father's footsteps, audible from his home study, but rather she steps into the footprint of the fugitive. Her identification with him rejects Francoism. Moncho's mother dresses him in his Sunday best, a suit that better resembles his father's than Don Gregorio's, for a display of distance from his teacher. Gonzalo's footwear makes possible his betrayal of Machuca. His Adidas shoes, a gift from his mother's married Argentine lover, denote his class membership and privileged exception from harassment. He becomes complicit with Pinochet's Chile. Cecilia is officially forced into submission to Argentina's last military dictatorship when she accepts her prize in crippling borrowed shoes. Juan/Ernesto, by contrast, shines shoes like a good soldier for Perón. Ofelia dons a new outfit with ruby booties, having muddied the formal wear gift from her stepfather, as Princess Moana. These child protagonists are outfitted with the combat footwear of the cinematic memory wars fought in the language of genre.

Notes

1. *Kamchatka* (Marcelo Piñeyro 2002 Argentina), *Valentín* (Alejandro Agresti 2002 Argentina), *Andrés no quiere dormir* (*Andrés Doesn't Want to Take a Nap*) (Daniel Bustamante 2009 Argentina), *El médico alemán* (*The German Doctor*) (Lucía Puenzo 2013 Argentina), *O Ano em Que Meus Pais Saíram de Férias* (*The Year My Parents Went on Vacation*) (Cao Hamburger 2006 Brazil), *Mutum* (Sandra Kogut 2007 Brazil), *Paisito* (*Small Country*) (Ana Díez 2008 Spain-Uruguay), *Viva Cuba* (Juan Carlos Cremata Alberti and Iraida Malberti Cabrera 2005 Cuba), *La edad de la peseta* (*The Silly Age*) (Pavel Giroud 2006 Cuba), *Habanastation* (Ian Padrón 2011 Cuba), *Voces inocentes* (*Innocent Voices*) (Luis Mandoki 2004 Mexico-El Salvador), *Paloma de papel* (*Paper Dove*) (Fabrizio Aguilar 2003 Peru), *Las malas intenciones* (*The Bad Intentions*) (Rosario García-Montero 2011 Peru) and *Pelo malo* (*Bad Hair*) (Mariana Rondón 2013 Venezuela). Julie Gavras's *Faute à Fidel* (*Blame it on Fidel!*) (2006) follows a young French girl's political awakening linked to anti-Franco and pro-Allende activism.

2. All translations to English in Chapter Eight are mine except those provided in the subtitles and published translations, which I denote with quotation marks around the text inside the brackets.

3. Birds also serve as symbols of the contrary and contradictory – retaliation or freedom – in *Cría cuervos* (*Raise Ravens*) (Carlos Saura 1976 Spain), *Pa negre* (*Black Bread*) (Agustí Villaronga 2010 Spain) and *El florido pénsil* (Juan José Porto 2002 Spain). *Cría cuervos* also has a Latin American sister, the Peruvian film *Las malas intenciones* (García-Montero 2011); see Thomas (2014).

4. In fact, *Machuca* has a dialogical relationship with Patricio Guzmán's *Battle of Chile* (Sorensen 2009: 86) and world cinema by virtue of intertext with French director Louis Malle's *Au revoir les enfants* (1987) (Park 2014: 124–6).

5. José Luis Cuerda adapted his film with Rafael Azcona from three stories from *¿Qué me quieres, amor?* (1996) by Manuel Rivas. I will focus on the adaptations of 'La lengua de las mariposas' and 'Un saxo en la niebla' rather than on 'Carmiña', in which the child characters participate to a lesser degree. Cuerda was born in Albacete in 1947 and has made more than eleven feature-length films (Quintana 1998: 264–5). Azcona (1926–2008) was born in Logroño and is one of the most respected and successful screenwriters in the history of Spanish cinema; his screenplay for *Belle Epoque* (Fernando Trueba 1992) was nominated for an Oscar (Torrerio Gómez 1998: 102–3). Rivas was born in A Coruña, Galicia in 1957 and has written in *gallego* and Spanish in the genres of journalistic articles, short stories, and novels. He interviewed Baltasar Garzón in Isabel Coixet's documentary *Escuchando al juez Garzón* (*Listening to Judge Garzón*) (2011). *Machuca* was co-written by Eliseo Altunaga, Roberto Brodsky, Mamoun Hassan, and Andrés Wood and based on Amante Eledín Parraguez's *Tres años para nacer* (2002), Roberto Brodsky's *Últimos días de la historia* (2001), and the experience of Eledín Parraguez and Wood as students at the St George School (Sorensen 2009: 83).

6. See Erin K. Hogan, 'A Politics of Listening in Isabel Coixet's *Listening to Judge Garzón* (2011)', *International Journal of Iberian Studies* 29.1 (2016): 65–79.

7. In this parenthetical citation, I direct readers to the Spanish and English publications of Machado's poetry.

8. *Viva Cuba* (Cremata and Malberti 2005) offers a counterpoint by illustrating the two Cubas through its ten-year-old boy and girl co-protagonists and by arguing for friendship and reconciliation. As both Operation Pedro Pan, the exile of approximately 14,000 Cuban children to the United States from 1960 to 1962, and the Elián González affair, in which the six-year-old emigrant was caught between the politics of Cuba and the United States in 1999 to 2000, demonstrate, the United States and Cuba have utilised the child as a political icon. Anita Casavantes Bradford follows 'Two Cubas': 'Between 1959 and the onset in 1999 of the Elián González custody battle, the politics of childhood in Havana and Miami would continue to articulate the processes of alienation, fragmentation, and reformation that led to the creation

of Two Cubas on opposite shores of the Straits of Florida' (2014: 184). *Viva Cuba* depicts the Two Cubas within Cuba; Malú (Malú Tarrau Broche) and Jorgito (Jorge Milo) come from families on the opposite ends of the political spectrum, but the children respond to the threat of Malú's leaving the country with her mother. Nevertheless, the film insists on the similarity in Cuban habits and customs; their mothers cast each other prejudicial glares when they simultaneously step out their front doors to call their children home for a meal. The parental generation is thoroughly embroiled but Malú and Jorge learn to value their unity in the film's proposal for Cuba's future. For more on *Viva Cuba*, see Dunja Fehimović, 'Not Child's Play: Tactics and Strategies in *Viva Cuba* and *Habanastation*', *Bulletin of Latin American Research* 34.4 (2015): 503–16.

9. Roberto Brodsky gave a talk on his screenwriting for *Machuca* and *Mi vida con Carlos* (Berger 2010) at the University of Maryland Baltimore County, entitled 'Baltimore, imágenes del pájaro y la jaula', on 14 April 2016 from 7 pm to 8:30 pm.

10. However, despite Don Gregorio's secular agenda, the teacher becomes a profane martyr. Three moments in the film support this reading: 1) Don Gregorio baptises Moncho in the river as a response to his asthma attack, 2) the teacher's followers deny and forsake him and as a result he is apprehended by authorities, and 3) the instructor is stoned by his pupil Moncho.

11. Other references include Moncho's uncle who left for America and the 1930 Cuban song, 'El manisero' by Moisés Simons, played during Carnival.

12. Hogan conducted an interview of José Luis Cuerda in Madrid on 19 November 2009.

13. Daniel Feierstein maps the terminology referring to the period: 'Dirty War' refers to the 'repression carried out by Argentina's last military government' and is used outside of Argentina and especially in academic literature written in English (2014: 131–2).

14. Child star crossings were fully realised with the young career of Pulgarcito (Cesáreo Quezadas Cubillas 1950–) from Mexican cinema. Also within Mexican cinema, Castro de Paz asserts that *En el balcón vacío* (Jomí García Ascot 1962) is the 'espíritu de la colmena' of Spanish Republican exile (Castro de Paz 2005: 381).

15. It is important to note, however, that the happy scene of reunification between father and daughter that Smith's Guadalajara Film Festival review discusses is absent in the DVD of *El premio* distributed by Global Film Initiative. Cecilia is not reunited with her father. According to co-producer Dankmar García (Elite Studios), many variations and endings were shot of the film and it was not presented in its final cut in Guadalajara nor at the Berlinale (e-mail, 11 August 2017).

16. The reception of *Viva Cuba* in the American Associated Press's (NBC's Today) interview of Cremata similarly, and I would argue erroneously, downplays politics. The article opens with a description and the director's

categorisation: 'Cuban film director Juan Carlos Cremata's new movie is about a young girl who runs away from home because her mother plans to leave Fidel Castro's Cuba and she doesn't want to go. But "Viva Cuba" isn't a political film – it's a human one. "It's not that the girl wants to stay in Cuba because of the Revolution," Cremata told the Associated Press in a recent interview. She wants to stay, he said, because Cuba "is where her friends are, where her school is, and above all, where her beloved grandmother is buried." Depoliticizing the subject of Cuban exiles is about as easy as taking the fruit out of an apple pie, but judging from the international reaction, Cremata has succeeded in moving beyond nationalism to reach a universal audience' (Anonymous 2006a: n.p.).

17. Shaw uploaded her Houston talk to her Academia.edu page (https://www. academia.edu/32306454/Reading_Pan_s_Labyrinth_in_the_era_of_neo-fascism).

18. There appears to be a typo in the body of the article, which repeats the title: 'Militancia no es sinónimo de muerte, sino de crecer.' *Página 12* staff were not available to clarify.

Conclusion
Spanish Movies: Genre, Nation and
Spanish Movie

How Does the *Panish* Movie Become the Spanish Movie?

The *Spanish Movie* house indeed is haunted. Ramira, Roberta, Ramona, Raimunda, or Rigoberta (Alexandra Jiménez) – it is so hard even for co-stars to keep the recurring characters in Spanish cinema straight – arrives to a mansion to care for photo-sensitive Simeón (Óscar Lara), but sends him for fresh air outside where he is charred to death by the sun. The medium Gerarda (Juana Cordero), named and modelled after Geraldine Chaplin's actual Spanish nickname and heavy accent (French rather than English here) and fictional character in *El orfanato* (Bayona 2007), tries to locate the disappeared boy. She asks: '¿Qué es un fantasma, Carlos?' ('What is a ghost, Carlos?'), invoking the central question and main character of *El espinazo del diablo* (Del Toro 2001).[1] Maligna (Teresa Lozano) may be responsible, like the suspect Benigna (Montserrat Carulla) from Bayona's film. Meanwhile, the pastime of Simeón's unconcerned sister Ofendia (Laia Alda) is to torture Faunofarfollas (Joaquín Reyes) and Hada (Michelle Jenner). Ramira, who incarnates many of Penélope Cruz's roles, falls in love with Pedro San Antón (Carlos Areces), who plays a number of Javier Bardem's award-winning parts. Perhaps this is why Pedro is bludgeoned with a Goya award statuette. Their *Mar adentro* (*Sea Inside*) (Amenábar 2004) – inspired love story culminates in a hybrid *Abre los ojos* (*Open Your Eyes*) (Amenábar 1997) – *La comunidad* (*Common Wealth*) (De la Iglesia 2000) sequence. *Spanish Movie* concludes with a deliberately unbelievable 'Hollywood' happy ending: Simeón is resurrected and the characters fly blissfully through the air together like superheroes.

Spanish Movie is, like the 'Faunofarfollas' named 'Ambrosio', an irreverent and entertaining salad of intertextual references and stock characters for Spanish cinema freaks. Ruiz Caldera's film illustrates many of the elements that form the *nuevo cine con niño* genre. *Spanish Movie* speaks to national cinema, the relationship between genre and nation, the intertextuality of genre cinema and its function. In Chapters Two, Four, and Five, I focus on continuities across the *cines con niño*, from the 1950s to the 2000s, arguing that similar narrative strategies serve the opposing political purposes and genre functions of the two Spains. I analysed the ideological function, Rick Altman's theorisation that follows Louis Althusser and reads genre as a vehicle for a regime's indoctrination (1999: 27), of the Francoist *cine con niño* in the most depth in Chapter Three. In Chapter Four, I discussed prosopopeia, a concept related to ventriloquism from Jacques Derrida by way of Karen Lury, with regards to the Gothic child protagonist's ability to connect with the marginalised. It now manifests on both the levels of genre whereby the hallmarks of the *nuevo cine con niño* repeatedly reappear as phantom intertexts across the cinematic landscape and in the character of the grotesque Gothic child. Jacques Derrida, we review from Chapter Seven, may consider *Spanish Movie* a phantom-text of Spanish filmmaking, where: '[i]n a phantom-text, these distinctions, these quotation marks, references, or citations become irremediably precarious; they leave only traces, and we shall never define the trace or the phantom without, ironically or allegorically, appealing from one to the other' (1986: 80). I underscore the traceability of phantom intertexts in *Spanish Movie* and the *cines con niño*. This dialogism is the key ontological feature for genre formation.

Genre film is the specialty of *Spanish Movie*'s director and writers Paco Cabezas and Eneko Lizarraga and it extends beyond Spanish cinema. *Spanish Movie*, just as Spanish film has, also draws from Hollywood film. The film's English-only title itself is an indication of external influences. *Spanish Movie* is a parody inspired by the *Scary Movie* (Keenan Ivory Wayans 2009) franchise and even features spoof-movie leading-man extraordinaire, Leslie Nielsen. Ruiz Caldera's movie channels the comedies of the Coen and Farrelly Brothers, *Superman* (Richard Donner 1978), and other films that may transgress the borders of Spanish cinema. *Spanish Movie* includes works by Alejandro Amenábar, a Spanish director who filmed *The Others* in English, and Guillermo del Toro, a Mexican filmmaker who made two features in Spain. The film's poster (Figure 9.1) features the characters that I describe above with a very curious spatial composition of its title. 'Spanish Movie' lies diagonally across the legs of a lounging 'Pan' of *Pan's Labyrinth* but its first letter coyly leans left in distinction from the rest of the vertical lettering. How does the *panish* movie become the Spanish movie, with a teetering capital S? (Figure 9.1)

Figure 9.1 *Spanish Movie* poster with its teetering capital S.

Ceci n'est pas un Spanish Movie?

Spanish Movie is a parodic frame narrative that not only reflects genre conventions but is also self-reflexive. In one sequence, Laura (Silvia Abril) plays the piano and sings a song of desire for her husband, modelled after Capitán Alatriste, who is away at war. First, we hear the soundtrack of deceptively diegetic music as we see within the film's frame a picture frame of Laura playing the piano (Figure 9.2). The camera zooms out to the true wide shot to reveal that picture only to be internal framing within the larger frame of the film and to identify the actual pianist of the diegetic music. This clip that lasts a mere fourteen seconds in the eighty-three-minute film provides us with the blueprint of the full-length feature. The mise-en-abyme structure provides the frame for the entire film whereby *The Others* and *The Orphanage* are the master frame within which other filmic texts intersect. Laura is a cross between Nicole Kidman's Grace and Belén Rueda's Laura.

I can now rephrase my central question regarding the transformation of the *panish* movie into the Spanish movie: Ceci n'est pas un Spanish Movie? This is not a Spanish Movie? The presence of surrealist artist René Magritte's 'Treachery of Images' (1922, 1926) is undeniable in *Spanish Movie*'s own exercise in textual mirroring. Magritte plays with word and image to, in Michel Foucault's estimation, dissociate similitude from resemblance (1982: 44). *Spanish Movie* resembles its source texts, for Foucault: 'resemblance has a "model," an original element that orders and hierarchizes the increasingly less faithful copies that can be struck from it. Resemblance presupposes a primary reference that prescribes and classes' (ibid.). Let us recall that it is a 'pan*ish*' movie, one that resembles *Pan's Labyrinth* (2006) and many other films through parody. According to *Spanish Movie*'s prescriptions and classifications: films set in Spain, by Spanish directors, or starring Spanish actors are Spanish movies. My theorisation emphasises that intertextuality is a defining feature of genre cinema. Therefore, I would have to agree with the filmmakers that this is, in fact, a Spanish Movie.

The sequence also demonstrates the film's relationship to parody. Linda Hutcheon's re-examination of the etymology of 'parody' sheds further light on the sequence. While Hutcheon notes that 'par-odia' has typically been described as a counter-song, she underscores that it can be best understood as beside the text within the context of twentieth, and I would add twenty-first, century art forms (1985: 32). Laura, of course, sings beside an image of herself (Figure 9.2) and we can best appreciate *Spanish Movie* alongside its source texts. Familiarity with source texts, however, does reveal that *Spanish Movie* provides its viewers with grotesque degradations and carnivalesque inversions of its characters, in other words figures that are counter or even opposite their originals. *Spanish Movie* belongs to a long tradition of dark humour in the Spanish arts and evidences an ingrained cultural impetus of benevolent self-deprecation and celebration of anti-heroes. Benigna becomes Maligna and Ofelia becomes Ofendia. The canted capital S of Spanish Movie from the poster is an early indication of its distortions.

Figure 9.2 *Spanish Movie*'s parodic homage to Magritte's 'Treachery of Images' (1922, 1926).

Spanish Movie calls attention to the repetitiveness of genre films and national cinema for comedic effect. What is true of *Scary Movie* may also be the case for *Spanish Movie*, according to Keenan Ivory Wayans: 'What happens in parody is, first there is a good movie, then there are fifty bad versions of that movie, and when the audience is tired of seeing those films, then that genre's right for parody' (Wayans cite in Alexander 2003: 144). Film scholar Rick Altman also notes the repetitiveness of genre film:

> Both intratextually and intertextually, the genre film uses the same material over and over again. A common complaint levelled against genre films, 'If you've seen one you've seen 'em all', correctly describes their *repetitive* nature. The same fundamental conflicts are resolved over and over again in similar fashion – the same shoot-out, the same sneak attack, the same love scene culminating in the same duet. Each film varies the details but leaves the basic pattern undisturbed, to the point where shots used in one film are often recycled in another. (Altman 1999: 25; emphasis in the original)

Spanish Movie highlights the repetition in recent Spanish cinema and the attitude towards it. '¡Otro cine español!' ('Another Spanish movie!'), is Ofendia's lament while viewing a trailer for *Los lunes alcohol* (poking fun at Fernando León de Aranoa's 2002 unemployment drama *Los lunes al sol* (*Mondays in the Sun*)). We repeat and review these observations now in our concluding examination.

A review of Ruiz Caldera's film in *El País* by comedian, journalist, and screenwriter Pepe Colubi relates genre and nation, discusses genre convention in terms of stereotypes, and echoes the blasé attitude that Altman parroted. Colubi dismisses cinematic repetition as a conglomeration of irritating stereotypes rather than as an indicator of genre formation. *Spanish Movie* parodies a number of genres in recent Spanish cinema from social realism to science-fiction and fantasy to horror to child-starred films retrospective of the Spanish Civil War and Francisco Franco's thirty-six-year dictatorship. Let us revisit Colubi's gripes:

> 'La Guerra Civil a través de los ojos de un niño. Por mucho que le pese a José Luis Cuerda, el cansino espectador medio español cataloga, por pura acumulación, las películas ambientadas en nuestra Guerra Civil y su posguerra como todo un subgénero ibérico con varios elementos comunes: ausencia de escenas bélicas, pre-adolescentes salidos, tristeza vital, algún curilla, graves penurias y Maribel Verdú.' (Colubi 2009: n.p.)

> [The Spanish Civil War through the eyes of a child. In spite of José Luis Cuerda [director of *Butterfly* and *Blind Sunflowers*], the tired and average Spanish spectator

catalogues, by pure accumulation, the films set during our Civil War and post-war as an Iberian subgenre with various common elements: absence of war scenes, horny preteens, vital sadness, a priest here or there, grave scarcities and Maribel Verdú.]

First, the tone of Colubi's critique is a very common one used towards genre films. Film scholar Leo Braudy accounts for the resistance to genre films, explaining that they 'offend our most common definition of artistic excellence: the uniqueness of the art object, whose value can in part be defined by its desire to be uncaused and unfamiliar, as much as possible unindebted to any tradition, popular or otherwise' (Braudy 1999: 613). Patterns and repetition that are central to genre filmmaking get old for Colubi, Wayans, Ofendia, and others. Second, these characteristics do appear to varying degrees in *El espíritu de la colmena*, *Secretos del corazón*, and *El laberinto del fauno*. However, in my monograph's inventory of *nuevo cine con niño* protagonists, I catalogue curious, rebellious, intrepid, heteronormative, and sexually naïve children who may either be victims of Francoism or the thorns in its side.

Spanish Movie's Grotesque Gothic Child

If we now take another look at the *Spanish Movie* poster (Figure 9.1), shifting our focus from the title to the figures at dead centre, we find that children are at the literal and metaphorical centre of Spanish movies. Ofendia, who also disguises herself as the hooded child from *The Orphanage*, actually appears twice at centre. Her alter ego, the hooded child, is roped and appears to be held hostage for *Spanish Movie*, perhaps calling to our minds Pepa Flores's charge of sequestration from Chapter Three. It is no coincidence that the frame narrative that houses this parody of recent Spanish cinema's most popular films is in the Gothic mode. These are the phantom intertexts of contemporary Spanish filmmaking. Simeón and Ofendia participate in the narrative thread that links new child-starred cinema in this mode: *The Others*, *The Orphanage*, and *Pan's Labyrinth*. According to Colubi's overview, child protagonists of films set during the Spanish Civil War and Franco's dictatorship have become synonymous with Spanish film: 'Del niño de la posguerra al terror que no se ve, repasamos los estereotipos que hacen país' (From the child of the post-war to unseen terror, we review the stereotypes that make a country). These characters are nation-making. Altman hints at the genre-nation connection:

> Genres and nations . . . are tied together in such a special way that, against all likelihood, genre theory might actually be a useful tool for analyzing relationships between populations and the texts they use, for whatever purpose they might use them. (Altman 1999: 206)

This is our position; genre and Spanish cinema are linked in no uncertain terms.

We now focus on the Gothic child, whose sensitivity and marginality allows him or her to empathise with the suffering of others and choose to serve as their advocate. However, this describes the earnest Gothic child from the original films we discussed in Chapter Five. *Spanish Movie*'s grotesque distortions turn *Pan's Labyrinth*'s Ofelia into a character more reminiscent of the fatalistic Wednesday Addams (Sonnenfeld 1991) who spoils the plot of *The Others* and *The Orphanage*: 'Estamos todos muertos' ('We are all dead'). Ofendia revels in the afflictions of others. Simeón does not suffer from acquired immune deficiency syndrome (AIDS) like *The Orphanage*'s Simón but rather from the infantile ailment from *The Others* – photosensitivity – and spontaneously combusts when locked outside by his nanny Ramira. To cover up the terrible incident, Ramira enlists the sixty-six-year-old former child actor Joselito (José Jiménez Fernández), who to this day is billed in the diminutive unlike Marisol-Pepa Flores, to perform as a child once more. *Spanish Movie* presents carnivalesque inversions of these characters, that is: grotesque Gothic children. The faun inspires apprehension and distrust in Ofelia but in *Spanish Movie* he becomes Ofendia's abused pet. An adult plays a child – although this also recalls the child roles that Joselito played well into his adolescence. We will focus on Joselito's star-text and context now.

There is more than meets the eye with Simeón's disappearance and Joselito's substitution for the boy. Knowledge of the history of the children of Franco on- and off-screen casts a darker shadow over the comedy. Let us first return to the source text. *The Orphanage* opens with Laura's adoption in 1975, the year of Franco's death. Benigna's institution is reminiscent of the Francoist abusive state orphanages, the Auxilio Social, where many children of Republicans were punished for their parents' political affiliations (Cenarro Lagunas 2006). In Bayona's film, unwed Benigna treated her son Tomás (Óscar Casas), who was born with a 'malformación', like a monster who had to be kept hidden and hooded in a downstairs basement and then poisoned the orphans involved in Tomás's accidental death. In the fantastic interpretation of *The Orphanage*, Simón is taken prisoner by the ghosts of Benigna's victims. Whether appropriated or disappeared, Simón goes missing.

Simón and then Siméon are akin to recent independent and art cinema's many missing children that Emma Wilson identifies in her monograph from 2003. For Wilson:

> The issue of the missing child enables films to mobilise questions about the protection and innocence of childhood, about parenthood and the family, about the past (as childhood is constructed in retrospect as nostalgic space of safety) and about the future (as fears for children reflect anxiety about the inheritance left to future generations). (Wilson 2003: 2)

I am compelled to modify Wilson's observations for the context of Francoist and post-Franco Spain where films retrospective of the dictatorship most certainly do not offer nostalgic visions of safety. They portray the contrary through the Gothic mode. However, the child's consistent and continued mobilisation for the future is quite relevant to contemporary Spanish cinema. Freud's interpretation of the dream of the burning child from *The Interpretation of Dreams* is key for Wilson's thesis on cinema's missing children. *Spanish Movie* provides us with the grotesque version of the burning child: Simeón smoulders in the sun. As in the dream, although through other mechanisms, parent and child are reunited. For Freud, the dream denotes the wish to deny a child's death (Wilson 2003: 5). For us, *Spanish Movie* and the *nuevo cine con niño* exhibit a desire to recover the child protagonist from an unjust, unpleasant, or deadly fate under Francoism and envision a better future for child and nation.

Spanish Movie goes to absurd lengths to recover the child protagonist from Francoism. Calling upon a senior Joselito, whom writer and film critic Terenci Moix has called a 'professional orphan' (Pavlović, Perriam, and Toribio 2013: 322–3; Moix 1993: 268), to step in as Simeón's understudy. Joselito himself, a star-text who signifies orphanhood and the Francoist *niño prodigio*, becomes a parody of the cinematic child protagonist. Joselito's wig and wardrobe are designed to resemble Simeón's (Figure 9.3). Joselito is parodic according to the composition of this frame. He appears physically beside Simeón's photo, which offers another instance of the internal framing we highlighted from Laura's song. Joselito's third age also pits him against Simeón's youth. He looks as pleased to be here as the faun was to be ridden by Ofendia. As I explored in Chapter Three, a certain model of childhood was imposed on the Francoist *niños prodigios*. Ramira quite literally imposes Simeón's likeness over Joselito's face. Joselito once again is the epitome of the malleable, Foucauldian docile body (Foucault 1979: 136). However, the grotesque does not improve but rather degrades. Eating in this sequence (sugary foods, no less) also triggers the grotesque and underscores Ramira's shortcomings as a caretaker.

Figure 9.3 Joselito (José Jiménez Fernández, on the right) parading as Simeón
(Óscar Lara, in photograph at the centre) at the breakfast table with Ramira
(Alexandra Jiménez, on the left).

Spanish Movie cracks a number of jokes at Joselito's expense with
regards to his age and diminutive stature but also recognises his indis-
pensability in Spanish popular cinema. His presence would also indicate
how Franco's child stars turned the silver screen into a smoke screen for
the abuse of children in the state orphanage system and beyond. Behind
the scenes, Joselito, and his female counterpart Marisol, complained
about his exploitation as a child star. Terenci Moix observes the 'sarcastic moral' of Francoism's child stars: 'al franquismo le salieron rana los
niños prodigio, portadores de "valores espirituales". Joselito, presunto
narcotraficante. Marisol, más roja que la Pasionaria. Y Rocío Dúrcal, agi-
tadora social' (Francoism's child stars, bearers of 'spiritual values,' went
pear-shaped. Joselito, an alleged drug dealer. Marisol, a bigger commie
than la Pasionaria. And Rocío Dúrcal, social agitator) (1993: 291). Their
Francoist educations were so radically counter-productive that they in
fact created their own opposition. Through their roles as Francoist cultural icons, they underwent grotesque distortion. Recall from Chapter
Three the malformations (bandaging of her chest and plastic surgery) of
Marisol's pubescent body. Joselito's reprisal of the child role may not only
be an indication of the difficult transition from child to adult actor but also
the seedier, tabloid elements of his adult star-text. Perhaps *Spanish Movie*
is also commenting on the former child star's deviations from his early
professional calling; he was arrested and imprisoned for drug dealing in
1991, he reportedly worked as a mercenary for Portugal in Africa (Bayarri
1991: n.p.; Manzano 2014: 191), and has appeared in the reality television show *Supervivientes: perdidos en Honduras* (2008) and the talk show
Sálvame (September 2011).

So, Then, How Does the *Panish* Movie Become the Spanish Movie?

This is a Spanish movie. But, how does the *panish* movie become the Spanish Movie? Ruiz Caldera's spoof film ventriloquates numerous filmic texts and star-texts to illuminate the most pervasive concerns of Spanish national cinema. The child protagonist and the nation's relationship to its dictatorial past are the concerns that we have examined in *The Two* cines. *Spanish Movie*'s intertexts extend beyond contemporary cinema in their inclusion of Joselito, a blast from Spanish cinema's past. The parodic film from 2009 makes light of national cinema's obsession with the past; one perplexed character understates: '¿Qué guerra?' ('What war?'). The movie appeared on the tails of the 2007 Law of Historical Memory that took a few tentative steps in the direction of recognising Francoist injustices.

In grotesque fashion, *Spanish Movie* recuperates Joselito from the Francoist *cine con niño*, but uses and abuses him again. Simeón's fate, coming back to life and reuniting with his mother but losing his arm again, is perhaps the happiest of grotesque endings. Carnivalesque inversions time and again produce *Spanish Movie*'s characters and even betray the irreverent movie's intertextual nod to Magritte's *The Treachery of Images* by calling into question its declarative statement. Ruiz Caldera's playful parody stands beside, aslant, and upside down its source texts. (Recall the exaggerated diagonal leanings of Ramira's drunk husband.) Despite its grotesque deformations, *Spanish Movie* maintains the *nuevo cine con niño*'s exercise in the ritual genre function. The child protagonist, worse for the wear, is indeed reunited with his family for a better (than death) future.

Spanish Movie reveals and demonstrates how genre cinema relates to film history and, I argue, to national history as well. The *panish* movie becomes Spanish through parodic intertext and engagement with the nation's cinematic and socio-political history. Child-starred cinema has persisted in more than fifty years of Spanish film because it expresses ongoing concerns of the nation's past, present, and future.

Note

1. All translations in the Conclusion are mine except those provided in the English subtitles to *Spanish Movie*, which I denote with quotation marks around the text inside the brackets.

Select Filmography

¡A mí no me mire usted!, film, directed by José Luis Sáenz de Heredia. Spain: Ernesto Giménez Caballero, Ernesto González, 1941.

Abre los ojos/Open Your Eyes, film, directed by Alejandro Amenábar. Spain: Canal+ España, 1997.

Addams Family, film, directed by Barry Sonnenfeld. USA: MGM, 1991.

Andrés no quiere dormir/Andrés Doesn't Want to Take a Nap, film, directed by Daniel Bustamante. Argentina: El Ansia Producciones, 2009.

Au revoir les enfants/Goodbye, Children, film, directed by Louis Malle. France: Nouvelle Éditions de Films, 1987.

Belle Epoque, film, directed by Fernando Trueba. Spain: Fernando Trueba Producciones Cinematográficas, 1992.

Bello recuerdo, film, directed by Antonio del Amo. Spain: Cesáreo González Producciones Cinematográficas, 1961.

¡Bienvenido Míster Marshall!/Welcome Mr. Marshall!, film, directed by José Luis García Berlanga. Spain: Unión industrial cinematográfica SL, 1953.

Bodas de sangre/Blood Wedding, film, directed by Carlos Saura. Spain: Emiliano Piedra, 1981.

Camino, film, directed by Javier Fesser. Spain: Mediapro, Películas Pendelton, 2008.

Cerca de la ciudad, film, directed by Luis Lucía. Spain: Goya Producciones Cinematográficas, 1952.

Cría cuervos/Raise Ravens, film, directed by Carlos Saura. Spain: Elías Querejeta Producciones Cinematográficas, 1976.

Crónica de un niño solo/Chronicle of a Boy Alone, film, directed by Leonardo Favio. Argentina: Luis de Stefano, Instituto Nacional de Cinematografía, 1965.

Demonios en el jardín/Demons in the Garden, film, directed by Manuel Gutiérrez Aragón. Spain: Luis Megino P.C., 1982.

El camino de la victoria, film, directed by Antonio del Amo. Spain: Partido Comunista de España, 1937.

El coche de pedales/The Pedal Push Car, film, directed by Ramón Barea. Spain: Alokatu S.L., 2004.

El corazón del bosque/Heart of the Forest, film, directed by Manuel Gutiérrez Aragón. Spain: Arándano S.A., 1979.

El embrujo de Shanghai/Shanghai Spell, film, directed by Fernando Trueba. Spain: Lola Films, 2002.

El espinazo del diablo / The Devil's Backbone, film, directed by Guillermo del Toro.
  Spain: El Deseo, Tequila Gang, Sogepaq, 2001.
El espíritu de la colmena / The Spirit of the Beehive, film, directed by Víctor Erice.
  Spain: Elías Querejeta Producciones Cinematográficas, 1973.
El florido pénsil, film, directed by Juan José Porto. Spain: Walt Disney Company
  Iberia, S.L., 2002.
El jardín de las delicias / The Garden of Delights, film, directed by Carlos Saura.
  Spain: Elías Querejeta Producciones, 1970.
El laberinto del fauno / Pan's Labyrinth, film, directed by Guillermo del Toro.
  Spain: Estudios Picasso, Tequila Gang, Esperanto Filmoj, 2006.
El mar / The Sea, film, directed by Agustí Villaronga. Spain: Cameo D.L, 2000.
El médico alemán / The German Doctor, film, directed by Lucía Puenzo. Argentina:
  Historias cinematográficas Cinemanía, 2013.
El niño de la luna, film, directed by Agustí Villaronga. Spain: Ganesh Producciones
  Cinematográficas, 1989.
El orfanato / The Orphanage, film, directed by José Antonio Bayona. Spain: Está
  Vivo! Laboratorio de Nuevos Talentos, Grupo Rodar, Rodar y Rodar Cine y
  Televisión, 2007.
El pequeño ruiseñor / The Little Nightingale, film, directed by Antonio del Amo.
  Spain: Argos S.L. P.C., 1956.
El premio / The Prize, film, directed by Paula Markovitch. Mexico: Elite Studios,
  2011.
El sur, film, directed by Víctor Erice. Spain: Elías Querejeta Producciones
  Cinematográficas, 1983.
El viaje de Carol / Carol's Journey, film, directed by Imanol Uribe. Spain: Aiete-
  Ariane Films, 2002.
Els nens perduts del franquisme / Franco's Forgotten Children, film, directed by
  Montse Armengou and Ricard Belis. Spain: Televisió de Catalunya, 2002.
En el balcón vacío / On the Empty Balcony, film, directed by Jomí García Ascot.
  Mexico: Ascot, Torre, 1962.
Esa mujer, film, directed by Mario Camus. Spain: Proesa, Cesáreo González
  Producciones Cinematográficas, 1969.
Escuchando al juez Garzón / Listening to Judge Garzón, film, directed by Isabel
  Coixet. Spain: Miss Wasabi, 2011
Faute à Fidel / Blame it on Fidel!, film, directed by Julie Gavras. France: Gaumont,
  Les Films du Worso, B Movies, 2006.
Frankenstein, film, directed by James Whale. USA: Universal Pictures, 1931.
Gringuito, film, directed by Sergio M. Castilla. Chile: Amor en el sur Films, 1998.
Ha llegado un ángel / An Angel Has Appeared, film, directed by Luis Lucía. Spain:
  Cesáreo González Rodríguez and Benito Perojo, 1961.
Habanastation, film, directed by Ian Padrón. Cuba: Quad Productions, DDC
  Films LLC, TVC Casa Productora, Instituto Cubano de Radio y Televisión,
  La colmenita, El ingenio, 2011.
Infancia clandestina / Clandestine Childhood, film, directed by Benjamín Ávila.

Argentina: Historias cinematográficas, Habitación 1520, RTA Radio y Televisión Argentina, 2011.

Kamchatka, film, directed by Marcelo Piñeyro. Argentina: Alquimia Cinema, 2002.

La batalla de Chile/The Battle of Chile, film, directed by Patricio Guzmán. Chile: Equipo Tercer Años, Instituto Cubano del Arte e Industrias Cinematográficas, 1975.

La camada negra/Black Litter, film, directed by Manuel Gutiérrez Aragón. Spain: El Imán cine y televisión SA, 1977.

La comunidad/Common Wealth, film, directed by Álex de la Iglesia. Spain: Antena 3 Televisión, Lolafilms, 2000.

La corrupción de Chris Miller/Behind the Shutters, film, directed by Juan Antonio Bardem. Spain: Javier Armet Xiol, 1973.

La edad de la peseta/The Silly Age, film, directed by Pavel Giroud. Cuba: Instituto Cubano del Arte e Industrias Cinematográficas, 2006.

La gran familia/The Big Family, film, directed by Fernando Palacios. Spain: Pedro Masó Producciones Cinematográficas, 1962.

La guerra de papá/Daddy's War, film, directed by Antonio Mercero. Spain: José Frade Producciones Cinematográficas, 1977.

La historia oficial/The Official Story, film, directed by Luis Puenzo. Argentina: Historias cinematográficas, 1985.

La lengua de las mariposas/Butterfly, film, directed by José Luis Cuerda. Spain: Canal+ España, Las Producciones del Escorpión, Sogetel, Televisión española, Televisión de Galicia, 1999.

La ley del deseo/Law of Desire, film, directed by Pedro Almodóvar. Spain: El Deseo, 1987.

La mala educación/Bad Education, film, directed by Pedro Almodóvar. Spain: El Deseo, 2004.

La nueva cenicienta/The New Cinderella, film, directed by George Sherman. Spain: Guión Producciones Cinematográficas, 1964.

La prima Angélica/Cousin Angelica, film, directed by Carlos Saura. Spain: Elías Querejeta Producciones, 1974.

La voz dormida/The Sleeping Voice, film, directed by Benito Zambrano. Spain: Maestranza Films, S.A., Audiovisual Aval SGR, Warner Brothers, 2011.

Largo viaje/A Long Journey, film, directed by Patricio Kaulen. Chile: Naranjo-Campos Menendez, 1967.

Las bicicletas son para el verano/Bicycles Are for the Summer, film, directed by Jaime Chávarri. Spain: Jet Films S.A., Impala, In-Cine, 1984.

Las largas vacaciones del '36/The Long Holidays of 1936, film, directed by Jaime Camino. Spain: José Frade Producciones Cinematográficas, 1976.

Las malas intenciones/The Bad Intentions, film, directed by Rosario García-Montero. Peru: Barry Films, Garmont Films, 2011.

Las trece rosas/13 Roses, film, directed by Emilio Martínez Lázaro. Spain:

Enrique Cerezo Producciones Cinematográficas, Pedro Costa Producciones Cinematográficas S.A., 2007.

Libertarias/Freedomfighters, film, directed by Vicente Aranda. Spain: Sogetel, Academy, Canal+ España, 1996.

Los días del pasado/The Days of the Past, film, directed by Mario Camus. Spain: Impala S.A., 1978.

Los girasoles ciegos/The Blind Sunflowers, film, directed by José Luis Cuerda. 2008. Spain: Sogecine, Estudios organizativos y proyectos cinematográficos, Producciones A Modiño, Producciones Labarouta, 2008.

Los lunes al sol/Mondays in the Sun, film, directed by Fernando León de Aranoa. Spain: Sogepaq, Elías Querejeta Producciones, Mediapro, 2002.

Los niños de Rusia/The Children of Russia, film, directed by Jaime Camino. Spain: Tibidabo Films, Televisió de Catalunya, Televisión Española, 2001.

Los otros/The Others, film, directed by Alejandro Amenábar. Spain: Cruise/Wagner Productions, Sogeine, Las Producciones del Escorpión, 2001.

Machuca, film, directed by Andrés Wood. Chile: Wood Producciones, Tornasol Films, Mamoun Hassan Productions, 2004.

Mar adentro/The Sea Inside, film, directed by Alejandro Amenábar. Spain: Sogepaq, Sogecine, Himenóptero, 2004.

Marcelino pan y vino/The Miracle of Marcelino, film, directed by Ladislao Vajda. Spain: Chamartín Producciones y Distribuciones, Falco Film, 1955.

Mi último tango/My Last Tango, film, directed by Luis César Amadori. Spain: Suevia Films, Cesáreo González Rodríguez, Producciones Benito Perojo, 1960.

Mi vida con Carlos/My Life with Carlos, film, directed by Germán Berger. Chile: Todo por las niñas, Cinedirecto Producciones, 2010.

Mutum, film, directed by Sandra Kogut. Brazil: Ravina Films, Gloria Films, 2007.

No Country for Old Men, film, directed by Ethan and Joel Coen. Spain: Paramount Vantage, Miramax, Scott Rudin Productions, 2007.

No-do/The Haunting, film, directed by Elio Quiroga. Spain: Eqlipse Producciones Cinematográficas, 2009.

Noches de Casablanca/Casablanca, Nest of Spies, film, directed by Henri Decoin. Spain: Finanziaria Cinematográfica Italiana, Intercontinental Productions, Producciones Cinematográficas Balcazar, 1963.

Nosotros somos así, film, directed by Valentín R. González. Spain: Sindicato de la industria cinematográfica, 1936.

O ano em que meus pais saíram de férias/The Year My Parents Went on Vacation, film, directed by Cao Hamburger. Brazil: Gullane, Caos Produções Cinematográficas, Miravista, 2006.

Ocho apellidos catalanes/Spanish Affair 2, film, directed by Emilio Martínez Lázaro. Spain: Lazona Films, Telecino Cinema, A.I.E., 2015.

Ocho apellidos vascos/Spanish Affair, film, directed by Emilio Martínez Lázaro. Spain: Snow Films A.I.E., Lazonafilms, Kowalski Films, 2014.

Pa negre/Black Bread, film, directed by Agustí Villaronga. Spain: Massa d'Or Produccions, 2010.

Paisito/Small Country, film, directed by Ana Díez. 2008. Uruguay, Spain, Argentina: Haddock Films, La Jolla Films, Tornasol Films, 2008.

Pájaros de papel/Paper Birds, film, directed by Emilio Aragón. Spain: Versátil Cinema S.L., Antena 3 Films, Canal+ España, Institut Català de les Indústries Culturals, Instituto de la Cinematografía y de las Artes Audiovisuales, 2010.

Paloma de papel/Paper Dove, film, directed by Fabrizio Aguilar. Peru: Luna Llena Films, 2003.

Pelo malo/Bad Hair, film, directed by Mariana Rondón. Venezuela: Artefactos, S.F., Hanfgarn & Ufer Film und TV Produktion, Imagen Latina, 2013.

Pepi, Luci, Bom y otras chicas del montón/Pepi, Luci, Bom and Other Girls on the Heap, film, directed by Pedro Almodóvar. Spain: Fígaro Films, 1980.

¿Qué he hecho yo para merecer esto!/What Have I Done to Deserve This?, film, directed by Pedro Almodóvar. Spain: Tesauro SA, Kaktus Producciones Cinematográficas, 1984.

¿Quién puede matar a un niño?/Who Can Kill a Child?, film, directed by Narciso Ibáñez Serrador. Spain: Penta Films, 1976.

Sanz y el secreto de su arte, film, directed by Francisco Sanz and Maximiliano Thous. Spain: Francisco Sanz Baldoví, 1918.

Scary Movie, film, directed by Keenan Ivory Wayans. USA: Wayans Brothers Entertainment, Gold/Miller Productions, Dimension Films, 2000.

Secretos del corazón, film, directed by by Montxo Armendáriz. Spain: Aiete-Ariane Films, Canal+ France, D.M.V.B Films, Eurimages, Euskal Media, Fábrica de Imagens, Instituto de la Cinematografía y de las Artes Audovisuales, Sogepaq, Mercury Films, 1997.

Spanish Movie, film, directed by Javier Ruiz Caldera. Spain: Telecinco Cinema, Mediaset, Think Studio, 2009.

Superman, film, directed by Richard Donner. USA: Dovemead Films, Film Export A.G., International Film Production, 1978.

Todo sobre mi madre/All about My Mother, film, directed by Pedro Almodóvar. Spain: El Deseo, Renn Productions, France 2 Cinéma, Vía Digital, 1999

Tómbola, film, directed by Luis Lucía. Spain: Guión Producciones Cinematográficas, 1962.

Tras el cristal/In a Glass Cage, film, directed by Agustí Villaronga. Spain: T.E.M. Productores, 1986.

Un rayo de luz, film, directed by Luis Lucía. Valladolid: Guión Producciones Cinematográficas, Producciones Benito Perojo, 1960.

Urte ilunak, film, directed by Arantxa Lazkano. Spain: José María Lara P.C., 1992.

Vacas/Cow, film, directed by Julio Medem. Spain: Departamento de cultura del Gobierno Vasco, Idea, Instituto de la Cinematografía y de las Artes Audiovisuales, Sogetel, 1992.

Valentín/Valentin, film, directed by Alejandro Agresti. Argentina: First Floor

Features, De Productie, RWA, Patagonik Film Group, DMVB Films, Duque
Films, Castelao Producciones, Surf Film, 2002.
Viridiana, film, directed by Luis Buñuel. Spain: Unión Industrial Cinematográfica,
Gustavo Alatriste, Films 59, 1961.
Viva Cuba, film, directed by Juan Carlos Cremata Alberti and Iraida Malberti
Cabrera. Cuba: Quad Producciones, DDC Films LLC, TVC Casa Productora,
Intituto Cubano de Radio y Televisión, La Colmenita, El Ingenio, 2005.
Voces inocentes/Innnocent Voices, film, directed by Luis Mandoki. Mexico:
Lawrence Bender Productions, MUVI Films, Organización Santo Domingo,
A Band Apart, Altavista Films, Santo Domingo Films, 2004.
Volver/To Return, film, directed by Pedro Almodóvar. Spain: El Deseo, 2006.

Shorts

Franco en Salamanca II, newsreel, Spain, 1937. https://www.youtube.com/
watch?v=q8ZzsEgHxJI (last accessed 28 July 2017).
Veo veo, film short, directed by Benjamín Ávila. Argentina: Habitación 1520
Producciones, 2011.

TV Series and Mini-series

Curso del 63. Spain: Zeppelin TV, 2009.
Curso del 73. Spain: Zeppelin TV, 2012.
Marisol, mini-series, directed by Manuel Palacios. Spain: Antena 3 Films,
Quiroptero films, Sagrerga TV, 2009.
Niños robados, mini-series, directed by Salvador Calvo. Spain: Mediaset España,
Mod Producciones, 2013.
Sálvame. Spain: Mediaset España Comunicación, La Fábrica de la Tele, 2011.
Supervivientes: perdidos en Honduras. Spain: Magnolia TV España, 2008.

Select Bibliography

Anonymous (1989), 'El rincón de la nostalgia: Adrianita, la niña del gato', *Revista Radiolandia*, 19 October.

Anonymous (1996), 'Marisol', *El Mundo Revista*, http://www.elmundo.es/lare vista/num185/textos/marisol1.html (last accessed 7 March 2018).

Anonymous (2003), 'Adiós a "La mala educación" de Pedro y su equipo', *El Periódico Extremadura*, 1 June, <http://www.elperiodicoextremadura.com/ noticias/caceres/adios-la-mala-educacion-pedro-equipo_56881.html> (last accessed 20 March 2017).

Anonymous (2006a), 'Cuban Director Reaches Out with "Viva Cuba"', *NBC News Today*, 27 January, <http://www.today.com/popculture/cuban-director-reaches-out-viva-cuba-wbna11062630> (last accessed 14 June 2017).

Anonymous (2006b), '*Pan's Labyrinth* Production Notes', *Visual Hollywood*, <http://visualhollywood.com/movies/PansLabyrinth/notes.pdf> (last accessed 28 July 2017).

Anonymous (2011), 'Denuncias de niños robados presentados ante la fiscalía', *El País*, 5 March, <http://elpais.com/elpais/2011/03/05/media/1299326234_ 720215.html> (last accessed 23 February 2017).

Anonymous (2012), 'Muere el escritor Emili Teixidor a los 78 años', *La Vanguardia*, 19 June, <http://www.lavanguardia.com/libros/20120619/ 54313582518/emili-teixidor.html> (last accessed 14 June 2017).

Anonymous (2014), 'Human Rights Abusers in Franco-era Spain Could Be Tried in Argentina', *The Guardian*, 2 November, <https://www.theguardian.com/ world/2014/nov/02/buenos-aires-spain-franco-argentina> (last accessed 27 June 2016).

Anonymous (2016), 'Canarias tramita ya la primera ley de niños robados de España', *Nueva Tribuna*, 8 November, <http://www.nuevatribuna.es/artic ulo/sociedad/canarias-tramita-primera-ley-ninhos-robados-espanha/201611 08173651133551.html> (last accessed 23 February 2017).

Abajo de Pablos, Juan Julio de (1998), *Mis charlas con Antonio del Amo*, Valladolid: Fancy Editores.

Abella, Rafael (1996), *La vida cotidiana bajo el régimen de Franco*, Madrid: Ediciones temas de hoy.

Acevedo Kanopa, Agustín (2012), 'Entrevista a Paula Markovitch, directora de *El premio*', *El pijama de Hepburn*, 4 April, <http://elpijamadehepburn.blogspot.

com/2012/04/entrevista-paula-markovitch-directora.html> (last accessed 6 July 2016).

Agamben, Giorgio (1993), *Infancy and History: The Destruction of Experience*, trans. Liz Heron, London: Verso.

Agamben, Giorgio (1998), *Homo Sacer*, trans. Marilene Raiola, Stanford: Stanford University Press.

Aguilar, José and Miguel Losada (2008), *Marisol*, Madrid: T&B Editores.

Aguirresarobe, Javier (2004), '*El viaje de Carol*: más allá que una mirada', in *Luces y sombras en el cine de Imanol Uribe*, Valladolid: Semana Internacional de Cine, pp. 208–21.

Aldana Reyes, Xavier (2017), *Spanish Gothic: National Identity, Collaboration and Cultural Adaptation*, London: Palgrave MacMillan.

Aldecoa, Josefina (1983), *Los niños de la guerra*, Madrid: Ediciones Generales Anaya.

Alexander, George (2003), 'Keenan Ivory Wayans', in *Why We Make Movies: Black Filmmakers Talk about the Magic of Cinema*, New York: Harlem Moon, pp. 133–53.

Allbritton, Dean (2014), 'Recovering Childhood: Virulence, Ghosts, and Black Bread', *Bulletin of Hispanic Studies*, 91: 6, 619–36.

Alted Vigil, Alicia (1996), 'Las consecuencias de la guerra civil española en los niños de la República: de la dispersión al exilio', *Espacio tiempo y forma. Serie V, Historia contemporánea* 9, pp. 207–28.

Altman, Rick (1999), *Film/Genre*, London: British Film Institute.

Álvarez Pérez, Antonio (1959), *Enciclopedia intuitiva, sintética y práctica ajustada al cuestionario oficial: primer grado*, Valladolid: Miñón.

Amago, Samuel (2013), *Spanish Cinema in the Global Context: Film on Film*, London and New York: Routledge.

Amatria, Isabel (1992), 'Todos los niños son actores', *Gente*, 37–8.

Archibald, David (2012), *The War that Won't Die: The Spanish Civil War in Cinema*, Manchester: Manchester University Press.

Armengou, Montse (2011), 'Niños robados', in *Diccionario de memoria histórica: Conceptos contra el olvido*, ed. Rafael Escudero Alday, Madrid: Los libros de la catarata, pp. 123–9.

Armengou, Monste and Ricard Belis (2016), *Los internados del miedo*, Barcelona: Ara Llibres.

Armengou, Montse, Ricard Belis, and Ricard Vinyes (2002), *Los niños perdidos del franquismo*, Barcelona: Plaza Janés.

Bakhtin, Mikhail Mikhaïlovich (1981), *The Dialogic Imagination: Four Essays*, trans Caryl Emerson and Michael Holquist, ed. Michael Holquist, Austin: University of Texas Press.

___(1984), *Rabelais and His World*, Bloomington: Indiana University Press.

Ballesteros, Isolina (1996), 'Las niñas del cine español: la evasión infantil en *El espíritu de la colmena*, *El sur* y *Los años oscuros*', *Revista hispánica moderna*, 49: 2, 232–42.

___(2009), 'Performing Identities in the Cinema of Pedro Almodóvar', in *All About Almodóvar: A Passion for Cinema*, eds Brad Epps and Despina Kakoudaki, Minneapolis: University of Minnesota Press, pp. 71–100.

Barreiro, Javier (1999), *Marisol frente a Pepa Flores*, Barcelona: Plaza & Janés.

Bayarri, Francesc (1991), 'La juez dicta prisión incondicional para el excantante Joselito', *El País*, 1 September, <http://elpais.com/diario/1991/09/01/espana/683676011_850215.html> (last accessed 31 May 2017).

Beck, Jay and Vicente Rodríguez Ortega (2008), *Contemporary Spanish Cinema and Genre*, Manchester: Manchester University Press.

Bonet, Blai (1958), *El Mar: Novel·la*, Barcelona: Aymà.

Boynton, Susan (1998), 'The Liturgical Role of Children in Monastic Customaries from the Central Middle Ages', *Studia Liturgica*, 28: 2, 194–209.

Braggio, Ana Karine, Alexandre Felipe Fiuza, and Marcia Magalhães Debiazi (2014), 'Educação e ditaduras: a memória traumática nos filmes *Machuca* e *La lengua de las mariposas*', *Educação Unisinos*, 18: 2, 193–201.

Brasó, Enrique (2003), 'Interview with Carlos Saura on *Cría cuervos* [*Raise Ravens*] and *Elisa, vida mía* [*Elisa, My Life*]', in *Carlos Saura Interviews*, ed. Linda M. Willem, Jackson: University of Mississippi Press, pp. 42–51.

Braudy, Leo (1999), 'From the World in a Frame, Genre: The Conventions of Connection', in *Film Theory and Criticism*, New York: Oxford University Press, pp. 613–29.

Brodsky, Roberto (2001), *Últimos días de la historia*, Santiago de Chile: Ediciones B.

Buckley, Christina A. (1998), '*Los años oscuros*: Silence against Micro/Macro-Nationalist Ideology', in *Cine-Lit III*, eds George Cabello-Castellet, Jaume Martí-Olivella, and Guy H. Wood, Corvallis: Oregon State University, pp. 131–43.

Burdeau, Emmanuel and Jean-Michel Frodon (2004), 'Pedro Almodóvar: "Il m'a fallu dix ans pour écrire ce scénario"', *Cahiers du Cinéma*, 590: 5, 24–8.

Burnett, Frances Hodgson (1996 [1885]), *Little Lord Fauntleroy*, Charlottesville: University of Virginia Library.

Bustelo, Eduardo S. (2007), *El recreo de la infancia: argumentos para otro comienzo*, Buenos Aires: Siglo XXI.

Camporesi, Valeria (2007), 'Para una historia de lo no nacional en el cine español: Ladislao Vajda y el caso de los huidos de las persecuciones antisemitas en España', in *Cine, nación y nacionalidad en España*, eds Nancy Berthier and Jean-Claude Seguin, Madrid: Casa de Velázquez, pp. 61–74.

Carrera, Javier (2016), 'El Doctor Vela decía que los niños no se podían enseñar a nadie porque eran hijos del pecado', *Cadena Ser*, 14 December, <http://cadenaser.com/programa/2016/12/14/hoy_por_hoy/1481710466_340212.html> (last accessed 23 February 2017).

Carrón, C. D. and L. Seoane (2011), 'Los Goya hablan catalán: *Pa negre* gana a De la Iglesia y Bollaín', *La Razón*, 16 February, <http://www.larazon.es/de

talle_hemeroteca/noticias/LA_RAZON_358590/661-alex-de-la-iglesia-ten go-unas-ganas-locas-de-conocer-al-proximo#.Ttt12V7R7be80r6> (last accessed 13 March 2014).

Cartmell, Deborah and Imelda Whelehan (2013), *Adaptations: From Text to Screen, Screen to Text*, London and New York: Routledge.

Casanova, Julián (2016), 'Disremembering Francoism: What is at Stake in Spain's Memory Wars?', in *Interrogating Francoism: History and Dictatorship in Twentieth-Century Spain*, trans. Linda Palfreeman and Helen Graham, ed. Helen Graham, London: Bloomsbury Publishing, pp. 203–22.

Casas, Romina (2013), 'La verdad de los lugares, con su terrible carga, complementa la ficción', *Centro Cultural de la Memoria Haroldo Conti*, 12 August 2013, <http://conti.derhuman.jus.gov.ar/2013/08/noticias-entrevista-paula-markovitch.shtml> (last accessed 6 July 2016).

Casavantes Bradford, Anita (2014), 'Epilogue: Understanding Elián', in *The Revolution is for the Children: The Politics of Childhood in Havana and Miami, 1959–1962*, Chapel Hill: University of North Carolina Press, pp. 184–212.

Castro, Rosalía de (1991), *Poems*, trans. Anna-Marie Aldaz, Barbara N. Gantt, and Anne C. Bromley, eds Anna-Marie Aldaz, Barbara N. Gantt, and Anne C. Bromley, Albany: State University of New York Press.

Castro de Paz, José Luis (2005), 'Raíces profundas (mito, guerra e infancia en el cine español)', in *El espíritu de la colmena . . . 31 años después*, ed. Julio Pérez Perucha, Valencia: Institut Valencià de Cinematografía Ricardo Muñoz Suay, pp. 359–88.

Cenarro Lagunas, Ángela (2006), *La sonrisa de Falange: Auxilio social en la guerra civil y en la posguerra*, Barcelona: Crítica.

Charnock, Greig, Thomas Purcell, and Ramon Ribera-Fumaz (2012), '¡Indígnate!: The 2011 Popular Protests and the Limits to Democracy in Spain', *Capital & Class*, 36: 1, 3–11.

Cirlot, Juan Eduardo (2002), *A Dictionary of Symbols*, trans. Jack Sage, Mineola: Dover Publications.

Ciuró, P. W. (1963), *La ventriloquía: este arte al alcance de todos*, Madrid: Artes gráficas.

Clark, Roger and Keith McDonald (2010), '"A Constant Transit of Finding": Fantasy as Realisation in *Pan's Labyrinth*', *Children's Literature in Education*, 41: 1, 52–63.

Colubi, Pepe (2009), 'Los tópicos de la españolada', *El País*, 4 December, <http://elpais.com/diario/2009/12/04/tentaciones/1259954575_850215.htm> (last accessed 23 August 2016).

Conde, Francisco Javier (1942), *Contribución a la doctrina del caudillaje*, Madrid: Ediciones de la Vicesecretaría de Educación Popular.

Connor, Steven (2001), 'Violence, Ventriloquism and the Vocalic Body', in *Psychoanalysis and Performance*, eds Patrick Campbell and Adrian Kear, London and New York: Routledge, pp. 75–93.

Córdoba García, David (2005), 'Teoría queer: reflexiones sobre sexo, sexualidad e identidad. Hacia una politización de la sexualidad', in *Teoría Queer: Políticas Bolleras, Maricas, Trans, Mestizas*, eds David Córdoba, Javier Sáez, and Paco Vidarte, Barcelona: Egales, pp. 21–66.

Craig, Ian (2001), *Children's Classics under Franco: Censorship of the* 'William' *Books and* The Adventures of Tom Sawyer, Bern: Peter Lang.

Cros, Edmond (1994), 'Lecture politique de *Demonios en el jardín*', *Sociocriticism*, 10: 19–20, 185–95.

Crumbaugh, Justin (2015), 'Spectacle as Spectralization, Untimely Timelessness: *Marcelino pan y vino* and Mid-1950s' Francoism', *Journal of Spanish Cultural Studies*, 15: 3, 337–50.

Curry, Richard (1996), 'Clarifying the Enigma: "Reading" Víctor Erice's *El espíritu de la colmena*', *Bulletin of Hispanic Studies*, 73: 3, 269–76.

Davies, Ann (2006), 'The Beautiful and the Monstrous Masculine: The Male Body and Horror in *El espinazo del diablo* (Guillermo Del Toro 2001)', *Studies in Hispanic Cinemas (New Title: Studies in Spanish & Latin American Cinemas)*, 3: 3, 135–47.

___(2009), 'Woman and Home: Gender and the Theorisation of Basque (National) Cinema', *Journal of Spanish Cultural Studies*, 10: 3, 359–72.

___(2011), 'The Final Girl and Monstrous Mother of *El Orfanato*', in *Spain on Screen*, Basingstoke: Palgrave, pp. 79–92.

___(2016), 'Spanish Gothic Cinema: The Hidden Continuities of a Hidden Genre', in *Global Genres, Local Films: The Transnational Dimension of Spanish Cinema*, eds Elena Oliete-Aldea, Beatriz Oria, and Juan A. Tarancón, London: Bloomsbury, pp. 115–26.

De Grandis, Rita (2011), 'The Innocent Eye', in *The Utopian Impulse in Latin America*, New York: Palgrave Macmillan, pp. 235–56.

Del Amo, Alfonso (1996a), *Catálogo general del cine de la Guerra Civil*, Madrid: Cátedra; Filmoteca Española.

Del Amo, Alfonso (1996b), 'Franco en Salamanca I y II', in *Catálogo general del cine de la guerra civil*, ed. Alfonso del Amo, Madrid: Cátedra; Filmoteca Española, pp. 449–50.

Delgado, María (2008), 'Yesterday's Children: The Young and the Damned', *Sight and Sound*, 18: 4, 45.

Demasi, Carlos and Aldo Marchesi (2004), 'Un repaso a la teoría de los dos demonios', in *El presente de la dictadura: estudios y reflexiones a 30 años del golpe de estado en Uruguay*, eds Aldo Marchesi, Vania Markarian, Álvaro Rico, and Jaime Yaffé, Montevideo: Ediciones Trilce, pp. 67–74.

Derrida, Jacques (1986), *The Art of Mémories*, New York: Columbia University Press.

Derrida, Jacques and Paul De Man (1989), *Memoires for Paul De Man: The Wellek Library Lectures at the University of California, Irvine*, New York: Columbia University Press.

Deveny, Thomas G. (1999), *Cain on Screen: Contemporary Spanish Cinema*. Lanham: The Scarecrow Press.

___(2012), '*Pa negre* (*Pan negro*): Bildungsroman/bildungsfilm de memoria histórica', *La nueva literatura hispánica*, 16, 397–416.

___(2014), 'Once upon a Time in Spain in 1944: The Morphology of *El laberinto del fauno*', *Cine y . . .*, 1: 1, 1–12.

Diestro-Dópido, Mar (2013), *Pan's Labyrinth*, London: Palgrave Macmillan.

D'Lugo, Marvin (1991), *The Films of Carlos Saura: The Practice of Seeing*, Princeton: Princeton University Press.

___(1997), *Guide to the Cinema of Spain*, Westport: Greenwood Publishing Group.

___ (2009), 'Postnostalgia in *Bad Education*: Written on the Body of Sara Montiel', in *All About Almodóvar: A Passion for Cinema*, eds Brad Epps and Despina Kakoudaki, Minneapolis: University of Minnesota Press, pp. 357–85.

Domínguez García, Javier (2009), 'St. James the Moor-Slayer, a New Challenge to Spanish National Discourse in the Twenty-first Century', *International Journal of Iberian Studies*, 22: 1, 69–78.

Duva, Jesús and Natalia Junquera (2011), *Vidas robadas: una investigación periodística rigurosa que arroja luz sobre el robo de niños en España y el papel de las instituciones. miles de vidas robadas*, Madrid: Santillana Ediciones.

Eagleton, Terry (2007), *Ideology: An Introduction*, London: Verso.

Edelman, Lee (2004), *No Future: Queer Theory and the Death Drive*, Durham, NC: Duke University Press.

Eledín Parraguez, Amante (2002), *Tres años para nacer*, Santiago de Chile: Del Gallo.

Elena, Alberto (2001), 'El cantor del cine Rex: una revisión del cine de Joselito', *Archivos de la Filmoteca: Revista de estudios históricos sobre la imagen*, 38, 48–61.

___(2010), *La llamada de África: estudios sobre el cine colonial español*, Barcelona: Edicions Bellaterra.

Erice, Víctor (2004), 'El latido del tiempo', *El País*, 23 January, <http://www.elpais.com/articulo/cine/latido/tiempo/elpepuculcin/20040123elpepicin_7/Te s> (last accessed 18 November 2007).

Esteso Poves, María José (2012), *Niños robados: de la represión franquista al negocio*, Madrid: Diagonal.

Evans, Peter W. (2004), 'Marisol: The Spanish Cinderella', in *Spanish Popular Cinema*, eds Antonio Lázaro Reboll and Andrew Willis, Manchester and New York: Manchester University Press, pp. 129–51.

Faulkner, Sally (2006), *A Cinema of Contradiction: Spanish Film in the 1960s*, Edinburgh: Edinburgh University Press.

Faulkner, Sally (2013), *A History of Spanish Film: Cinema and Society 1910–2010*, London: Bloomsbury Publishing.

Fehimović, Dunja (2015), 'Not Child's Play: Tactics and Strategies in *Viva Cuba* and *Habanastation*', *Bulletin of Latin American Research*, 34: 4, 503–16.

Feierstein, Daniel (2014), *Genocide as Social Practice: Reorganizing Society under the Nazis and Argentina's Military Juntas*, New Brunswick, NJ: Rutgers University Press.

Fernández Santos, Ángel and Víctor Erice (1976), *El espíritu de la colmena*, Madrid: Elías Querejeta Ediciones.

Foucault, Michel (1976), *History of Sexuality, Volume 1: An Introduction*, trans. Robert Hurley, New York: Random House.

___(1979), *Discipline & Punish*, New York: Vintage Books.

___(1982), *This is Not a Pipe*, trans. James Harkness, Berkeley: University of California Press.

___(2003), '*Society Must be Defended': Lectures at the Collège de France, 1975–76*, New York: Picador.

Fouz-Hernández, Santiago (2004), 'Identity without Limits: Queer Debates and Representation in Contemporary Spain', *Journal of Iberian and Latin American Research*, 10: 1, 63–81.

Fuentes, Víctor (2009), '*Bad Education*: Fictional Autobiography and Meta-film Noir', in *All about Almodóvar: A Passion for Cinema*, eds Brad Epps and Despina Kakoudaki, Minneapolis: University of Minnesota Press, pp. 429–45.

García Lorca, Federico (1963), 'Retablillo de Don Cristóbal', in *Obras Completas*, ed. Arturo Del Hoyo, Madrid: Aguilar, pp. 1,019–43.

García Roldán, Ángel (1988), *A boca de noche*, Barcelona: Plaza & Janés.

___ (2002), 'El viaje del guión', in *El viaje de Carol*, Madrid: Ocho y medio libros de cine, pp. 7–12.

Garibotto, Verónica Inés (2015), 'Private Narratives and Infant Views: Iconizing 1970s Militancy in Contemporary Argentine Cinema', *Hispanic Research Journal*, 16: 3, 257–72.

Gavela Ramos, Yvonne (2011), 'El acto colectivo de recordar: historia y fantasía en *El espíritu de la colmena* y *El laberinto del fauno*', *Bulletin of Hispanic Studies*, 88: 2, 179–96.

Gavilán Sánchez, Juan Antonio (2002), 'Conversación con Carlos Saura', in *Conversaciones con cineastas españoles*, Córdoba: Universidad de Córdoba, pp. 47–89.

Georgieva, Margarita (2013), *The Gothic Child*, Basingstoke: Palgrave Macmillan.

Gibson, Ian (2006), *La vida de Antonio Machado: ligero de equipaje*, Madrid: Santillana Ediciones.

Gil Poisa, María (2016), '¿Qué es un fantasma? Trauma pasado y fantasía en el cine contemporáneo sobre la Guerra Civil española: el cine de Guillermo Del Toro', *Hispania*, 99: 1, 128–36.

Gillespie, Richard (2008), *Soldados de Perón: historia crítica sobre los montoneros*, trans. Antoni Pigrau, Buenos Aires: Editorial Sudamericana.

Golob, Stephanie R. (2008), '*Volver*: The Return of/to Transitional Justice Politics in Spain', *Journal of Spanish Cultural Studies*, 9: 2, 127–41.

Gómez, Concha (1998), 'Montxo Armendáriz', in *Diccionario del cine español*, eds José Luis Borau, Carlos F. Heredero, and María Pastor, Madrid: Alianza Editorial, pp. 83–4.

Gómez, José Martí (1995), *La España del estraperlo, 1936–1952*, Barcelona: Planeta.

Gómez López-Quiñones, Antonio (2012), 'Fairies, Maquis, and Children without

Schools', in *Representing History, Class, and Gender in Spain and Latin America: Children and Adolescents in Film*, eds Carolina Rocha and Georgia Seminet, New York: Palgrave Macmillan, pp. 49–62.

González Portilla, Manuel and José Urrutikoetxea Lizarraga (2012), 'El pan del franquismo: primer franquismo, mercado negro y "venganza social"', in *La dictadura franquista: la institucionalització d'un règim*, eds Antoni Segura, Andreu Mayayo, and Teresa Abelló, Barcelona: Universitat de Barcelona, pp. 237–59.

Goody, Jack (2010), *Myth, Ritual and the Oral*, Cambridge: Cambridge University Press.

Graham, Helen (2004), 'Coming to Terms with the Past: Spain's Memory Wars', *History Today*, 5, 29–31.

___(2012), *War and its Shadow: Spain's Civil War in Europe's Long Twentieth Century*, Brighton: Sussex Academic Press.

Grantham, Barry (2001), *Playing Commedia: A Training Guide to Commedia Techniques*, Portsmouth, NH: Heinemann Educational Books, 2001.

Griswold, Jerome (1996), 'Motherland, Fatherland, or Oedipal Politics: *Little Lord Fauntleroy*', in *The Classic American Children's Story*, New York: Penguin, pp. 93–103.

Gubern, Román (2001), 'Teoría y práctica del star-system infantil', *Archivos de la Filmoteca*, 38, 9–15.

Gubern, Román, José Enrique Monterde, Julio Pérez Perucha, Esteve Riambau, and Casimiro Torreiro (1995), *Historia del cine español*, Madrid: Cátedra.

Haberman, Clyde (2015), 'Children of Argentina's "Disappeared" Reclaim Past, with Help', *The New York Times*, 11 October, http://www.nytimes.com/2015/10/12/us/children-of-argentinas-disappeared-reclaim-past-with-help.html?_r=0 (last accessed 22 September 2016).

Haddu, Miriam (2014), 'Reflected Horrors: Violence, War, and the Image in Guillermo del Toro's *El espinazo del diablo/The Devil's Backbone* (2001)', in *The Transnational Fantasies of Guillermo Del Toro*, eds Ann Davies, Deborah Shaw, and Dolores Tierney, New York: Palgrave Macmillan, pp. 143–59.

Halberstam, Judith (2005), *In a Queer Time and Place*, New York: New York University Press.

Hart, Stephen M. (2015), *Latin American Cinema*, London: Reaktion Books.

Heredero, Carlos F. (1993), 'Los niños del estrellato', in *Las huellas del tiempo: cine español 1951–1961*, Valencia: Filmoteca de la Generalitat Valenciana, pp. 226–34.

___(1998), 'Erice, Víctor', in *Diccionario del cine español*, eds José Luis Borau, Carlos F. Heredero, Julio Pérez Perucha, and Esteve Riambau, Madrid: Alianza Editorial, pp. 312–13.

___ (1998), *Historias de vida y de ficción: el cine según Manuel Gutiérrez Aragón*, Huesca: Festival de Cine de Huesca.

Hirschberg, Lynn (2004), 'The Redeemer', *The New York Times Magazine*, 5 September, <http://www.nytimes.com/2004/09/05/magazine/the-redeemer.html?_r=0> (last accessed 14 January 2016).

Hogan, Erin (2011), *La patria es la infancia: The Vocalization and Ventriloquism of Spanish Civil War and Post-war Children in the* cine con niño *and* nuevo cine con niño *(1973–2010)*, University of California Los Angeles.

___ (2012), 'Tomando partido: Soccer and Political Opposition in *O ano em que meus pais saíram de férias* (Cao Hamburger 2006) and *Paisito* (Ana Díez 2008)', *Transnationality in the Luso-Hispanic World*, eds Anamaria Buzatu, Covadonga Lamar Prieto, Hilary Larson, Moira Nardi, Brenda Ortiz, Chase W. Raymond, and Belén Villarreal, University of California eScholarship, pp. 51–60.

___(2013), 'The Voice, Body and Ventriloquism of Marisol in *Tómbola* (Lucía, 1962)', *Studies in Spanish & Latin American Cinemas*, 10: 1, 101–15.

___ (2016a), 'A Politics of Listening in Isabel Coixet's *Escuchando al juez Garzón* (2011)', *International Journal of Iberian Studies*, 29: 1, 65–79.

___(2016b), 'Queering Post-war Childhood: *Pa negre* (Agustí Villaronga, Spain 2010)', *Hispanic Research Journal*, 17: 1, 1–18.

Holquist, Michael (2002), *Dialogism: Bakhtin and His World*, London: Routledge.

Hopewell, John (1986), *Out of the Past: Spanish Cinema after Franco*, London: British Film Institute.

Hubner, Laura (2010), '*Pan's Labyrinth*, Fear and the Fairy Tale', in *Fear itself: Reasoning the Unreasonable*, eds Stephen Hessel and Michèle Huppert, Amsterdam: Rodopi, pp. 45–62.

Hutcheon, Linda (1985), *A Theory of Parody: The Teachings of Twentieth-Century Art Forms*, New York: Methuen.

___(2013), *A Theory of Adaptation* (second edition), Oxon: Routledge.

Izquierdo Anrubia, José (n.d.), 'Francisco Sanz Baldovi', Historia de Anna siglo XIX, <http://www.historiadeanna.com/SXIX/sanz.pdf> (last accessed 15 June 2017).

Jabois, Manuel (2015), 'Carmencita Franco y el amor', *El País*, 22 November, <http://politica.elpais.com/politica/2015/11/20/actualidad/1448035561_476032> (last accessed 6 June 2017).

Jenkins, David (2006), 'Guillermo Del Toro: Interview', *Timeout*, 11 August 2008, <https://www.timeout.com/london/film/guillermo-del-toro-intervi ew-3> (last accessed 15 June 2017).

Jolivet, Anne-Marie (2003), *La pantalla subliminal:* Marcelino pan y vino *según Vajda*, Valencia: Ediciones de la Filmoteca, Institut Valencià de Cinematografia Ricardo Muñoz Suay.

Jones, Tanya (2010), *Studying Pan's Labyrinth*, Leighton Buzzard: Auteur.

Jordan, Barry and Mark Allinson (2005), *Spanish Cinema: A Student's Guide*, London: Hodder Arnold.

Jordan, Barry and Rikki Morgan-Tamosunas (1998), *Contemporary Spanish Cinema*, Manchester: Manchester University Press.

Juliá, Santos (2004), *Historias de las dos Españas*, Madrid: Taurus.

Junquera, Natalia (2011), 'Más de 200 personas piden a la puerta de la fiscalía que investigue el robo de niños durante el franquismo', *El País*, 27 January, <http://

www.elpais.com/articulo/espana/200/personas/piden/puerta/fiscalia/
investigue/robo/ninos/durante/franquismo/elpepisoc/20110127elpepunac_
8/Tes> (last accessed 13 January).

Karesh, Sara E. and Mitchell M. Hurvitz (2006), *Encyclopedia of Judaism*, New York: Facts on File.

Kinder, Marsha (1983), 'The Children of Franco in the New Spanish Cinema', *Quarterly Review of Film & Video*, 8: 2, 57–76.

Kristeva, Julia (1982), *Powers of Horror: An Essay on Abjection*, trans. Leon S. Roudiez, New York: Columbia University Press.

Labanyi, Jo (1998), *Rescuing the Living Dead from the Dustbin of History: Popular Memory and Postwar Trauma in Contemporary Spanish Film and Fiction*, Bristol: University of Bristol, Department of Hispanic, Portuguese and Latin American Studies Bristol.

___(2007), 'Memory and Modernity in Democratic Spain: The Difficulty of Coming to Terms with the Spanish Civil War', *Poetics Today*, 28: 1, 89–116.

Larrosa, Jorge (2007), 'El rostro engimático de la infancia: a modo de presentación', in *Miradas cinematográficas sobre la infancia: niños atrevesando el paisaje*, eds Jorge Larrosa, Inês A. de Castro, and José de Sousa, Madrid: Miño y Dávila, pp. 17–24.

Lázaro-Reboll, Antonio (2007), 'The Transnational Reception of *El espinazo del diablo* (Guillermo Del Toro 2001)', *Hispanic Research Journal*, 8: 1, 39–51.

___ (2012), *Spanish Horror Film*, Edinburgh: Edinburgh University Press.

Lebeau, Vicky (2008), *Childhood and Cinema*, London: Reaktion Books.

León Solís, Fernando (2003), *Negotiating Spain and Catalonia: Competing Narratives of National Identity*, Bristol: Intellect Books.

Lie, Nadia (2009), 'Monstruos y espectros en el imaginario cinematográfico de la posguerra civil española: *El espíritu de la colmena* y *El laberinto del fauno*', *Romanica Gandensia* Alianzas entre historia y ficción: homenaje a Patrick Collard, 37, 259–69.

Lindsay, Richard (2012), 'Menstruation as Heroine's Journey in *Pan's Labyrinth*', *Journal of Religion & Film*, 1: 1, 1–27.

Lury, Karen (2010), *The Child in Film: Tears, Fears and Fairy Tales*, London: I. B. Tauris.

Machado, Antonio (1977), *Poesías*, Buenos Aires: Editorial Losada.

___(1982), *Selected Poems*, trans. Alan S. Trueblood, Cambridge, MA: Harvard University Press.

___(1983), *Times Alone: Selected Poems of Antonio Machado*, trans. Robert Bly, Middletown: Wesleyan University Press.

___(1998), *Campos de Castilla*, Madrid: Editorial Biblioteca Nueva.

MacKenzie, Suzie (2004), 'All about My Father', in *Pedro Almodóvar Interviews*, ed. Paula Willoquet-Maricondi, Jackson: University of Mississippi Press, pp. 154–61.

MacLeod, Anne Scott (1994), 'Good Democrats: *Ragged Dick* and *Little Lord*

Fauntleroy', in *American Childhood: Essays on Children's Literature of the Nineteenth and Twentieth Centuries*, Athens, GA: University of Georgia Press, pp. 77–86.

Maguire, Geoffrey (2017), *The Politics of Postmemory: Violence and Victimhood in Contemporary Argentine Culture*, Cham, Switzerland: Palgrave Macmillan.

Manzano, Valeria (2014), *The Age of Youth in Argentina: Culture, Politics, and Sexuality from Perón to Videla*, Chapel Hill: University of North Carolina Press Books.

Maqua Lara, Javier (1998), 'Marcelino pan y vino', in *Diccionario del cine español*, eds José Luis Borau, Carlos F. Heredero, and María Pastor, Madrid: Alianza Editorial, p. 539.

Martín, Annabel (2005), 'Basque Postnationalism, Identity Politics, and the Reconfiguration of Transgression in *Urte Ilunak*', *Chasqui*, 34, 95–108.

Martín-Cabrera, Luis (2011), *Radical Justice: Spain and the Southern Cone beyond Market and State*, Lewisburg, PA: Bucknell University Press.

Martín-Cabrera, Luis and Daniel Noemi Voionmaa (2007), 'Class Conflict, State of Exception and Radical Justice in *Machuca* by Andrés Wood', *Journal of Latin American Cultural Studies*, 16: 1, 63–80.

Martín Gaite, Carmen (1987), *Usos amorosos de la postguerra española*, Barcelona: Editorial Anagrama.

Martí-Olivella, Jaume (1997), 'Regendering Spain's Political Bodies: Nationality and Gender in the Films of Pilar Miró and Arantxa Lazcano', in *Refiguring Spain: Cinema / Media / Representation*, ed. Marsha Kinder, Durham, NC: Duke University Press, pp. 215–38.

___(2003), *Basque Cinema: An Introduction. Vol. 7*, Reno: University of Nevada Press.

Martin-Márquez, Susan (2008), *Disorientations: Spanish Colonialism in Africa and the Performance of Identity*, New Haven: Yale University Press.

Marzal Felici, Javier (2006), 'Una poética del silencio: relato mítico y aprendizaje del tiempo', in *El espíritu de la colmena . . . 31 años después*, ed. Julio Pérez Perucha, Valencia: Institut Valenciá de Cinematografía (I.V.A.C.); Asociación Española de Historiadores del Cine (A.E.H.C.); Fundación Autor, pp. 35–52.

Matute, Ana María (2011), *Primera Memoria*, Barcelona: Destino.

Mayora, Jon (1992), 'Me gusta la ficción', *El correo español: El pueblo vasco*, 23 November, 6.

Miles, Robert J. (2011), 'Reclaiming Revelation: *Pan's Labyrinth* and the *Spirit of the Beehive*', *Quarterly Review of Film and Video*, 28, 195–203.

Moix, Terenci (1993), *Suspiros de España*, Barcelona: Plaza & Janés.

Morales, José Luis (1979), 'Marisol nos cuenta su vida', *Interviú*, 4: 169, 24–8.

Muir, Edward (2005), 'Rites of Passage', in *Ritual in Early Modern Europe*, Cambridge: Cambridge University Press, pp. 21–61.

Muñoz, Pedro M. and Marcelino C. Marcos (2010), *España ayer y hoy*, Upper Saddle River: Pearson.

Núñez Prieto, Iván (2003), *La ENU entre dos siglos: ensayo histórico sobre la Escuela Nacional Unificada*, Santiago: LOM Ediciones.

Ofer, Inbal (2009), *Señoritas in Blue: The Making of a Female Political Elite in Franco's Spain*, Brighton: Sussex Academic Press.

Otero, Luis (2004), *La sección femenina*, Madrid: Editorial Edaf.

Park, Moisés (2014), 'Capítulo 4 iniciación sexual y política: paraíso perdido y reconsideraciones del duelo en *Machuca* de Andrés Wood', in *Figuraciones del deseo y coyunturas generacionales en literatura y cine postdictatorial*, New York: Peter Lang, pp. 115–54.

Pavlović, Tatjana (2011), *The Mobile Nation: España cambia de piel (1954–1964)*, Bristol: Intellect Books.

Pavlović, Tatjana, Chris Perriam, and Nuria Triana Toribio (2013), 'Stars, Modernity, and Celebrity Culture', in *A Companion to Spanish Cinema*, eds Jo Labanyi and Tatjana Pavlović, Chichester: Wiley-Blackwell, pp. 319–42.

Pavlović, Tatjana, Inmaculada Alvarez, Rosana Blanco-Cano, Anitra Grisales, Alejandra Osorio, and Alejandra Sánchez (2009), *100 Years of Spanish Cinema*, West Sussex: John Wiley & Sons.

Pedraza, Pilar (2007), *Agustí Villaronga*. Madrid: Ediciones AKAL.

Pelauzy, María Antonia (1978), 'Elements of Popular Theater', in *Spanish Folk Crafts*, eds María Antonia Pelauzy and Francesc Català Roca, Barcelona: Editorial Blume, pp. 185–93.

Pereira-Muro, Carmen (2003), *Culturas de España*, Stamford: Cengage Learning.

Pereira Zazo, Óscar (2002), 'Cuestión de puntos de vista: la mirada infantil en *El espíritu de la colmena y Secretos del corazón*', in *La cultura mediàtica: modes de representació i estratègies discursives*, eds Gavaldà Roca, Josep V., Carmen Gregori Signes, and Ramón X. Rosselló Ivars, Valencia: Universitat de València, pp. 227–37.

Pérez, Jorge (2011), 'The Queer Children of Almodóvar: *La mala educación* and the Re-sexualization of Biopolitical Bodies', *Studies in Hispanic Cinemas (New Title: Studies in Spanish & Latin American Cinemas)*, 8: 2, 145–57.

Pérez Gómez, Miguel A. (2010), '*Tómbola* como paradigma del cine con niño español', *Frame*, 6, 146–58.

Pérez-Sánchez, Gema (2007), *Queer Transitions in Contemporary Spanish Culture*, Albany: State University of New York Press.

Pozas, Alberto (2017), 'Primera petición de cárcel contra un médico por el robo de bebés', *Cadena Ser*, 12 January, <http://cadenaser.com/ser/2017/01/12/tribunales/1484183007_852407.html> (last accessed 23 February 2017).

Pramaggiore, Maria (2017), '*Suspendido en el tiempo*: Children and Contemporary Spanish Horror', in *Tracing the Borders of Spanish Horror Cinema and Television*, ed. Jorge Marí, New York: Routledge, pp. 67–87.

Preston, Paul (1999), 'Italy and Spain in Civil War and World War, 1936–1943', in *Spain and the Great Powers in the Twentieth Century*, eds Sebastian Balfour and Paul Preston, London: Routledge, pp. 151–84.

___(2001), Prólogo: la guerrilla de los años cuarenta', in *La resistencia armada contra Franco*, ed. Francisco Moreno Gómez, Barcelona: Editorial Crítica, pp. vii–xiv.

Prout, Ryan (2005), 'Marcelino Pan y vino/Miracle of Marcelino', in *The Cinema of Spain and Portugal*, ed. Alberto Mira, London and New York: Wallflower, pp. 148–56.

Puelles Benítez, Manuel de (1986), *Educación e ideología en la España contemporánea* (2nd edition), Barcelona: Editorial Labor.

Quintana, Ángel (1998), 'Cuerda, José Luis', in *Diccionario del cine español*, eds José Luis Borau, Carlos F. Heredero, Julio Pérez Perucha, and Esteve Riambau, Madrid: Alianza Editorial, pp. 264–5.

Ramos Altamira, Ignacio (2010), *El mejor ventrílocuo del mundo. Paco Sanz en los teatros madrileños (1906–1935)*, San Vicente: Editorial Club Universitario.

Ranzani, Oscar (2012), 'Militancia no es sinónimo de muerte, sino de crecer', *Página 12*, 20 May, <http://www.pagina12.com.ar/diario/suplementos/espectaculos/2-25270-2012-05-20.html> (last accessed 13 February 2017).

Rey Reguillo, Antonia del (2004), 'Entre el documental y la ficción, o las fantasías de un ventrílocuo', in *Encuentro de historiadores: en torno al cine aficionado*, Guadalajara: Diputación Provincial de Guadalajara/CEFIHGU, pp. 225–37.

Riley, Edward C. (1984), 'The Story of Ana in *El espíritu de la colmena*', *Bulletin of Hispanic Studies*, 61: 4, 491–7.

Rivas, Manuel (2000), *Butterfly's Tongue*, trans Margaret Jull Costa and Jonathan Dunne, London: The Harvill Press.

___ (2006), *¿Qué me quieres, amor?* Madrid: Punto de lectura.

Rocha, Carolina (2011), 'Introduction: "Children in Hispanic Cinema"', *Studies in Hispanic Cinemas (New Title: Studies in Spanish & Latin American Cinemas)*, 8: 2, 123–30.

___ (2014), 'Can Children Speak in Film?: Children's Subjectivity in *Mutum* (2007) and *O Contador De Histórias* (2009)', *Luso-Brazilian Review*, 51: 2, 1–16.

Rocha, Carolina and Georgia Seminet (eds) (2012), 'Introduction', in *Representing History, Class, and Gender in Spain and Latin America: Children and Adolescents in Film*, New York: Palgrave Macmillan, pp. 1–29.

Rodríguez, María Pilar (2002), 'Nación e infancia en la etapa franquista: *Urte Ilunak* de Arantxa Lazcano y *Secretos del corazón* de Montxo Armendáriz', in *Mundos en conflicto: aproximaciones al cine vasco de los noventa*, San Sebastián: Universidad de Deusto, pp. 35–72.

Rodríguez, Pepe (2003), *Pederastia en la iglesia católica: delitos sexuales del clero contra menores, un drama silenciado y encubierto por los obispos*, Madrid: Ediciones B.

Rodríguez Pérez, M. (2002), *Mundos en conflicto: aproximaciones al cine vasco de los noventa*, Bilbao: Universidad de Deusto.

Rubio, Miguel, Jose Oliver, Manuel Matji, and Víctor Erice (1976), 'Entrevista con Víctor Erice', in *El espíritu de la colmena*, Madrid: Elías Querejeta Ediciones, pp. 137–50.

Rudlin, John (2002), *Commedia Dell'Arte: An Actor's Handbook*, London and New York: Routledge.

Ryan, Lorraine (2016), 'Memory, Transnational Justice, and Recession in Contemporary Spain', *European Review*, 24: 4, 1–12.

Sánchez, Francisco J. (2012), 'A Post-national Spanish Imaginary. A Case-study: *Pan's Labyrinth*', *The Comparatist*, 36: 1, 137–46.

Sánchez Noriega, José Luis (2004), 'Infancia', in *Diccionario temático del cine*, Madrid: Ediciones Cátedra, pp. 269–73.

Sanders, Julie (2006), *Adaptation and Appropriation*, London and New York: Routledge.

Savater, Fernando (1976), 'Riesgos de la iniciación al espíritu', in *El espíritu de la colmena*, Madrid: Elías Querejeta Ediciones, pp. 9–26.

Scarry, Elaine (1999), 'The Difficulty of Imagining Other Persons', in *Human Rights in Political Transitions: Gettysburg to Bosnia*, eds Carla Hesse and Robert Post, New York: Zone Books, pp. 277–309.

Segal, Naomi (1998), *André Gide: Pederasty and Pedagogy*, Oxford and New York: Clarendon Press.

Seguin, Jean-Claude (1990), 'Joselito: La voix inhumaine: du genre au corpus, du corpus à l'acteur', PhD diss., University of Bordeaux.

Serrano, Secundio (2001), *Maquis. historia de la guerrilla antifranquista*, Madrid: Ediciones temas de hoy.

Shaw, Deborah (2013), *The Three Amigos: The Transnational Films of Guillermo Del Toro, Alejandro González Iñárritu, and Alfonso Cuarón*, Manchester: Manchester University Press.

Sierra Blas, Verónica (2009), *Palabras huérfanas: los niños y la guerra civil*, Madrid: Santillana Ediciones Generales.

Skidmore, Thomas, Peter H. Smith, and James N. Green (2014), *Modern Latin America* (8th edition), New York: Oxford University Press.

Smith, Angel (1996), 'National Catholicism', in *Historical Dictionary of Spain*, Lanham: The Scarecrow Press, pp. 249–50.

Smith, Paul Julian (1999), 'Between Metaphysics and Scientism: Rehistoricizing Víctor Erice's *El espíritu de la colmena* (1973)', in *Spanish Cinema: The Auteurist Tradition*, ed. Peter Evans, Oxford: Oxford University Press, pp. 93–114.

___(2007), 'Pan's Labyrinth (El laberinto del fauno)', *Film Quarterly*, 60: 4, 4–9.

___(2014), *Mexican Screen Fiction: Between Cinema and Television*, Cambridge: Polity.

Soliño, María Elena (2002), *Women and Children First: Spanish Women Writers and the Fairy Tale Tradition*, Potomac: Scripta Humanistica.

Sontag, Susan (1978), *Illness as Metaphor*, New York: Farrar, Straus, and Giroux.

Sorensen, Kristin (2009), 'The *Machuca* Phenomenon', in *Media, Memory, and Human Rights in Chile*, New York: Palgrave Macmillan, pp. 75–103.

Soriano, Mar (2011), 'Entrevista con Mar Soriano', *El País*, 8 March, <http://politica.elpais.com/politica/2011/03/08/actualidad/1299603600_12996113 78.html> (last accessed 23 February 2017).

Souto, Luz Celestina (2013), 'Las narrativas sobre la apropiación de menores en las dictaduras española y argentina. El relato de la memoria y el de la identidad', *Olivar*, 14: 20, 221–43.

Stockton, Kathryn Bond (2009), *The Queer Child, Or Growing Sideways in the Twentieth Century*, Durham, NC: Duke University Press.

Stone, Rob (2002), 'Spirits and Secrets: Four Films about Childhood', in *Spanish Cinema*, Harlow: Longman, pp. 85–109.

___(2012), 'Song-shaped Cinema: The Performance of Gypsy and Basque Songs in Relation to Film Form', in *Screening Songs in Hispanic and Lusophone Cinema*, eds Lisa Shaw and Rob Stone, Manchester: Manchester University Press, pp. 114–33.

Swier, Patricia and Julia Riordan-Goncalves (2013), *Dictatorships in the Hispanic World: Transatlantic and Transnational Perspectives*, Madison: Fairleigh Dickinson University Press.

Tal, Tzvi (2005), 'Alegorías de memoria y olvido en películas de iniciación: *Machuca* y *Kamchatka*', *Aisthesis: revista chilena de investigaciones estéticas*, 38, 134–49.

Teixidor, Emili (1975), *Sic Transit Gloria Swanson: i altres narracions*, Barcelona: Laia.

___(1987), *Retrat d'un assassí d'ocells*, Barcelona: Edicions Proa.

___(2011), *Pa negre*, Barcelona: Editorial Seix Barral.

Thau, Eric M. (2011), 'The Eyes of Ana Torrent', *Studies in Hispanic Cinemas (New Title: Studies in Spanish & Latin American Cinemas)*, 8: 2, 131–43.

Thomas, Sarah (2014), 'Yo no soy invisible: Imaginative Agency in *Las malas intenciones*', in *Screening Minors in Latin American Cinema*, eds Carolina Rocha and Georgia Seminet, Lanham: Lexington Books, pp. 53–68.

___ (2015), 'Rupture and Reparation: Postmemory, the Child Seer and Graphic Violence in *Infancia Clandestina* (Benjamín Ávila, 2012)', *Studies in Spanish & Latin American Cinemas*, 12: 3, 235–54.

Torreiro Gómez, Casimiro (1998), 'Azcona, Rafael', in *Diccionario del cine español*, eds José Luis Borau, Carlos F. Heredero, Julio Pérez Perucha, and Esteve Riambau, Madrid: Alianza Editorial, pp. 101–3.

Torres, Maruja (2004), 'Pedro Almodóvar: Life is a Bolero', in *Pedro Almodóvar Interviews*, ed. Paula Willoquet-Maricondi, Jackson: University Press of Mississippi, pp. 9–16.

Torrús, Alejandro (2017), 'Querella en México por un bebé robado en el franquismo que salpica a la Iglesia católica', *Público*, 16 February, <http://www.publico.es/politica/amnistia-internacional-querella-mexico-bebe.html> (last accessed 23 February 2017).

Triana-Toribio, Núria (2003), *Spanish National Cinema*, London: Routledge.

Vallejo Nágera, Antonio (1938), *Política racial del nuevo estado*, San Sebastián: Editorial española S.A.

Vargas, Juan Carlos (2014), 'Between Fantasy and Reality: The Child's Vision and Fairy Tales in Guillermo del Toro's Hispanic Trilogy', in *The Transnational*

Fantasies of Guillermo Del Toro, eds Ann Davies, Deborah Shaw, and Dolores Tierney, New York: Palgrave Macmillan, pp. 183–97.

Vázquez Montalbán, Manuel (1977), *Diccionario del franquismo*, Barcelona: Dopesa.

Vernon, Kathleen M. (2009), 'Queer Sound: Musical Otherness in Three Films by Pedro Almodóvar', in *All about Almodóvar: A Passion for Cinema*, eds Brad Epps and Despina Kakoudaki, Minneapolis: University of Minnesota Press, pp. 51–70.

Vidal Estévez, Manuel (1998), 'Ladislao Vajda', in *Diccionario del cine español*, eds José Luis Borau, Carlos F. Heredero, and María Pastor, Madrid: Alianza Editorial, pp. 883–5.

Vilarós, Teresa M. (2005), 'Banalidad y biopolítica: la transición española y el nuevo orden del mundo', in *Desacuerdos 2: sobre arte, políticas y esfera pública en el estado español*, ed. Jesús Carrillo, Barcelona: Arteleku, Gipuzkoako Foru Aldundia, MACBA, Museu d'Art Contemporani de Barcelona, Universidad Internacional de Andalucía, UNIA arteypensamiento, pp. 29–56.

Washabaugh, William (2012), *Flamenco Music and National Identity in Spain*, London: Ashgate Publishing Ltd.

Willem, Linda M. (1996), 'Highlighting the Hidden: Visual Representation in Gutiérrez Aragón's *Demonios en el jardín*', *RLA: Romance Languages Annual*, 8, 678–80.

Wilson, Anna (1996), '*Little Lord Fauntleroy*: The Darling of Mothers and the Abomination of a Generation', *American Literary History*, 8: 2, 232–58.

Wilson, Emma (2003), *Cinema's Missing Children*, London: Wallflower Press.

Wright, Sarah (2000), *The Trickster-Function in the Theatre of García Lorca*, London: Tamesis.

___ (2013), *The Child in Spanish Cinema*, Manchester: Manchester University Press.

Yim, Ho-Joon (2017), 'La infancia como mito e historia en *La lengua de las mariposas* (1999) y *Machuca* (2004)', *Bulletin of Hispanic Studies*, 94: 2, 199–214.

Zubiaur Gorozika, Nekane Erritte (2013), 'La perversión de la infancia. Ser y parecer en *Pa negre* de Agustí Villaronga (2010)', *Archivos de la Filmoteca*, XIX–XXIX.

Zumalde Arregi, Imanol (2013), 'El laberíntico caso del fauno. A propósito de la identidad nacional de las películas', *Zer*, 18: 34, 195–209.

Index

EU Authorised Representative:

Easy Access System Europe Mustamäe tee 50, 10621 Tallinn, Estonia

gpsr.requests@easproject.com

Printed and bound by CPI Group (UK) Ltd, Croydon, CR0 4YY

24/02/2026

02059257-0011